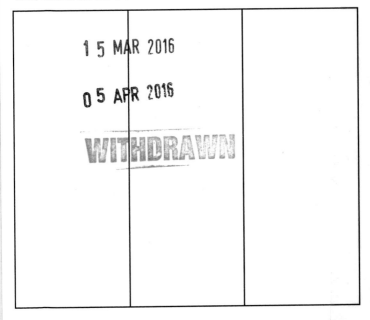

## ALSO BY ELENA GOROKHOVA

*A Mountain of Crumbs*

# Russian Tattoo

## A Memoir

### Elena Gorokhova

**WINDMILL BOOKS**

Published by Windmill Books 2015

2 4 6 8 10 9 7 5 3 1

Copyright © Elena Gorokhova 2015

Elena Gorokhova has asserted her right under the Copyright, Designs and
Patents Act, 1988, to be identified as the author of this work.

This book is based on the life, experiences and recollections of the author.
In some cases certain names and identifying characteristics have been
changed, some people are composites, and certain events have
been reordered and/or compressed.

First published in the United States in 2015 by Simon & Schuster

First published in Great Britain in 2015 by
Windmill Books
The Random House Group Limited
20 Vauxhall Bridge Road, London SW1V 2SA

Addresses for companies within The Random House Group Limited can be found at:
www.randomhouse.co.uk/offices.htm

The Random House Group Limited Reg. No. 954009

www.randomhouse.co.uk

A CIP catalogue record for this book
is available from the British Library

ISBN 9780099592051

Interior design by Aline C. Pace

Printed and bound by CPI Group (UK) Ltd, Croydon, CR0 4YY

*For Andy and Laurenka*

Cut yourself free of what you love and hope that the wound heals.

—J. M. COETZEE, *SUMMERTIME*

# Russian Tattoo

# PART 1

# *Robert*

# *One*

I wish I could clear my mind and focus on my imminent American future. I am twelve kilometers up in the air—forty thousand feet, according to the new, nonmetric system I have yet to learn. Every time I glance at the overhead television screen that shows the position of my Aeroflot flight, this future is getting closer. The miniature airplane is like a needle over the Atlantic, stitching the two hemispheres together with the thread of our route. I wish I could get ready and dredge my mind of all the silt of my previous life. But I can't. I can't help but think of my mother's crumpled face back in Leningrad airport, of her gaze, open, like a fresh wound, of her smells of the apple jam from our dacha mixed with the sharp odor of formaldehyde she'd brought home from the medical school where she teaches anatomy. I can't help but think of my sister Marina's tight embrace and her hair the color of apricots, one fruit that failed to grow in our dacha garden my grandfather planted. Ten hours earlier, I said good-bye to both of them.

In my Leningrad courtyard, where a taxi was waiting to take us to the airport, a small girl with braids had crouched on the ledge of a sandbox: green eyes, slightly slanted, betraying the drop of Tatar ancestry in every Russian; faint freckles, as if someone had splashed muddy water onto her skin. As the plane taxied past evergreen forests and riveted itself into the low Russian sky, I longed to be that girl, not ready to leave, still comfortable on the ledge of her childhood sandbox.

When I am not watching the plane advance westward on the screen, I talk to my neighbor, a morose-looking American with thin-rimmed glasses and a plastic cup of vodka in his hand. He has just warned me, between sips of Stolichnaya, that I will never find a teaching job in the United States. He is a former professor of Russian literature, bitter and disillusioned, and, as we glide over Greenland, he dismisses my approaching American future with a single wave of his hand. "You should go back home," he says, staring into his glass and rattling the ice cubes. "It's 1980, and what you're looking for in the U.S. no longer exists. You'll be happier with your family in Russia."

My family in Russia would applaud this statement—especially my mother, who thinks I'll be begging on the streets and sleeping under a bridge, as *Pravda* has informed her.

I know I should tell this Russian expert that my new American husband is waiting for me at the airport, probably with a list of teaching jobs in his pocket. I should tell him to mind his own business. I should tell him that no one in Russia puts ice in drinks or ever sips vodka. But I don't. I am a docile ex–Young Pioneer who only this morning left the Soviet Union, a ravaged suitcase on the KGB inspector's table with twenty kilograms of what used to be my life.

∞

In the sterile maze of Washington Dulles International Airport, an official pulls me into a little room, tells me to sit down, and points a camera at my face. A flash goes off and I blink. Another man in uniform dips my index finger in ink and presses it to paper. "Sign and date here." He points to a line, and I write my name and the date, August 10, 1980. "Here is your green card," he says and hands me a small rectangular piece of plastic. I don't know why he calls it a green card. It is white, with a fingerprint in the middle to certify that the bewildered face is mine.

I feel as if I were inside an aquarium, sensing everything through layers of water, clear and still and deeper than I know, with real life happening to other people behind the glass. They are pulling suitcases that roll magically behind them; they are waiting for their flights in docile, passive lines—all without color or sound, like a silent film. With a new identity bestowed on me by the card between my fingers, I float out of the immigration office, the weight of my suitcase strangely diminished, as though the value of my Russian possessions has instantly shrunk with the strike of the immigration stamp. The sign in front of me points an arrow to something called RESTROOM, although I can see it is not going to dispense any rest. The floor gleams here, the hand dryers whir, and the faucets sparkle—*restroom* is a perfect word for this luxury that seems to have emerged straight from the spotless future of science fiction. I think of the rusty toilets of Pulkovo International Airport I just left, of their corroded pipes and sad, hanging pull chains that never release enough water to wash away the lowly feeling of barely being human.

In the waiting crowd I make out Robert, my new American husband, a man I barely know. He is peering in my direction through his thick glasses, not yet able to see me among the exiting passengers. It feels odd to apply the word *husband* to a tall stranger in corduroy jeans and tight springs of black hair around his waiting face. And what about me? Do I want to be a wife, the word that in Russia mostly conjures standing: on lines, at bus stops, by the stove?

Five months earlier, Robert came to Leningrad to marry me, to my mother's horror. We stood in the wedding hall of the Acts of Marriage Palace on the Neva embankment—a small flock of my mortified relatives and close friends—in front of a woman in a red dress with a wide red ribbon across her chest, who recited a speech about the creation of a new society cell. The speech was modified for international marriages: there was no reference to our future contributions to the Soviet cause or to the bright dawn of communism.

To be honest, the possibility of leaving Russia was never as thrilling as the prospect of leaving my mother. My mother, a mirror image of my Motherland—overbearing and protective, controlling and nurturing—had spun a tangle of conflicted feelings as interlaced as the nerves and muscles in her anatomy charts I'd copied since I was eight. Our apartment on Maklina Prospekt was the seat of the politburo; my mother, its permanent chairman. She presided in our kitchen over a pot of borsch, ordering me to eat in the same voice that made her anatomy students quiver. She sheltered me from dangers, experience, and life itself by an embrace so tight that it left me innocent and gasping for air and that sent me fumbling through the first ordeals of adulthood. She had survived the famine, Stalin's terror, and the Great Patriotic War, and she controlled and protected, ferociously. What had happened to her was not going to happen to Marina and me.

Robert and I met last summer, during the six-week Russian program for American students at Leningrad University, where I was teaching. For the last two weeks of classes—the time we spent walking around the city—I showed him my real hometown, those places too ordinary to be included among the glossy snapshots of bronze statues and golden domes. We walked along the cracked asphalt side streets where crumbling arches lead into mazes of courtyards, those wells out of Dostoyevsky that depress the spirit and twist the soul into a truly miserable Russian knot. If the director of the program, or her KGB husband, had known I was spending time with an American, I wouldn't now be gawking at the splendor of the airport in Washington, DC. After four months of letters, Robert came back to Leningrad in December to offer to marry me if I wanted to leave the country—on one condition: I had to understand that he wasn't ready to get married.

He wasn't ready to settle down with one person, Robert said. He wanted to continue seeing other women, particularly his colleague Karen, who taught Russian in Austin, where he was working on his PhD in physics. We would have an open marriage, he said. "An open marriage?" I repeated as we were walking toward my apartment building in Leningrad. It was minus twenty-five degrees Celsius and the air was so cold it felt like shards of glass scraping inside my throat as we clutched onto each other because the sidewalk was solid ice.

I didn't know *marriage* could be paired with an adjective gutting the essence of the word's meaning, but then I didn't know lots of things. I didn't know, for example, that my mother, who has always been in love with propriety and order, had two marriages before she met my father—two short-lived, hasty unions, of which neither one seemed perfect or even good. I didn't know, before my university friends told me, that it was legal to marry a foreigner and leave the country. My mother had diligently sheltered me from the realities of Russian life; my Motherland had kept all other ways of life away from everyone within its borders. We were crowded on the Soviet side of the Iron Curtain, clad in ill-fitting garb and ignorant about the rest of the world.

"I understand," I said to Robert on that frosty day in Leningrad— words that hung in the air in a small cloud of frozen breath—although I really didn't.

# Two

Robert and I are walking around the airy rooms of the Smithsonian Institution in Washington, DC. The Air and Space Museum is full of planes suspended from the ceiling, boasting their antiquated, propeller innocence. We are staring at space capsules where you can sit in a cosmonaut's chair and pretend you are flying through space. "I'm Yuri Gagarin," says Robert in Russian and pushes the buttons on the dashboard, making me giggle.

This morning, as the plane was descending over the unfamiliar contours of my new country's capital, I tried to conjure up my husband, a word that sounds strange when applied to the man showing me all these space wonders. What if he had been absent from the crowd at the airport? What if he'd come to his senses and realized, as the surly Russian literature professor on the plane informed me, that my prospects here are not very promising?

For a week before our wedding in March, Robert and I had stayed at the apartment of Galya, my half sister from my father's earlier marriage, not without the silent comment of compressed lips from my mother, who pointed out how inappropriate it was for two people to live in one place prior to the moment the state pronounces them officially married. I loved that week of being away from my family, of pretending to be married to someone so exotic and unknown. I even thought I loved Robert. When we first found ourselves in bed, we were both tentative, as if afraid to discover in each other something alien and ghastly. But the only foreign part of American sex turned out to be a supply of prophylactics.

Back in Leningrad, I loved Robert's foreignness. I loved that he represented the forbidden and the unknown, that his nationality made people gasp. I loved that Robert had lifted me above the collective and I could be the opposite of what we all were in Russia, cynical and meek. The opposite of what our souls had become, cleaved and schizophrenic. I could heal and fuse the two parts of me together, I thought. I would no longer be a yearning Soviet teenage Pioneer vying for state-sanctioned approval, or a little sister begging Marina to take me backstage, or a docile grown-up marching in step with everybody else.

The air of the museum is cool and odorless. The cool, I know, comes from air-conditioning, a capitalist invention I read about in an American novel, but why are there no smells? Russia assaults you in your nostrils: milk always on the verge of turning sour, the wet wool of winter coats we wear every day for five months, rubber phone booth tiles buckled with urine, exhaust from trucks that run on leaded gasoline, mothballs, yesterday's soup. Here, despite thirty-four degrees Celsius outside (ninety-three Fahrenheit, says Robert)—a temperature I know only from books on the Soviet republics of Central Asia—it smells of nothing. People who pass by don't trail the odor of unwashed clothes, and the museum cafeteria where we stop to have lunch doesn't reek of boiled cabbage and dishrags made from old stockings crisscrossed by runs beyond repair.

I don't even know if I should call the antiseptic space with the sparkly floor and smiling cashiers a cafeteria. Where are the bread crumbs and the dried puddles of cabbage soup? Where are the empty napkin holders—napkins stolen for toilet paper—and where are the flies? And what is a gleaming ketchup bottle doing on every table, open to anyone's cravings?

"What would you like?" asks Robert, a simple question I can't answer since the menu on the wall contains no words I recognize. I stand in front of the counter, dumb and mute and wishing for a miraculous hand to pluck me out of this awkward silence. I squeeze out a mousy "I don't know," as if this were my first American test and I have instantly failed it. Should I admit to Robert that I've never heard of burgers, hot dogs, or French fries? Should I say I'm not hungry and simply ask for tea? Robert shrugs and says something to the girl behind the counter. A few minutes later, she hands him two paper boxes and he motions for me to sit at one of the spotless tables. We haven't yet eaten together, just the two of us, and I am hoping for this to be good, the first meal of our marriage, even if it isn't quite a real marriage.

Robert opens the packages and they reveal something that looks like a small loaf of bread stuffed with layers of meat and salad. I don't know how to approach this bread concoction, so I stare at it without moving.

"It's a hamburger," says Robert. "You eat it like a sandwich."

"Like a ham sandwich," I say, happy to finally understand something.

"No, not like a ham sandwich," says Robert and shakes his head. "That's just its name, a hamburger. Try it."

I don't know how to try it. It looks so imposing sitting there in its own container, staring back at me as I try to figure out how to wrap my mouth around it. I cast a furtive glance to see if anyone is using a knife and a fork. No one is. Robert takes his hamburger out of its box, presses the bread down with his fingers, and takes a bite. When I do the same, a rivulet of ketchup squirts out and pulls with it some bits of lettuce, which land on my sundress. A woman at the next table stops eating and gives me a pitiful glance.

"I'm sorry," I mumble with my mouth full, not knowing what else to say, not knowing whether I should say anything at all, as I get up and head for the restroom to wash off the ketchup. I am wearing the only dress I own, and I can't afford to have it stained.

When I come back, after scrubbing the stains off with hand soap and then holding my skirt up to the dryer, Robert has already finished his hamburger and asks me if I want to finish mine. I weigh in my mind if a few bites of food are worth risking another round of scrubbing and drying. They aren't, so I shake my head. He scoops up our boxes, his empty one and mine with most of my hamburger still in, and drops them into a trash bin. Our table is as gleaming as it was before we sat down. I look back at the perfectly aligned chairs painted in light blue and rust colors, at a young man in uniform sliding a mop around the immaculate tile floor. A tide of questions swirls in my head, stupid questions I'll never have the nerve to ask. Is every hamburger here so special that it deserves its own individual container? What else in this country is as disposable as these paper boxes? Why would anyone toss perfectly good food into the trash?

&#8500;

On my first full day in the United States, I wake up to unreality, emerging from a dream about my father's funeral. He died fourteen years ago, when I was ten. "Smoked since he was nine," my mother lamented to a neighbor on that day. "So what do you expect?" I didn't know what she'd hoped for, but I expected him to stay alive. In our neighbor's apartment, after the funeral, his friends from the Leningrad Technical School drank vodka toasts to his shining memory, to his party leadership, to my mother, my sisters, and me. Uncle Volodya, my father's driver, asked everyone to drink to my father's fishing. "The greatest happiness of his life was sitting in a boat with his line cast," he said, long bags under his eyes making his face even sadder as my mother pursed her lips because she probably considered herself to have been the greatest happiness of his life.

I thought of the Renaissance paintings in the Hermitage, where our third-grade teacher, Vera Pavlovna, had taken our class the previous spring, of souls fluttering in the clouds alongside harp-playing angels. "We no longer believe in heaven," she announced, standing next to an icon, and a week later, as if to make the point, arranged a school trip to the Museum of Religion and Atheism at Kazan Cathedral. As we stood in front of the gilded altar, Vera Pavlovna condemned the atavisms of the tsarist past as backward beliefs about heaven and afterlife.

"Heaven is church mythology made up in an effort to suppress the populace," she said. "To distract their attention from everyday struggles."

I liked the Hermitage elongated angels and Leonardo da Vinci's Madonna with a fat baby in her arms. But our teacher told us to think of all those floating souls in the densely populated skies as nothing but symbols, the way a snake under the feet of Peter the Great's horse in the Bronze Horseman monument on the Neva River was a symbol of all the tsar's enemies who didn't want him to build a city on a cold swamp infested with mosquitoes. The same way Pushkin's poems teemed with speaking souls and fiery prophets. And though I hated to agree with our teacher who demanded that we marched in step with the school collective, I found it difficult to believe that anyone could still hope to rise to heaven after death. You died in a hospital, like my father, and then you were buried in the ground.

In a dream I had about my father's funeral, Uncle Volodya announced he was leaving. I got up and lurked in the doorway between the living room and the entrance hallway so he would notice me, because in my mind he was directly linked to my father.

"He was a good man," said Uncle Volodya and patted me on the cheek.

I wondered if I would ever see Uncle Volodya again, and that thought suddenly made me so sad that I could feel the tears rising, but I swallowed hard and pretended I was coughing. Uncle Volodya put on a raincoat and a hat, his skin hanging under his eyes and around his mouth as if tired of holding on to his face. Then the heavy double doors locked behind him and he was gone.

I tried not to think about Uncle Volodya anymore; I tried not to think about my father. I stood in the hallway's soft dusk under a coatrack, trying not to think at all, but thoughts marched in, like columns of the suppressed populace protesting the church's mythology of heaven. I thought of the only time I went fishing with my father: a slippery perch glistening in my hands, a purple worm squiggling in an inch of water on the bottom of the boat, my father's fingers, black from dirt, hooking it onto the end of my fishing rod.

∽

As I wake up, unfamiliar images float in through gummy eyes: a bulky dresser with a giant television, a floor covered with something soft and beige, a wool blanket without a duvet cover. The walls are naked, too, not sheathed with wallpaper.

I can almost smell the woody musk of our Leningrad armoire in the room where my mother and I slept, the dusty air of Marina's room with the two pieces of furniture required for every respectable home: a cupboard filled with cut crystal and a piano called Red October. I hated dusting the cupboard and the piano. I hated practicing the piano, too, and this double aversion kept me away from my sister's room, which suited us both. But now my Leningrad bed next to my mother's, with its white duvet and square pillow, floats in my memory, feathery and warm, next to an undusted sideboard full of porcelain ballerinas and a bottle of my mother's sweet perfume called Red Moscow. I used to sit in front of her triple mirror, where nothing interesting was ever reflected, and wonder whether I could ever leave. And now, half a world away, I can smell that perfume.

It takes a few minutes for alien objects to come into focus, until one thing becomes sharp and real: I am no longer home.

∽

It is early morning, and we go down to the kitchen full of strange bottles on the counter and cardboard boxes in the cabinets. The house belongs to a former professor of Robert's, who let us stay here for two days before we drive to New Jersey, where Robert's mother lives. The professor is round and balding and doesn't look at all professorial.

Robert asks him something, and the professor launches into what sounds like a lecture, most of which I don't understand. The words stream out of his mouth—words that sound vaguely familiar, yet distorted with the yawning vowels and the r's that have broken out of control in their mad attempt to take over other sounds. And the unseemly intonation: a wild rhythm galloping in all directions, like unbroken horses in Westerns I have yet to see. American English—all wrong, as my British-trained professors warned me back home. I spent fifteen years trying to master proper British English—the language no one seems to speak here.

In my family, no one spoke a foreign language, especially one as foreign as English. My mother knew the names of all the body parts in Latin, but Latin wasn't exotic; it was ancient and dead. My father spoke nothing but Russian. Marina studied French at her Moscow drama school, but French was so ingrained in Russian history that even my provincial aunt Muza sometimes said, *"Merci beaucoup."* English was regal and mesmerizing, unknown and rarely heard. It was my way out of the ordinary life—the same escape my sister found in theater and acting. When I was ten, the year my father died, I insisted on learning English the same way Marina had earlier insisted on auditioning for the Moscow drama school.

Every day, for the three months of summer, I took a streetcar to a tutor's apartment to contort my mouth around unfamiliar sounds until it hurt, to learn the twelve tricky tenses, to make the bewildering discovery that Russian had no word for *privacy*. Thirteen years of English classes later, I'd been selected to teach Russian to visiting American students at the Leningrad University summer program. Robert was in my friend Nina's class. That was exactly a year ago.

I look around Robert's professor's kitchen as if it were another museum. "Would you like some cereal?" asks his wife, tall and broad-boned, not interested in her husband's lecture.

I imagine a pot with steaming farina, *mannaya kasha,* the cereal my sister refused to swallow when she was little. Marina would hold the kasha in her mouth for hours, her cheeks bulging, not letting even a drop slide down her throat. Unlike my sister, I've always liked farina, hot and gooey, made with milk and lots of sugar, a cube of butter slowly dissolving in the center of a steaming heap. But the professor's wife reaches for a cardboard box with a picture of brown flakes and raisins, and the mixture rattles into my bowl with the same sound you'd hear if you poured a handful of nails.

∞

This is our last day in the capital of my new country because this evening we are driving to Robert's mother's house in New Jersey. The car Robert used to pick me up at the airport belongs to his father, he said with a glimmer of pride in his eyes at being the only American who doesn't own a vehicle.

The Washington air trembles with heat as we walk along a rectangular pool that seems to be steaming. Low, uniform buildings, a tall obelisk, huge expanses of space so strange in a major city. Jefferson Memorial, Lincoln Memorial, Washington Monument. I should've brushed up on American history, as my university dean told me to do during his harangue about my betrayal of Leningrad University and the entire Soviet Union because I married an American.

I compare what I see to our capital, Moscow, where the scale of everything is so much grander. I think of our May 1, Labor Day, marches and Victory Day parades that are supposed to energize us with their rows of tanks and lines of rockets rolling past the Lenin Mausoleum; of endless lines for Czech mascara, bologna, and Polish boots. We cannot afford to smile at every customer in Russia or wrap each sandwich, even if we had the meat or the paper, even if we had a word for *service*.

"Let's stop for iced tea," says Robert and points to a café entrance.

I am stunned that you can simply stop for a drink here—a random detour, a result of an individual's whim—and no one is going to yell at you for trying to be special, for standing out from the collective. But I am even more astonished at the notion of iced tea. What kind of sacrilege is this? Everyone knows that tea must be served scalding hot. I don't say anything to Robert as I consider this just American ignorance. But I also think of the waitress who didn't scowl at us as we sat at her table and who pretended that our order of iced tea was exactly what she'd been waiting for. It was so utterly un-Soviet in its cheeriness that it made me giggle.

"Life's a kopek," my mother would always say, and now I think I am beginning to understand what our most popular proverb really means.

How am I going to get used to all this sudden worthiness?

# *Three*

My new mother-in-law lives in a *pomestie* nestled in the woods called Princeton, New Jersey. A *pomestie* is a sprawling country house with land, a kind of dwelling surrounded by an orchard as thick as a forest, where many of Chekhov's characters lamented their lives and yearned for Moscow. At first glance, my mother-in-law didn't seem to lament anything. She pressed me to her soft T-shirt that said WOMEN UNITE and we had sweet drinks made from a dark cordial I'd never seen. My tongue wouldn't contort to calling the woman I'd just met *mother*, so I call her Millie.

As I explored the vast premises of Millie's estate, I knew my real mother was fretting in our Leningrad kitchen across from my older sister, wondering if I'd already settled down to live under a bridge or was begging on the street, like most Americans. We all saw a recent Soviet documentary shot in New York and broadcast on our TV at least three times before I left. *A Man from Fifth Ave.* showed men and women sleeping on the pavement amid a crowd of indifferent capitalists on their way to restaurants and stores. I haven't yet seen the real Fifth Avenue, with half its population begging for scraps, so what I can write back home has no relevance to anyone in Leningrad. What can I possibly tell my family that they would understand? That roads in New Jersey are jammed with cars they've never seen? That supermarkets nearby are the size of stadiums, brimming with foods they couldn't even dream up? That no matter how hard I look, I haven't seen even one line?

I wrote in my letter that Robert had caught a cold and I was treating him with tea and honey, in the absence of raspberry jam from the dacha. I wrote that Millie appreciated the set of painted spoons and the shawl with roses my mother had procured through her medical connections. I wrote nothing about the aquarium feeling of unreality that has settled inside me since I stepped off the plane in Washington.

Millie is a psychotherapist, said Robert, a profession mysterious to everyone raised on the other side of the Iron Curtain. In a second house that hides behind thick rhododendron bushes, she runs something called the Academy for Experiential Development. I know about rhododendrons from a Fitzgerald novel, but I've never seen the word *experiential* before, so I thought that the sign said "experimental development." It makes me wonder, as I look across the lawn trying to peer through the thicket of branches, what kinds of psychological experiments Millie carries out there on her patients. I could ask Robert about the experiments, but I don't want to sound more clueless than I must already seem. I don't want to pester him to explain psychotherapy, in addition to everything else he has to explain to me. Back home we had physical therapists and medical therapists to deal with various malfunctions of the body, but our psyches—the products of our bright future and heroic past—were all supposed to be uniform and healthy. When they were not, we called our friends and sat in their kitchens until the blackness behind the window became diluted with the first rays of gray dawn. We talked about love and parents, drinking acidic wine and exchanging homegrown advice not based on any theories, especially those of Freud, whose books were safely locked away in secret vaults of the Central Library, away from most readers' eyes.

With her professional power to analyze the human mind, Millie has quickly figured out that I need a new pair of shoes. The only pair I brought with me, the best shoes I've ever owned—thanks to a friend with connections—is Hungarian and made of real leather. They have black laces in the front and thick rubber soles perfect for April in Leningrad, when the snow turns into dirty porridge and walking becomes wading. But now it is August in Princeton, and with the sun melting the asphalt behind the window, they look out of place.

On the third day after our arrival at her house, Millie takes me to a shoe store. Alarmingly, it is full of shoes. Loafers, espadrilles, ballerina slippers, pumps, clogs, flip-flops, sandals—in colors that bring to mind Matisse paintings hanging in the Hermitage; with heels, skinny and solid, high and low, and with no heels at all—are perched on gleaming plastic stands that radiate from the center of the room for as far as my eyes can see.

"What do you like?" Millie asks and smiles from above her glasses. She is shorter than I am, with a haircut that would look boyish if her hair weren't graying. As she patiently waits, pretending to examine a pair of pumps with stiletto heels no one could possibly walk on, I realize she wants me to make a choice. My heart sinks. I desperately look around, and a saleswoman promptly sidles up to us. "How may I help you?" she asks in a syrupy voice that makes my stomach queasy. They are both looking at me now, waiting for an answer with the same frustration Robert must have felt when he ordered me a hamburger, expecting me to choose one perfect drop in a glittering ocean of footwear. They wait and wait as the ocean rises to my nostrils and threatens to drown me. I take a deep breath as if it were my last. What can I possibly say to them? That Leningrad shoe stores had two models on the floor, both made from rubberized plastic that mangles feet, both produced by the Bolshevik Woman factory in Minsk? That I have no idea how much any of these shimmering shoes cost and how their prices correlate with my new mother-in-law's budget? That I don't even know what American shoe size I wear?

Millie finally says something to the saleswoman, who vanishes and then reappears holding a hefty metal gauge with end pieces that look like teeth. The word *torture* rushes to the surface of my mind and freezes there. The woman motions for me to take off my Hungarian shoes and step onto the cold surface of her metal instrument. I cringe as I unlace, baring my hot, sweaty foot. The teeth lurch forward, then stop. Seven and a half, says the woman and grins. Back home I wore size thirty-six, which makes me think of my sister's joke: the Soviet Union proudly announced to the world that it produced the biggest of everything—the largest microchip, the tallest dwarf. I see Millie holding a pair of sandals—a half-inch sole with an elegant band across the instep—that wrap perfectly around my feet. The saleswoman curls her lips in a smile and nods her head in satisfaction, as if she was the one who cobbled those sandals together and made them fit.

"Why don't you wear them out of the store?" suggests Millie, a question I don't understand. Wear them out? They are brand-new, American, leather, perfectly fitting sandals that have to be revered. How can I wear them out? How can I trivialize a pair of shoes that are going to replace my Hungarian wonders? These are shoes that have to be celebrated, tried on in front of a mirror at home, admired, and exalted before I can slip my feet into their perfect straps and announce them to the world.

"No, let's take them with us," I say, putting back on my old shoes, which suddenly begin to pinch. I can't see the saleswoman's face, but I am sure she is bemused. As Millie pays, I glance in the mirror, conveniently attached to one of the shoe pedestals. What I see is sorrowful and depressing: my previously glamorous Hungarian shoes have instantly lost their luster; the words BOLSHEVIK WOMAN might as well be scrawled all over their surface. I hobble out of the store with the boxed sandals in my hands, Millie trotting behind me, probably questioning her son's sanity as I am questioning my own. Why, despite all logical reasons, couldn't I bring myself to take the new sandals out of the box and wear them, as people here obviously do, as I should have done if I ever want to learn to fit in? Why am I so stubborn, so foolish, so unable to conform? Why am I so utterly un-American? My old shoes pull on my feet like lead weights as I walk out into the foreign heat, doubting my whole future in this glimmering land of glut.

⌘

On Wednesday a woman in her early forties spends most of the day in Millie's house vacuuming, dusting, and scrubbing. I don't know her first name because Millie calls her Mrs. Conover.

Mrs. Conover is the first black person I have ever met. Back in Leningrad, a handful of students from African nations studied at our universities, attracting astonished stares that quickly turned to mild disgust on the faces of passersby who had never seen a live person with skin so much darker than their own. Among the foreign students in my mother's anatomy class was Amir, a young man from Kenya, who spent his school vacations on trips to Paris to stock up on a new wardrobe. "He just took off for France, for two days," my mother used to say with reproach that seemed to apply more to the trips' brevity than to their destination. I'd never seen Amir, and when I tried to conjure him up, there was nothing to anchor the image. I had no idea what good clothes looked like, so all I could think of was a university poster where a muscular Negro in chains was trampled on by a tiny fat white man in a top hat. My aunt Muza from the provinces couldn't understand why a black man who, according to *Pravda*, is supposed to be ruthlessly exploited by societies that—unlike us—haven't yet tasted equality, was flying twice a year to France to buy suits.

"He is a prince," explained my mother, repeating Amir's words. "Related to the king of his country."

"Related to the king of the jungle, maybe," said my provincial aunt, more attuned to what most Russians thought about nonwhites. "And where in the jungle could he even learn about

Paris?" My aunt Muza, an obstetrician in a small town on the Volga River, delivered these words with unquestionable certainty that filled every corner of our kitchen. Although my aunt herself would never be allowed to cross the border to visit any European capital, even one in the Soviet bloc, she undoubtedly knew more about Paris than some brazen African prince who had the arrogance to get on an intercontinental flight to replenish his wardrobe on the Champs-Elysées.

Mrs. Conover, as I sense, is far from going on shopping sprees in Paris. She arrives by bus, wearing a plaid shirt and pants with an elastic waist, reticent and efficient in what she's been doing every week for probably longer than I've been learning English.

"So how are you?" she asks me when she enters. I am surprised by her desire to know about the life of someone she'd never met, but I dutifully recite what we did this past week: a bus trip to New York and a walk along Fifth Avenue, where no one was begging, a stroll around the Gothic towers of Princeton, my first horror film on television, where a fifteen-foot-tall bear kept popping out of the woods to terrorize a summer camp. I loved that movie, I say, proud of the newly acquired American word for what I knew as *film*.

"Here is a can of tuna if you'd like some lunch, Mrs. Conover," Millie murmurs, interrupting me. "And coffee, and a Danish, although it's a little stale." She smiles apologetically at her failure to run to the store this morning for a fresh piece of pastry.

Robert says he's never seen Mrs. Conover take a sip of coffee or open a tuna can, but Millie is persistent. She wants to be fair to the domestic help, he says, and that's why she calls her cleaning lady by her last name. He also tells me I don't have to answer the simple question of "How are you?" with a story of my life.

Robert sits on a kitchen stool next to me, watching in amazement as I shake a bottle of ketchup over a bar of cream cheese. I am on a tasting spree of all the foods I've never had. Yesterday I gobbled spoonfuls of whipped cream, and the day before I fished out olives from a tall, thin jar I found in the door of Millie's refrigerator.

Mrs. Conover is bending over a vacuum cleaner, pulling it up the stairs in vigorous spasms, making me think of the poster that hung in the Leningrad University hallway.

"Yet another example of capitalist exploitation," I say to Robert, scooping a spoonful of cream cheese into my mouth, nodding toward Mrs. Conover, who is jerking the vacuum cleaner up to the second floor.

Robert squints at me, confused. He silently regards the cream cheese with ketchup I've been eating, the same way he earlier looked at the old Hungarian shoes I wore in ninety-five-degree heat.

"She's paid well for this work," he says finally, thinking that I'm serious, that he needs to vouch for his mother's social integrity.

I wonder if my mother ever thought of buying fresh pastry for the woman who used to help around our apartment when I was little. She called her Nelka, a diminutive of Nelly, and I am sure the thought of using her patronymic for respect never crossed my mother's mind. The formality of Nelly Ivanovna or Nelly Petrovna would sound preposterous in our dilapidated kitchen, not nearly big enough for such magnanimity. Every day except Sunday, Nelka stayed with me in our apartment until I turned five and was admitted to nursery school. All day, while my mother taught anatomy at her medical institute, Nelka shuttled between our refrigerator and our stove, whipping up panfuls of fried potatoes with onions and buckets of cabbage soup, pouring kettles of hot water over the dishes in the sink before she washed them with an old stocking. She boiled milk in a dented, blackened pot and made me drink a cup with breakfast and lunch. As it cooled, the milk would form a film on top, like a layer of skin, and I would beg Nelka to skim it off because its grainy, papery texture would make me gag. "I hate boiled milk! I hate the skin on top!" I wailed, knowing that Nelka would always relent.

Of course, my mother, who is hard to fool, quickly figured out her own truth. "Nelka taught you to hate it on purpose. She skimmed it off and ate it herself," my mother said, her fists on her hips. "You can't trust those know-nothing plumbers' offspring," she added. "You have to watch their every step."

I didn't remember Nelka ever eating the skimmed-off skin, so I couldn't argue with my mother about my nanny's milk transgressions, as I normally would have. My mother has always been suspicious of other people's intentions, always weary of all those *chuzhoi,* those not part of the family. There were only so many soup bones, or beets, or bottles of milk to go around, and if you didn't make sure that your own, *svoi,* had hoarded enough for today and tomorrow, you might as well skim the top off every pot of milk and serve it to every Nelka on a silver platter.

"When I was little, my mother had a *domrabotnitsa,*" I say to Robert. "She didn't like her much."

He looks at me quizzically, and I realize he has never heard the word.

"*Domrabotnitsa* means a domestic worker, the feminine form. You know that nouns have a gender, right?" I ask as he nods, annoyed that I am questioning his knowledge of such basic grammar. "It's always the feminine form," I say, giving him a little Russian lesson, trying to make myself useful beyond reducing the supplies of cream cheese and ketchup in Millie's kitchen.

"*Domrabotnitsa,*" Robert repeats, and I know he has filed the word into his brain. "When we get to Texas, you must give me some more lessons."

"Sure," I say, although I am not sure at all, because I think of other lessons he may get from Karen the Russian professor, the woman in Austin who is keeping the door of this marriage open.

# *Four*

I sit on the floor in front of a fan in Austin, Texas. It is the end of August, the hottest August people around here say they remember, and the house where we live has no air-conditioning. Robert and I flew here last week from New Jersey, my first flight on an American airline, where smiling flight attendants walked around the cabin, offering drinks and serving salad topped with raw mushrooms. Two weeks earlier, I came from the mushroom capital of the world, our dacha thirty kilometers away from Leningrad, where everyone knew that mushrooms must always be cooked. I stared at the tray in front of me, white mushroom slices glaring up from the bowl, menacing in their rawness. No one else seemed alarmed at the prospect of sudden death. A passenger across the aisle leisurely poked at his salad with a plastic fork, and Robert was busy tearing a corner off the small rectangle of oil, ready to pour it onto his mound of poison.

"Can you really eat mushrooms uncooked?" I whispered, not to alarm the other passengers.

Robert turned his head, his stare revealing that my question made no sense to him. "Why not?" he said, shrugging. It was a dismissive shrug, unworthy of someone who had been to our stores and eaten at the Leningrad University cafeteria, with its smells of steamed cabbage and burned sunflower oil, someone who said he understood Russia. But Robert was home now, back in the land of smiling salesclerks and strawberries in December.

I thought—with a sudden sadness—of all those baskets full of wild mushrooms Marina, my mother, and I used to bring from the woods to our dacha every August and September. We would lay the mushrooms out on newspaper spread all over the kitchen floor: the best chocolate brown caps to be sautéed with sour cream or hung over the stove to dry for the winter, long-legged gray caps with slimy tops to use in soups, and purplish second-rate mushrooms with wheel spokes under their caps, only good for salting. Everyone—even the worst hooligan and failing *dvoechnik* in my school—knew you couldn't eat any of them raw.

I turned around to look at the doomed planeload of people, unconcerned about the hazards speared onto the tines of their forks. They were cheerfully thumbing through newspapers and books, chatting. A stewardess was already clearing trays from the front rows, where not a single person was doubled over with pain or beginning to spasm with convulsions. Everyone was still alive.

I poked at the shreds of salad leaves, aiming my fork between the mushroom slices. It was obvious everyone around me knew something I didn't, something they probably learned along with their first letters of the English alphabet. They were all privy to the knowledge that these mushrooms were altogether different— perhaps artificially grown in a hothouse or manufactured in a factory from capitalist synthetics. The only one who didn't know this was me.

But there was another, more depressing truth staring back at me from the bowl with raw mushrooms. I realized that what may have seemed interesting to Robert in Russia—my exotic ignorance—was now silly and annoying, a liability rather than a charm.

∞

Every day, Robert goes to the university, where he researches black holes and teaches math to freshmen. I stay in the house we share with a roommate and sit in front of a fan. Our roommate, Sagar, is in Robert's PhD program, and they leave the house together in Sagar's little Volkswagen when their teaching schedules coincide. Sagar is Indian, born in Bombay, and this makes me think of a typewritten yoga manual I borrowed, when I was eighteen, from tall, blond Anton, who designed posters at the Leningrad House of Friendship and Peace, where I was a secretary. For two years after I met him, I practiced yoga poses in our apartment on a rug in front of an armoire, thinking that I was intrigued by Eastern philosophy and its connection between mind and body, while I was really intrigued by Anton. Dreaming of mastering all the asanas, I imagined traveling to India with him to get close to the yoga teachings and, I hoped, to Anton himself. When I announced I was no longer eating meat, my mother launched into a story of standing on an hour-long line for a stick of bologna—after six hours of teaching anatomy—which was supposed to make me feel guilty for rejecting such a hard-earned offering. For two years I ignored her calls for sanity, picking gristle out of my cabbage soup, until one morning, passing my desk, Anton casually told me that he was leaving for a Crimean vacation with his new friend Raisa. "But what about the yoga?" I wanted to ask, as the air in the room seemed to have turned to lead. Anton, oblivious to my mute question, waved and muttered "so long" while I sat there with my spine stiff and my mouth open, a pose for which my yoga manual had yet to find a name.

Sagar doesn't resemble Anton in any way. He is not tall or blond, and he wears glasses that often slide to the middle of his nose. He speaks with an intonation that rises and falls like the little ripples of ocean surf, and his consonants are all soft, like the fine sand underneath. I don't know if he is interested in yoga or if he eats meat. Except for a bowl of cereal in the morning, he and Robert eat at the university, between their freshman math classes and whatever else they do to advance cosmic research. There, at the university, in addition to the research, Robert writes science fiction books and takes Russian lessons from Karen, whose name he hasn't mentioned even once.

Yesterday Sagar showed me photographs spilling out of an envelope covered with colorful Indian stamps that had arrived in the mail earlier that day. Young women with red dots on their foreheads, serious and coquettish, with deep black eyes, wearing gold-threaded saris, stared from the pictures as if in a beauty contest, waiting to be judged.

"It's my mother," said Sagar. "She has nothing better to do. She sits in her house, trying to find me a wife."

"Really?" I said. I couldn't believe that there were still marriages arranged by parents at the end of the twentieth century, as I couldn't believe that Sagar's mother had managed to occupy a greater area of control than mine.

"She wants me to marry an Indian girl from a good family," said Sagar and smirked. "She thinks I'll be more comfortable with one of our own."

"That's what my mother wanted me to do," I said. "Marry a Russian boy, a nice university graduate. Our own." *Svoi.*

"I'm already too spoiled for one of my own," said Sagar. "My life has moved on, I'm too Western. I wouldn't know what I'd do with any of these girls."

I wondered if Sagar was a bit too cavalier dismissing his Indian-ness, pegging himself so unquestionably into a Western lifestyle. But maybe he wasn't. Maybe, in his years of graduate school, he had already gone through whatever it takes to become American, his brain cells boasting new strings of DNA that didn't relate to women wrapped in saris. Maybe I should ask him for a lesson or two.

"My mother's going to be crushed," he said and shook his head. His glasses sat in the middle of his nose, and his eyes above them glistened with sadness.

"Look at this one," I said, lifting a picture out of the beauty pageant display. "She's ravishing." I turned the picture over and read what was written on the other side. " 'Dipti Kumar. Graduating from Oxford in May.' Graduating from Oxford! You wouldn't know what to do with *her*?"

"You sound like my mother," said Sagar, and it just then hit me that I probably did. Even worse, I sounded like *my* mother, and—because I simultaneously missed and resented my mother—the thought irked me and also made me grin.

&#8451;

In the afternoon I walk to the supermarket, where it is cool, and stare at the endless shelves that climb all the way to the ceiling, parading an infinite number of different brands of frozen pizza, pasta sauce, and flavored yogurts I never knew existed. I have always lived with my family, so I never had to shop for food, or cook, or stretch ten rubles until payday to make five more meals. Back in Leningrad, there was always a pot of something waiting under a pot warmer Marina had sewn from the remnants of cotton she'd collected over the years of making clothes. The pot warmer was made to look like a chicken, with a head and body stuffed with old rags, and underneath I always found sour cabbage soup, or macaroni with ground beef, or grated carrots stewed in tomato sauce, waiting patiently for me to remove the lid and scoop up whatever was there onto a plate my mother had left on the kitchen table, a spoon and fork next to it. Dinners in my kitchen had always been there, like water gurgling out of the faucet, like heat hissing through the radiators under the windows. They were simply a part of life, and it never occurred to me, in the twenty-four years I lived there, to think of where they came from.

Without my mother and sister, the job of shopping and cooking falls on me. I creep past shelves of cut-up beef and pork and poultry sheathed in plastic, feeling I am inside the aquarium again, gazing at the real life through the glass. All that meat—chopped in pieces for your convenience, big and small, displayed on plastic trays called Styrofoam, for soup, or stew, or other recipes I don't know how to make. It was easier to shop in Leningrad: lines always led to food available at the moment, eliminating the necessity of making a choice.

Among all these packages one attracts my attention. It looks like what I once saw under a glass display in Leningrad, although this meat is neatly arranged under plastic, fat and bones removed, rather than tossed onto a bloody sheet of paper hanging off a butcher's scale. It looks luxuriously expensive, although it isn't— something you would normally see at a special Party store if you were a high-ranking official with a pass to get in. I don't know what I am going to do with this hunk of meat, but it looks familiar, so I buy it.

Back in the house, Robert looks at the package I brought. "What is this?" he asks, regarding the meat from above his glasses. "It's chuck or something . . ." he says, wrinkling his nose.

I am not sure if I should feel guilty for not knowing what to buy or if I should tell Robert that at a supermarket the size of the Hermitage I was lucky to have found the meat section at all. Or maybe I should muster up some courage and announce that chuck, whatever it is, was precisely what I had in mind. Should I have asked Robert what he wanted from the supermarket, what he wanted for dinner tonight? Is this what married people—or those pretending to be married—do?

Yet it is clear that Robert saw right to the core of the matter: I have no idea what to do with this meat. I am as inept a shopper as I am a cook—and this might as well be burnt into my forehead. I bought something alien and awful, something only ignorant immigrants could try to turn into a meal in the twilight of their basements.

"What was I supposed to buy?" I ask.

"Minute steak," he says.

At first I'm not sure I heard him right. I'm not sure if he said "minute" or "mini steak." I don't know if he wants a tiny piece of steak or steak that is somehow connected to the clock. The truth, as my mother warned me, is staring me in the face: I've always been *egoistka*, always busy typing banned poetry through four sheets of carbon paper—so that five friends could read books my country wouldn't sanction—instead of learning how to keep house and make *blini*.

I wish Robert, instead of telling me what I should have bought, had gone to the supermarket with me to shed light on all those mysterious cuts of meat. I wish he could tell me about the exhibits in the supermarket Hermitage and the department store Hermitage, the way Nina taught him about Russian verbs, the way I showed him Leningrad courtyards. I wish he would stop practicing his violin, descend from his university lectern, and look at me the same way he used to look at me in Leningrad.

# *Five*

I am at the kitchen table writing a letter home, telling my mother and sister about my roommate's bride candidates from India, when the front door opens and Sagar walks in with a girl. "Roxana," she says as she extends her hand, strong and assertive. Roxana is tall, at least as tall as Sagar, with long, dark hair that falls down her shoulder blades in big, lazy curls. She is definitely not Indian, but not American, either. She speaks with a sharp accent that is different from Sagar's—gliding vowels and harsh *r*'s—an intonation I can't place.

They linger in the living room, and I don't know if I should offer them something to drink. I don't know if I should welcome Roxana into our house or be an indifferent roommate and go back to the room I share with Robert and shut the door. I know what my mother would do—hover over the visitors so she could later complain that they have left dirty footprints all over the hallway or haven't hung up their coats on the hook by the door—so I do the opposite and go to my room. But then I remember Sagar's expression when I saw him standing in the doorway next to Roxana, an expression of his wanting me to see her. As if she were a bride candidate and I were his mother evaluating his choice.

I go back, pretending that I was simply taking a detour on my way to the kitchen to offer them tea. But the idea of tea, something

I would offer guests back home, seems absurd in this heat, and a quick survey of the refrigerator results in my finding only little dregs on the bottom of an orange juice container and a bottle of something called root beer. Cold beer would be all right, I decide, and bring out the bottle and three glasses.

"Would you like some beer?" I ask Sagar and Roxana, who are sitting on the couch leafing through a brochure of the weekly sales I brought from the supermarket. They seem awkward around each other, as if they've just met and don't yet have enough to share.

They nod and I pour. The beer foams in the glasses, as beer should do, but when I take a drink, it is pure formaldehyde rushing up my nostrils, my mother's anatomy department with its organs, bones, and cadavers, distilled into a glass. I gag, spew it back with a noise unworthy of a hostess, and run into the kitchen for paper towels.

When I return, Sagar and Roxana are on their feet, looking bewildered.

"I thought it was beer," I say, feeling like an idiot. "But it smells like formaldehyde."

They smile, smelling their drinks, not finding anything unusual about root beer. It occurs to me that they have never come in contact with formaldehyde, that no one but me could have such a visceral dislike of root beer, that our reactions are triggered by bits of memory that float under the radar of consciousness, moving us still further apart from one another.

"Where are you from?" I ask Roxana as I wipe the table and the floor.

"Cuba," she says. "Havana, the capital," she adds. When she says "Havana," a spark of pride glints in her eyes, the same little flame that burns in my throat when I say "Leningrad."

"See," I tell Sagar, who can't stop staring at Roxana with a soft, unprotected gaze. "Cuba and Russia. This is a plot. You're surrounded by communists."

∞

My mother would be happy, I think, to find all this order, *poryadok*, here. No one jumps in front of you on a line because there are no lines. Buses course along their routes, with no passengers hanging out of their doors. Stores are brimming with products and all you need to do is buy them.

Yet everything was more understandable back home. All emotions were out in the open, from salespeople's resentment to bureaucrats' indifference. With the absence of social courtesy, you knew when a cashier had had a bad day because she gave you a stony stare and angrily tossed the change into a plastic tray when it took you longer than a second to open your wallet. You knew that a saleswoman in a stained white gown thought you brazenly overstepped your bounds when she glared at your request to slice your half a kilo of bologna. "Slice it?" she would repeat to the people waiting on line, inviting them to join in teaching you a lesson. "Would you also like me to wash your dirty underwear?" she would ask, fists on her hips. You got the message that a wiry babushka behind you on a bus was getting off when her elbow knifed into your kidney. Things were clearly delineated so we always knew what to expect. We felt happy when we were handed the log of bologna we would wrap in newspaper and carefully place in a string bag next to a loaf of black bread, still warm. We could easily slice them both at home, after all.

Rudeness was ordinary and familiar, a way of life adopted by people who were continuously deprived of the most basic things. Salesclerks glowered and customers cowered. Bureaucrats ordered and the rest of us complied. Life was predictable if you played the pretending game called *vranyo*, the game I learned in nursery school from Aunt Polya, who was in charge of the kitchen and who wasn't really my aunt. She loomed over us with a pitcher of warm milk and slices of buttered bread that had absorbed all the rancid smells of the kitchen, watching closely to make sure we ate and drank properly. We all knew she was watching us, she knew that we knew, and we knew she knew that we knew. She gave us surprise glances, and we chewed diligently, pretending we didn't expect her to look.

We all played the game: my parents played it at work and my sister Marina played it at school. We all pretended to do something, and those who watched us pretended that they were seriously watching us and didn't know we were only pretending. Life was simple if you sliced your soul in half, as you were supposed to. One half—for yourself, your family, and your close friends; the other—for all the salesclerks, teachers, and officials, who didn't need to know what you thought.

I have a sense that there is a different reality here simmering underneath all this sterility and order, a life bubbling under the courtesy and politeness. This liquid center, red and hot, is the heart that pumps blood to make it all work, to motivate what people do here. That heart is still months away, hidden deep under protective layers of tissue and bone, and I am not at all sure if I'll ever see it.

છ

I am in a pizzeria, standing next to Sagar and Roxana. Slices behind the counter are hot, cheesy, and cheap, and the toppings kept in metal containers personalize every order, making me think I am eating something different from what I had yesterday. Sagar's eyes are also fixed on the onions and peppers behind the glass, but I know he is thinking about something else because his glasses are down at the tip of his nose and his eyebrows are mashed together in a frown. A letter arrived from India yesterday and, instead of sending more bride pictures, his mother announced that she was coming to Austin to see him and discuss the matter in person. "She's already bought a ticket," said Sagar in a grave voice. "She still thinks I'm twelve."

The only two people interested in pizza toppings are Roxana and a three-year-old girl in front of us, whose mother has picked her up so the girl can see the containers. "What do you want on your pizza, sweetie?" asks the woman. "Olives? Pepperoni? Mushrooms?" she says, pointing to each one.

I don't know why the woman is asking a three-year-old what she wants to eat. I don't know what a three-year-old can possibly know about pizza toppings. Isn't it up to her mother to make these decisions? Back in Leningrad, I ate what was left for me under the chicken pot warmer. I think of my nursery school again and of Aunt Polya, her eyebrows penciled in carbon, who made us sit at tables pushed together and drink warm milk out of thick ribbed glasses. "Eat your soup, Gorokhova, or you'll die!" she shouted in her kitchen voice you could hear all the way on the street.

"Do olives look good?" the mother in the pizzeria line persists. "Or would you rather have sausage?"

I sympathize with the girl, who leans over the counter, peering through the glass, trying to figure out if green peppers trump meatballs. Wouldn't she be happier with toppings her mother ordered, not burdened with having to examine the containers, safe in the knowledge that her mother knows what she needs?

I think of my own mother, an apron with flowers over her housedress, cranking the metal handle of a meat grinder until its face erupts in red twists of beef squeezing into a bowl underneath. She adds egg and stale bread softened in water, mashes the mixture with a fork, and from her palms come perfect ovals of *kotlety* she drops into a frying pan, where they begin to brown and sizzle. Now I know why I bought that package of meat Robert hated: it looked like what my mother used to stuff down the throat of the meat grinder for *kotlety*, infrequently available and juicy, stored in a red pot on the refrigerator's top shelf, one per person for the next three days.

"Mushrooms," the girl says. "And pepperoni. And olives. And extra cheese."

The mother orders, and I can hear in her voice that she knows her daughter won't eat all the toppings she says she wants.

"Did your mother give you all these choices?" I whisper to Roxana.

She shakes her head and sighs. "I wish she was here now to choose the toppings for me. She would choose meatballs, I think. Just like the ones she used to make." The self-confidence I've been envying in Roxana has evaporated, and her eyes have turned fragile, pooled with sadness. Roxana and Sagar are both pensive and serious now, for reasons that are diametrically opposite. One is dreading his mother's visit; the other longs for her mother to be close.

And what about me? I am here because I married Robert—someone I knew for a total of four weeks, someone I thought I was in love with—to escape both my mother and my Motherland.

When my turn comes, I don't ask for any toppings. Plain, I say. Plain as our Leningrad kitchen, as our store counters, as our food. Plain as my realization that I am—and will always be—a stranger here.

# Six

R obert says I must look for a job. He is a graduate student and his stipend from the university barely pays our rent.

"How do I look for a job?" I ask him.

"Classifieds," he says and goes back to leafing through his notebook.

I don't know what classifieds are or where to find them.

"Look in the newspaper," Robert says, reading my puzzled face. "That's where they advertise job openings."

The idea of looking for a job in a newspaper makes me giggle. The newspapers I am familiar with are *Pravda* and *Izvestiya*— *Truth* and *News*—and there is an old joke about no truth in the *News* and no news in the *Truth*. Both papers fill every line of their four pages with articles about the biggest-ever harvests of grain in the Ukraine or the worst-ever unemployment anywhere west of Bulgaria. They offer imperious descriptions of NATO's bullying tactics and fiery accusations of fraudulent voting in Latin American countries that don't celebrate Cuban Liberation Day. On the bottoms of their last pages, they pour salt on the Zionist ulcers of Israel, where at least ten of my friends now reside. Everyone knows that newspapers report news, real or concocted, to enlighten and educate the citizens about current politics. Why would they lower themselves to such an inglorious function as listing job openings?

The next day Robert brings home a paper called *The Austin Times* to show me the classifieds. We lean over the tiny print announcing available positions: a certified teacher for grades K–5 (what kind of grade is K?); a manager for a restaurant (experience required); a receptionist for Texas Instruments (apply in person).

I don't know what a receptionist is, but I imagine a big factory called Texas Instruments, not unlike the secret boat factory with no hint of any boats where I worked for two months after high school. I copied drafts of what could only be warship design and carried them to production rooms with bawdy men who whistled when I passed.

"Go there and apply in person," Robert says. "It isn't far from the university," he adds, looking at the address. "A few blocks north of the student union."

"What's a receptionist?" I ask, although I don't know what a student union is, either.

"A receptionist?" he repeats incredulously, as if I'd asked him what a shoe or a slice of bread is. "It's a secretary, basically. Someone who says 'May I help you' when you call on the phone with a question or a complaint."

I am terrified of making phone calls, always expecting to be admonished for thinking that dialing a set of numbers from home could resolve an issue or answer a question. And what kind of perverse justice would place me on the other side of this exchange, without making me mute and paralyzed with fear?

But Robert doesn't know this. He has an American brain that is not wired to harbor phone paranoia, so I pretend that I want to be a receptionist and am not at all petrified by the possibility of answering questions or mediating phone complaints from the Texas Instruments customers who speak an English I can barely understand.

Robert doesn't know this and I feel I shouldn't tell him since I already hear a trace of irritation in his voice. He is busy and doesn't have time, his tone seems to say, for such mundane things as food shopping or helping me to find a job, or simply holding my hand and telling me everything will be all right.

၄

The next day I walk to a bus stop and wait for a bus to take me to Texas Instruments. I stand outside the glass bus shelter, hoping to catch a sigh of wind. A bus appears from around the corner and roars past without slowing down. This seems odd, but maybe it is off duty, I think. Ten minutes later, another bus appears and, just like the first one, rolls past the bus stop, washing the little shelter with scorching fumes. A doubt creeps into my head: Is this really a bus stop and not a rain shelter? Do American buses make their rounds at off-peak hours? Do I look so different they don't want to allow me onboard? When the third bus leaves me there standing in its wake, I begin to suspect that the reason these buses refuse to stop here must be me. I imagine these bus drivers taking one look at me—standing there alone, scared, in a sundress my sister had sewn out of a batch of Soviet cotton with a blue cornflower print—and knowing immediately I look undeserving of an air-conditioned American bus ride. Maybe they can even tell I resent interviewing for a receptionist's job.

I unfold my Austin pocket map, find Texas Instruments, and start walking. I walk for about an hour, the top of my sundress drenched with sweat. When the Texas Instruments sign finally appears in the distance, I walk past a field of gleaming cars, past a bed with straggly flowers, past a building with no signs that doesn't look like a factory. There is no one to ask directions. Whatever Texas Instruments is, it is eerily empty and quiet outside, as if this were a Ray Bradbury story and the entire population had been wiped out by the poisonous gas of an alien invasion—everybody except me, an alien.

Doors have no signs; windows are covered with uniform blinds.

Could this be a secret factory, after all? I summon up all my courage and push open one of the doors. The temperature drops thirty degrees, and I am in a corridor with more doors and a man in a suit waiting by an elevator.

"Excuse me," I say sheepishly, both glad and uneasy to see a human being. "Where do I apply in person?"

The man stares at me, his hard eyes on my sweaty sundress.

I pull *The Austin Times* out of my bag and point to the receptionist ad.

"Oh, Personnel," he says and points to the depth of the corridor. "Room 153." As I start walking, I can sense the man's disdainful stare on my back.

A woman in her forties with rich blond hair points to a chair on the other side of her desk. In her gray eyes gleams the same bemused contempt I saw in the suited man near the elevator. She is wearing a tailored blouse and a gold bracelet, her nails as red as her lipstick, and the homemade sundress I considered elegant enough to lug to the other side of the Atlantic suddenly looks unseemly in this office with the strange name *Personnel*.

The woman, coldly polite, asks me to fill out a one-page form. She doesn't ask what skills I have to be a receptionist. She doesn't ask me anything, not even the standard question of where I come from, because my sundress must have already answered all her inquiries.

&

Back home I tell Robert about my bus and my interview fiasco.

"Did you flag down the bus?" he asks.

"I was standing at the bus stop," I say. "Who else would be standing at a bus stop except someone waiting for a bus?"

Robert puts his arm around my shoulder and draws me closer, but it's an awkward gesture and I almost trip. He looks uncomfortable, as if he knows he needs to hold me but doesn't know how.

"*Bednaya devochka,*" he says in Russian, "you poor girl."

It feels good to be called *bednaya devochka*, despite the fact that I'm balancing on one foot, ready to tip over. It feels good to think that it is Texas Instruments's loss not to hire me as their reception-ist, that I would have probably gotten the job if I'd known how to flag down a bus.

"You know what?" says Robert and releases his embrace. "Let's celebrate your first interview. Let's go out."

I am just about to open my mouth and say that there is nothing to celebrate, but Robert has a gleam in his eyes, the look he wears when he has made a decision. I like this look, and it makes me forget about the nonstop buses and the frosty offices of Texas Instruments.

He asks Sagar to borrow his Volkswagen and we drive to some-where in the center of Austin, a place where stores are so clumped together that people don't have to walk outside in the heat. All the buildings are low and tidy, just like the center of Washington. Eye-pleasing and functional.

We park and I follow Robert to a place called Olives. A young woman seats us at a small table near a window. She is long-limbed and beautiful, and I can't believe that a perfect specimen like this has to host in a restaurant rather than open programs on television.

"What's the only thing worse than being dead in Texas?" asks Robert when the woman departs, and from the way his mouth crin-kles at the corners I know it's a joke. I make big eyes and shrug, to play along.

"Being ugly." Robert chuckles, pleased with his sense of humor.

The woman comes to our table to take our order, stunning in her faultlessness, and I feel even worse than I did before: I don't have her beauty; I can't speak English as she does, natively; and I'm not as friendly and charming, in either language.

I can't decipher the dishes Olives has to offer, so I close the menu and ask Robert to order for me.

Fifteen minutes later a plate arrives with something full of red sauce smothered with melted cheese.

"Lasagna," announces Robert proudly.

I start eating the lasagna carefully, poking with a knife and fork under all those mysterious layers.

"How is it?" asks Robert, and because it was his choice I say I love it. He nods, satisfied, and focuses on his own plate, chewing his chicken with total self-absorption, the same way he seems to deal with people. Concentrated on himself, turned inward. He moves his head from side to side rhythmically, as if replaying in his mind Berlioz's *Symphonie Fantastique,* which he was listening to when I returned from my failed job search.

We eat silently, and the perfect woman removes the ruins of our dinner.

# *Seven*

Robert says I should go to an agency.

"An agency?" I ask.

"They'll help you find a job," he says and sighs.

I try to imagine what Robert could be thinking right now, a painstaking and ungrateful task. A little less than a year ago, he nobly offered to marry a Russian to save her from the clutches of the Soviet state. He was going to bring her to the land of capitalism and freedom, where she would immediately feel at ease since she was already fluent in English. She would live with him for the first few months before she'd find a teaching job, helping him with his Russian grammar and pronunciation, listening to him practice the violin, cooking minute steak. Maybe she would even continue to live with him, providing Karen the Russian professor didn't mind this arrangement, providing the new foreign wife didn't become a stone around his neck, dragging him down the slope of routine existence from the heights of classical music and cosmic research.

She seemed mature and independent, cynical of the Soviet circus around her, eager and ready to make a new life. She seemed learned and well read. He thought she would look around, get used to the eight-hour time difference, and plunge into the culture, just like he did on his six-week stay in Leningrad.

All by himself, last summer he ventured into a *gastronom* near the university dorm in search of yogurt, puzzling the potbellied woman behind the counter, who didn't seem to know the word. He was pronouncing it correctly, he was sure of that, rolling the tongue against his front upper teeth, just as his Swarthmore professor had taught him. Nevertheless, the woman stared at him with annoyance, her arms folded across her stained, white-coated stomach. Yogurt, he repeated again, only to watch her shrug and turn away. He found another store and asked again because he was persistent and unafraid. He even befriended a black marketeer who had approached him at a metro station entrance, asking to exchange dollars into rubles at a rate of one to three. The black marketeer, Valery, invited him to his apartment at the end of the metro line, where his wife was doing the laundry in a Finnish washing machine—Valery's pride—parked in the living room, which, as it turned out, wasn't really a living room but a bedroom with a folding table and a sleeper couch against the wall. There are no living rooms in Russia, said Valery, a little culture lesson Robert immediately tucked away.

A year later, back in Austin, Robert couldn't understand why this Russian he brought here wasn't asking questions, making friends, trying to blend in. He felt disappointed in her. He felt trapped. How could a smart, English-speaking woman with a green card and a roof over her head not be able to figure out how to find a job or what to buy in a supermarket to make dinner? A supermarket so much better stocked than any yogurt-deficient *gastronom* in Leningrad.

ဢ

In a room with fat folders stacked on shelves along the walls, I sit on the other side of one of the four desks. Across from me is a woman with hurried movements and nervous eyes, a cup of coffee next to the form she's filling out, a pencil she is holding like a cigarette in her left hand.

"First you have to sign this," she says and points to the bottom of a page filled with tiny single-spaced print.

I try to read a few lines, but the words refuse to make sense. "What is it?" I ask.

"Just a standard agreement," says the woman. "You agree to pay the agency your first paycheck and ten percent of your salary thereafter for a year."

I have no idea if this is a regular practice in employment agencies or a ploy to enslave a newcomer ignorant of the rules. I don't know what constitutes a paycheck here or how much people make. I run my eyes over the document again, the words staring back at me in their indiscernible force, like linked rows of black fences. With her fixed gaze, the woman lets me know that at this moment my possible future employment hinges on my signature, so I pick up a pen and sign my name at the bottom of the page.

"Good girl," she says, plucking the paper away. As she files it into a folder, I see a small name plaque on the desk, STELLA CONROY. With her nervous eyes and nails bitten down to the flesh of her fingertips, she doesn't look like a Stella.

"What are your skills?" she asks me.

From her dismissive voice it is immediately obvious she knows that I don't possess the skills required in the application. What are my skills? I was a lab assistant in my mother's anatomy department, where I pulled rabbits out of their cages in the basement, strapped them to a centrifuge, and spun them at near cosmic speed as a contribution to animal research for the Soviet space program. I shuffled work orders at the Leningrad House of Friendship and Peace and wrote phony letters to get myself out of the university exams on Scientific Communism. I taught English at Leningrad University and Russian at the summer program where I met Robert.

"I can teach English grammar," I say to Stella Conroy.

She stops fidgeting with her pencil, takes a sip of her coffee, and tosses the cup into a wastebasket under her desk. "Can you type?" she asks.

I think of my Erika portable typewriter probably still sitting on my desk in Leningrad. But this woman is obviously not interested in my Russian typing skills. Can I type in English? Since typewriters with Latin keyboards were as scarce as copying machines in the Soviet Union, the answer should be no.

"Yes, I can," I say.

"How many words per minute?" she asks, her pen hovering over a box in the form.

I don't know if I can type at all, and I certainly don't know how many words a minute I'd type if I could.

I shake my head and shrug.

"Forty? Fifty? Sixty?" she offers, impatient to put a number in the box.

I try to calculate in my mind how fast that would make me type. A word a second seems meteoric, especially considering I am not familiar with the keyboard.

"Twenty or thirty," I say. "Maybe."

Stella sways the pencil in her left hand, looking at it longingly, as if it were a cigarette. She puts down her pen, gets up, and reaches for one of the files on the shelf above her desk.

"Here's a spelling test," she says, pulling a page out of a thick file. "Cross out all incorrect spellings."

I stare at the two columns of words on the page. The first one is *verbatim*, a word I've never seen. It doesn't look like an English word to me, so I cross it out. As my eyes run down the columns of words, I realize that I don't know about one third of them.

Stella looks at the page I hand her and says I didn't pass.

"Can you do anything else except typing?" she asks.

I can teach English grammar, I want to say, but I don't.

�

When I get back to the house, I squeeze into the corner of the couch and stare at a linoleum square by a coffee table leg, then out the window, where a couple of rickety bushes separate the front of the house from the empty street. This house in Austin is as quiet as our dacha near Leningrad, but infinitely more sterile. I can't believe that I am almost longing for our dacha, the place where I spent every spring Sunday ankle-deep in cold, soggy dirt, turning up beds for future cucumbers and dill with a spade rusted over the winter, yanking dandelions out of strawberry bushes later in June, lugging string bags full of apples to our Leningrad apartment to make jam for the winter. Why am I even thinking about that shack? Maybe because it was the deep well of smells that still tingle my nostrils: mushrooms we picked in the woods and spread on newspaper on the kitchen floor, strawberries sighing in big copper pots on the wood-burning kitchen stove, moldy sheets that survived a long winter in a house without heat.

This town, Austin, is flat and antiseptic, a padlocked gate with no chinks between the boards to peek inside the fence. It is just like Robert—impenetrable and foreign. All these immaculate roads, one-story houses, and bushes scorched by the heat may as well be scenery in a play about life on another planet, one of those alien universes Robert invents in his science fiction stories. It feels like a bad dream I've had so many times: the curtain opens, I am onstage, and no words come out of my mouth because I don't know my part.

# *Eight*

To do all this walking I need a pair of sneakers, says Robert. He points to the white and blue shoes he wears to walk to the university every morning. Sneakers, he repeats, so I'll know what to ask for when I get to a store.

After peering into the windows of several stores on a shopping street near the university, I finally see sneakers displayed on a wall in orderly rows. The store is small, and a man behind the counter looks bored. He springs into action when I ask him for sneakers, size seven and a half, vanishing into the back of the store, then reappearing with the pair I've selected. He is cheerful, his balding head gleaming under the neon light. I don't know why I chose sneakers with white and green stripes made of what looks like suede; maybe they reminded me of the shoes I once glimpsed in a magazine called *England* left open on my boss's desk at the Leningrad House of Friendship and Peace.

The salesman points to a stool for me to sit down on as he kneels, a sneaker in his palm like an offering. Please, I plead silently, don't put these shoes on my feet. I am not ready for this, having just arrived from a land that had no shoes at all. Twenty-four years of nothing have warped me, and now I am stupefied by all this enthusiasm and kneeling.

The man takes hold of my foot and slides on the shoe.

I walk around the store, supple suede enveloping my feet.

"They look great!" exclaims the man, watching me turn in front of a store mirror.

I think so, too, but how do I ask him about the price? When do customers ask salespeople here how much a product costs? Should I have asked before he knelt in front of me, thus possibly preventing all this cheerful prancing around?

As soon as I take off the white and green sneakers, the man scoops them up and puts them back in the box. "Terrific," he cries out, another word I don't know. "So we're all set here," he says and heads toward the cash register.

I can no longer delay the agony. "How much are they?" I ask.

He looks at the box label. "Forty-four ninety-five."

I open my Russian wallet, not big enough for dollar bills, and examine its contents. One twenty, three fives, and a couple of singles. I pour the bills onto the counter where the man is already writing out a receipt. "This is all I have," I force myself to utter.

The man stops writing and looks at me as if I've suddenly turned into Grishka, a drunk with a battered face who used to sleep under my Leningrad courtyard archway. He picks up the bills and counts them, already knowing that it is eight dollars less than the amount on the box. There is annoyance in his eyes, but also suspicion.

"Don't you have a credit card?" he asks curtly.

I don't know what he's talking about.

"Visa?" he says and peers from above his glasses.

"I have a visa," I assure him. "I am a resident alien," I say and pull out my green card.

The man throws up his hands in frustration, probably lamenting the moment he knelt before me, his balding head glistening with drops of sweat. I feel guilty for entering this place, for sauntering before a mirror in sneakers I couldn't afford.

"Take them," sputters the man, nodding toward the box. "And go," he adds and waves me out of his store.

I walk home slowly, the box with the sneakers weighing on my arm, a reminder of the most recent humiliation. The streets are empty, and people only come outside when they leave the stores and stride through the heat to their cars. I walk and walk until a car pulls to a stop a few feet ahead. The driver rolls down the window, and a whiff of arctic air escapes together with the man's voice.

"Do you want a ride?" he asks and smiles, baring his perfect teeth. He is sun-tanned and middle-aged, and in my mind he fits perfectly into the empty corridors of Texas Instruments. No one in Leningrad, I know, would bother to pull over their Lada or Moskvich and offer a ride to a total stranger lumbering through one of the hottest days of the decade. They would all be busy honking at streetcars and pedestrians, asserting their rights among fume-spewing public buses and state-owned trucks with creaky cabs and wobbling tires. Austin cars don't have to worry about any of this, gliding on roads that don't look like jagged slabs of concrete tossed together by a deranged giant, on tires with enough tread to take them all the way to New Jersey, with windshield wipers that don't have to be removed once the car is parked, as a precaution against theft.

I know, of course, that the man is not a kind stranger looking to give rides to foreigners on foot. From the way the tip of his tongue touches the corner of his mouth I can tell what he really wants.

"Thank you, but I don't have too far to go," I lie.

"Where are you from?" asks the man, leaning his elbow on the open window. "England?" he ventures, squinting a little. "Scandinavia?"

Despite the man's pedestrian intentions, I wish I could say I were from Britain or Sweden.

"Russia," I say. "Leningrad. Former St. Petersburg," I add because the man is just staring at me, silent. His fingers stop rapping on the window frame, and I can read nothing behind his watery gray, foreign eyes.

"Well, as you wish," he finally says and rolls up his window.

As the car starts moving, I see him gazing at me in the rearview mirror.

I stand there, awash in the exhaust fumes, as his car turns a corner and disappears from view. The street is completely empty now, the low evening sun burning its last rays onto the brown patches of grass. I start walking again, the only human soul as far as I can see. I walk one block, then the next, and then another one, as if I were in a science fiction film, a survivor of an attack aimed at the entire humanity traveling by foot. I see myself the way the man in the car must have seen me—unmoored, unattached to a vehicle, utterly alone.

# Nine

Robert asks if we could read a Russian book together. To practice his Russian, he says. This is a good sign, I think, that he is asking for Russian practice. Maybe it means he hasn't been seeing Karen.

Robert never mentions Karen, and I never ask. Yet, in my mind, she is always there with us, somewhere in the corner of the room, quietly observing everything that goes on, like an ever-present ghost. I can't quite make out her features or pull her into focus. But I know that she sits there and watches us: undressing in the dark, fumbling for each other dutifully, making ordinary love. Her presence is palpable and discomforting; she is a membrane between Robert and me, like a full-body prophylactic that keeps this relationship sterile of emotion. Without ever seeing her, I hate her.

I sit on a couch in the living room and try to think what parts of Russian grammar Karen would teach Robert. But instead I think of my courtyard friend Masha, the object of my childhood envy, who went to a special English school and who lived in an apartment with a living room. My Leningrad apartment had two rooms where we slept and a kitchen, where we ate. The idea of a room with no apparent function and a coffee table where no one drank coffee seemed truly decadent, and I was jealous of Masha's English skills and her apartment luxury. Should I feel happy now, sitting on a couch in a rented living room on the foreign side of the world?

Robert lingers in front of a shelf, picks a book, and sits down close so we can both see the text. CHEKHOV, I read on the front. PLAYS. As he turns the pages to *The Three Sisters*, I don't know if I should correct his pronunciation like a diligent teacher or cheer his fluency and ignore a foreign accent, like a supportive wife. Which role should I now play? Since Robert wasn't in my class in the Leningrad Russian Program, I don't even know how good his Russian reading is. But then I don't know most things about Robert.

He turns the pages and stops at a scene in Act 2. "This work is without poetry, without thought," he reads Irina's words. "My dear God, I dream of Moscow every night; I've almost lost my mind."

"I've almost lost my mind," I repeat to accentuate the palatalized consonants but also to add the drama and urgency missing from his voice. "We will be in Moscow," I continue, jumping to the next scene.

"In Moscow," repeats Robert, trying to flatten his tongue against the roof of his mouth, as Nina taught him last summer in her phonetics class.

"Softer," I say, "softer. And the stress is on the end, like in the word *toska*," a word I think of but don't translate for him.

This is what gnaws at the three sisters all the time, even when their cheerful military friends come calling with stories about their past, cherished life in Moscow. The sisters wallow in *toska*, wearing black dresses, loving inappropriately, and cowering before a new sister-in-law who blossoms from a shy philistine to a full-fledged bully by the time the sisters realize that there is no escape. How could the provincial town where they live, a place with one school and one post office and no one to talk to, compare to the culture and splendor of the city they left behind?

*Toska*, I say so that Robert hears how the *o* sounds like an *a* because the stress falls on the end of the word.

"Definition of *toska*?" Robert asks, ready to file the meaning into a compartment of his scientific brain.

If I could recite the definition of *toska*, in English or Russian, there would probably be no Chekhov or *The Three Sisters,* or the entire pantheon of Russian literature Robert is so keen on deciphering. It is a paradox, really: for him to understand Russian literature, he needs to know the definition of *toska*, while it is precisely trying to shoehorn *toska* into a definition that guarantees the failure of that understanding.

*Toska* is a combination of melancholy and longing, I say. It's a deep sadness and the awareness that something has been lost. It's what you find in every Russian book published before 1917, I explain, the year when melancholy and sadness were outlawed in favor of general optimism and enthusiasm for our bright future. But there are also other ingredients in *toska* for which I don't have words, things submerged deeply under the layers of silt on the soft bottom of the Russian soul.

What does Robert think of me? I can't read much behind his thick-lens glasses, behind his all-day absence at the university doing research that is as dark to me as the cosmic matter he is studying. Should I sit in on a freshman class he teaches and try to understand his personality along with the basics of college math? Or maybe I should buy some real beer, catch Sagar off guard one evening, and ask him for any insight on his roommate he can offer?

I know one thing about Robert: he doesn't seem to need people. He spent a year in Afghanistan on his own, without human contact, if you don't count a local doctor who wanted to inject him with a rusty syringe when he was bitten by a scorpion. Robert seems to treat people the same way he wants to be treated himself: he leaves them alone. In our first week in Princeton, he invited two high school friends to his mother's house, a small gathering Millie and I planned together. Half an hour after they arrived Robert disappeared—a grave offense at any Russian party, leaving before the guests get tipsy enough to forget about the host. I went up and down the stairs, looking in every room of the house, until I found him on the third floor sitting under the rafters in a rocking chair, thinking. I don't remember what I said—what could I possibly say, still in a fog of jet lag and culture shock? He just sat there, rocking slightly, legs crossed, glasses in his lap. I thought frantically of what I was going to tell his friends downstairs. I thought that if I were in their place I would leave and never see him again.

I probably said something like "Your friends are downstairs to see you. Why are you here, in the attic?"

"Because they bore me," Robert probably answered.

"But you invited them," I said, and he simply shrugged, going back inside his head, where more exciting things were happening.

ꙮ

Back in Leningrad, Robert had seemed as mysterious as the world he came from. He was a writer with a published novel, a violin player, a lover of the Russian language. He was also a physicist who understood cosmic laws, which made him as enigmatic as the world he had invented on the page. Robert had met Sakharov on his previous trip to Moscow. He'd read more Russian classics in the original than any neighbor I knew in our apartment building. But my knees had never gone weak when I looked at him. So I felt guilty when, a week after I tutored him in Chekhov, he tried to resuscitate our nonexisting chemistry by filling a bathtub with pine-smelling, bubbly water and inviting me to join him. The whole room smelled of spruce, and it made me think of our New Year in Leningrad—a white sheet of fake snow under a three-foot scrawny tree, a bottle of sweet champagne called Sovietskoye, and the midnight glow of a television that softened my mother's face and made everything seem right. The Austin tub was too small for two people, Robert and I splashing awkwardly, soaking the bathroom mat with water.

I thought of my gut melting when Boris from Kiev rolled up a blanket and we climbed into the mountains in the Crimea during one month we spent on a remote Black Sea beach. Boris's eyes were so blue that a silly smile stretched across my lips every time he looked in my direction. He had a cinnamon tan and hair bleached by the sun to peroxide white, and I felt happy standing on a cliff, watching his body through the green prism of water shimmering along the rocks as he hunted for crabs. It was simple being with Boris, as uncomplicated as elbowing in line for tomatoes at a local store, as basic as living on the beach.

I thought of Robert's former girlfriend's apartment in Manhattan, where we spent a night just a month ago. The former girlfriend and her husband both worked for some American corporations, so we saw them only late that night, when we came back after walking up and down the city. Robert and I slept on the living room floor, turned away from each other, pretending we didn't hear the former girlfriend and her husband's lovemaking behind a thin wall only ten feet away.

I felt guilty for not being more attracted to Robert, for not loving him with every nerve ending of my body, the same way I loved Boris. By the time the water in the bathtub cooled, I felt guilty for saying farewell to Boris on a slushy Leningrad street, for abandoning my mother and sister, for leaving behind the curved façades and lace ironwork of Leningrad. I felt guilty for leaving my father lying in the cemetery on the other side of the Neva under the snow and rain, with Baltic winds slowly erasing his picture from the headstone. By the time I climbed out and dried off, I felt so guilty that the only right thing to do seemed to be to pack my sundress and my sandals and get on the first flight back home.

The truth was I didn't even know what awaited me back home if I decided to return. What if Boris had been right when he tried, just before my scheduled wedding with Robert, to convince me not to leave the country? He ignored his Kiev engineering duties and rushed all the way to Leningrad to tell me I was making a terrible mistake. "You'd be marked," he warned, as we were sitting in a

Georgian restaurant on Nevsky Prospekt, gulping champagne, then cognac. "Nobody would want to be around you. Even your closest friends." The dizzier I got from the cognac the more eerie his words felt, until I saw myself as *vrag naroda*, enemy of the people. I'll be just like my mother's uncle Volya, who was arrested in 1937 and never heard from again, I thought, as we staggered out into the icy wind of Nevsky Prospekt. I'll be a person with a dubious past and certainly one without a future.

# *Ten*

Soon after my employment agency fiasco, I find work in a small sandwich shop owned by a young man from Vietnam. He is my age, or a few years older, perhaps, and he has probably also been damaged by his communist motherland. Yet his smile is open and his movements unstrained, and he walks around his just-about-to-be-opened eatery as if he has never heard of a state factory cafeteria or a five-year plan. His name is Truong, but he tells everyone he is Terry. Terry is easier, he says, for Americans.

Maybe Terry is right and I should also tweak my name and introduce myself as Helen, or Elaine, or Ellen, which is easier for Americans. And what about my patronymic of Ilyinichna, written into documents as my middle name, as unpronounceable as Gorokhova?

Terry and I get the place ready: he composes the menu and brings loads of paper products, and I mop the floor. His older sister, whose name is Fuoc, comes to help, introducing herself as Fanny.

"Nice to meet you," I say to her, proud to use the phrase I have just learned.

Fanny smiles and tells me to go clean the toilet because she just inspected it and found some rust stains. She says something in Vietnamese, pointing at the dining area, and Terry obediently walks around the counter where he was drawing pictures of his sandwiches on a billboard and starts moving the tables closer together. I don't know what Fanny did when she was Fuoc, but I imagine her in the Leningrad House of Friendship and Peace, where I worked at eighteen, giving orders to everyone below her in rank, just like Tatiana Vasilievna, the coordinator of the English-speaking countries and thus of the entire civilized world. Every morning, Tatiana Vasilievna sailed into the reception area, where I sat behind a desk, and handed thick batches of paper to the typist and reams of unneeded advice to everyone who happened to be there.

I go to the bathroom to scrub the toilet. I am on my knees, leaning on the sponge because the rust stains don't want to disappear. The more I rub the lower my spirits plunge until they can't plunge any lower.

"How you doing?" asks Fanny. I look up at her where she stands, framed by the bathroom doorway, with the dining room lights bright behind her, as though posing for a portrait.

For a moment, I consider letting Fanny know exactly how I'm doing and what it feels like to kneel in front of a rusty toilet bowl, being ordered around by a Tatiana Vasilievna from Vietnam. But then I think of my previous job searches and say that I'm doing fine.

A few days later, Terry and I stand behind the glass counter and take orders. The pictures of his sandwiches, along with their descriptions, are on the wall behind us, drawn meticulously by Terry's artistic hand. I am grateful that the sandwiches are numbered; I still don't understand American pronunciation, so different from what I heard on my university tapes recorded by British professors.

For a week, there is a line to our counter at lunchtime. Terry whistles unfamiliar tunes when he smokes in the back and asks me if Americans eat sandwiches for dinner. Should I stay open till ten? he wonders.

I don't know if Americans eat sandwiches for dinner. Until a week ago, I didn't even know they ate sandwiches for lunch. I know that Terry is ignoring the fact that I am not an American and he couldn't have found a more uninformed listener to test his business plan.

But I like Terry's drawings and I'd never tell him what I really think. I don't want to disappoint him, so I answer his question the way he wants me to.

"Sure," I say. "You can stay open for dinner. These are excellent sandwiches. I could eat them all day long," I add, another lie. This feels like the old Soviet *vranyo*—the pretending game we played with the state. I wonder if Terry had to play the same game in Vietnam. I wonder if he knows that I am pretending, praising his sandwiches as my favorite food; I wonder if he knows that I know that he knows I am not telling the truth.

I pretend. Five days a week I pretend to be excited about sandwiches. In the stores I pretend to examine the products as if I knew what to do with them. I pretend Robert is the same Robert he was in Leningrad. I pretend there is no Karen. If I look at my present job as a role, it makes it easier to feel okay when Fanny shows up and orders me to move the tables around or mop the floor or rub the glass surface of the display case until it sparkles.

As our lunch lines grow shorter, she shows up more frequently and orders me to do more cleaning and moving. Terry goes outside to smoke more often, especially when she is around. He paints a sign that says 50% OFF WITH COUPON and adds another sandwich to the menu, a fluffy concoction where the main ingredient is whipped cream. I don't know what a coupon is, but the sign, despite its unquestionable artistic value, fails to bring people to the store.

Two weeks later, there are no lines at all. For a day we sit at one of the tables staring at the front door. It opens once or twice, not enough to wipe the frown off Terry's forehead.

The next day Fanny shows up and tells me they no longer need help.

෨

The first and only paycheck I received from the sandwich shop had a three-digit figure on the front, $162.46, the biggest dollar sum I've ever seen. From the way Robert's face lit up when I handed it to him I knew I could no longer stay home, look at the pictures of Sagar's brides, and watch horror films on TV.

Across the street from Terry's sandwich shop is Milto's Pizzeria. When I worked at Terry's, I used to watch a short man in his forties walk around the tables spilling onto the street and shout orders back to someone inside the restaurant. I cross the street and ask Milto if he can give me a job.

"What are you making at the sandwich shop?" Milto asks.

I give him the number, which one of Robert's friends referred to as minimum wage. Since Terry's store is still in business, Milto cannot know that I've been laid off and must think that I am looking for a better-paying job.

"I'll pay you ten cents an hour more," says Milto and shakes a cigarette out of a pack, giving me time to respond.

"Good," I say, as proud of my luck as Milto is of his shrewdness, thinking he's just outbid a business rival.

The following day I am at Milto's Pizzeria moving tables around and mopping floors. Every morning, Milto explains, I must take the tables from the indoor restaurant where they are stacked for the night, set them outside, and plant an umbrella in the middle of each one. I try to figure out how heavy each table is, using a common unit of weight, the same way back home the values of things were measured by the price of a ubiquitous half-liter bottle of vodka. "The yarn is so damn expensive these days," my sister would complain, returning from a farm market with skeins of wool to knit herself a sweater, "ten half liters a kilo." Does each table weigh two twenty-kilogram suitcases like the one I brought from Leningrad, or three? I don't know the answer, but I know it is definitely more than one because my arm still remembers the weight, and it takes me half an hour to drag all of the tables outside, one by one, as they screech on the asphalt, announcing the beginning of Milto's lunch.

In addition to moving and mopping, I am entrusted with standing behind the counter and taking orders, then placing toppings on pizza slices and sliding them into the big steel oven behind me. Once the slices are in, I start thinking of my old Leningrad courtyard or my upcoming test called a GRE, which usually makes me forget about the oven until a customer comes up to the counter and inquires why it's taking so long. At that point the slice has been so shrunken and charred that I have to go through the process again, under the customer's angry stare, hoping that Milto is elsewhere, unable to witness my inadequacy.

The good thing is that I can eat all the pizza I want and even take a few slices home and reheat them for Robert's dinner. Compared to what he is probably getting from Karen, a few slices of reheated pizza isn't much, but I don't know what else I can give.

ဆ

An airmail envelope from Leningrad arrives in the mailbox, our address carefully made out in my mother's square handwriting.

*Our dearest Lenochka and Robert,* she writes.

*I just returned from the post office where they told me I couldn't send you the nesting doll, matryoshka, I'd bought because it's made with pieces of inlaid wood. I also wanted to send a souvenir salt dish Marina brought from her theater trip to Armenia, but it isn't allowed in the foreign mail, either. So I sent you two bars of chocolate instead. At least, something sweet. Everything is all right here. We had a scare when a man came from the district housing office to announce that, since you'd left, we had too many square meters per inhabitant, which meant they were going to take one room away from us and move another family in.*

*Of course, Marina got very angry and yelled at the man, but he wouldn't budge; he must have heard arguments like that before. "Start moving your stuff out of this room," he said and pointed to the piano. "We'll see about that," I replied and pointed to the front door. "That's just great," barked Marina in her stage voice when the door banged shut. "Back to the paradise of communal living, with some idiots from the provinces making pickles in our bathtub." But then I remembered that my brother-in-law from Kineshma went on vacation at a Volga sanatorium for free every year because he was a war veteran. I am a war veteran, too, I reminded Marina, and I've never had a free vacation, so maybe I could claim the ten extra square meters of my apartment as a veteran's perk. So I went to the district office, stood on line, and wrote a request according to the form hanging on the wall under glass. Yesterday we heard the good news: my request was approved. So we don't have to move the piano and the couch out and no strange family from the provinces will be moving in.*

I stare at the rows of Coca-Cola bottles behind the glass of a refrigerated cabinet. What would I do if they hadn't approved my mother's request? If our Leningrad home had been turned into a communal apartment because I decided to marry a foreigner and leave? And what would my mother say if she knew I worked in a pizzeria moving tables and burning pizza slices?

America is the mouth of the shark, she'd say. She warned me many times, but I wouldn't listen because, as she'd always pointed out, I am stubborn as a goat.

I write back that I am planning to enter graduate school at the University of Texas next semester, studying Russian literature, although I have no idea what literature or language possibilities the university has to offer. All I know is that I have to take a test before I can even apply, a strange test called the GRE. Robert and I went to a bookstore the other day and bought a thick volume called *GRE Practice Tests.*

"It's pretty simple," said Robert as I stood by the bookshelf, leafing through the tome in my hands. "Take all the sample tests and you'll do just fine."

Standing at Milto's counter, I think of all the tests I had to take at Leningrad University. We would draw a card from the examiner's table, read the three questions written on the paper, prepare for twenty minutes, and then face a bored and exhausted professor. We had to speak succinctly yet eloquently about the topics we'd drawn, plugging in all the relevant facts we could remember to convince the examiner that we deserved a decent grade. Those much dreaded exams were always subject-specific and required intensive book searches, scrupulous note taking, and blunt memorization.

I don't understand the principle of the GRE practice tests. Why are we given five possible answers to each question? And the questions: what exactly are they aiming at? It isn't literature, or language, or history, or any other subject I am familiar with. The test paragraphs are short, trivial, and boring. They have words I don't know and they test things I can't figure out.

"It's multiple choice," says Robert, and although I know the meaning of every word separately, I can't figure out the overall phrase. "Only one answer out of the five is right," he says. The paragraph in front of me describes the changes in the population of some neighborhoods in Detroit. I don't know what the Detroit population has to do with linguistics or literature and how my choosing the correct answer will help the head of the Russian department make a decision as to whether I will be a good candidate to study the works of Nabokov and Mandelstam.

"Just take the practice tests," says Robert, unable to give me better advice. He stands in the middle of our living room, his hands in the pockets of his corduroy jeans. I don't know what he is really thinking. All I know is his calm tone does not reassure me.

I do the first test and get half of the answers wrong.

There is a wall calendar in Sagar's room, a countdown to his mother's visit. "Four weeks and three days," he says and looks at the date circled in black Magic Marker, pushing his glasses up his nose as though to make sure he counted correctly. "I haven't told Roxana," he adds. "I don't even know how to bring it up."

"Tell her your mother is coming for a visit," I suggest with a giggle. I know I shouldn't trivialize this with a giggle, but I imagine my mother arriving in Austin, carrying string bags of homemade *pirozhki* and cardboard boxes with samovars inside them, ready to advise me on a life she has never seen. "Roxana will be thrilled your mother is coming," I say, trying to be convincing. "She'll envy you."

Why is it, I wonder, that the mothers who are wanted can't make it here while those who aren't are hopping on the first plane? I know, of course, that the real torment for Sagar is not how to tell Roxana about his mother but how to tell his mother about Roxana. The mother who is coming all the way from India with a suitcase full of Kodak brides.

# *Eleven*

I hate working in the pizzeria," I say to Robert. "I forget about slices in the oven, I can't understand what people are asking for. I don't even like pizza anymore."

But what I hate most is the feeling of worthlessness. "It makes me sick," I say. "Going there every day, moving the tables out, then rolling them back in. Having to pretend that I'm someone I don't even know."

Robert takes off his glasses and starts rubbing the lenses with his shirt.

"Back in my insane Motherland," I say, "waiters waited and teachers taught. Everything was permanent, everything made sense. If you moved tables, you knew nothing about books or theater. If you punched out cash register receipts, you thought that Pasternak was an herb."

"But you know about theater and books." Robert's voice is now louder and higher. "You're not in Soviet Russia anymore." He is logical, as usual. "You know who you are."

Do all Americans know who they are? Maybe in this country people are born with an inherent knowledge about themselves as individuals—not as part of various collectives—an identity that doesn't get incinerated, as they grow up, by the rays of the bright future no one is promised here.

"Look, this is only temporary," says Robert. "Here are the numbers: in August I had a thousand dollars in my bank account; now I'm down to one seventy-five."

"Maybe I can do translations," I say. "Does anyone in Austin need anything translated into Russian?" For a moment, the idea seems to make sense and I look at Robert with hope, but he doesn't say anything and I know the answer even before he shrugs and shakes his head.

"Russian lessons?" I ask, but he still sits silently, frowning.

If I were as open and unafraid as my actress sister, I would tell Robert that life here rushes at me like a flood of indecipherable information, a constant pitch of senseless noise, a cruel language-immersion program with no trace of human teachers. I would tell him to break out of his self-absorption—his black holes, his violin, his science fiction—and show me how to buy a pair of shoes without humiliating myself. But I am not my actress sister.

Instead, I say something meaningless. "I found a dollar on the sidewalk this morning," I mumble and pull a crumpled bill out of my pocket.

"Lucky you," says Robert and sighs.

ॐ

I am in a university auditorium taking the GRE test. We sit at single desks with pencils hovering over the multiple-choice question booklet. I read paragraphs I don't understand; I fill the little circles of the answers as I'm required. When the proctor warns us we have five minutes left, I realize I am still three pages away from the end of section one.

When I first fell in love with English, it was the middle of July in Leningrad, the summer I was ten and my father lay in bed at home, watching soccer on television, his skin shrink-wrapped around his bones. Every weekday, in my tutor's apartment, I heard the musical sounds of English and memorized words and grammar to pass an entrance exam to a special school that would continue to teach me this mysterious language. But now—when I thought I'd learned it—I can't find a trace of magic in the five answers to each question the GRE booklet offers.

The math part is easier, although I still don't understand why I need to figure out the unknowns in algebra equations and calculate perimeters of triangles to apply to graduate school to study literature. I don't understand why, instead of solving each problem and posting the correct answer, we need to be distracted by four erroneous choices. And I don't know how all this—whether I get into the Austin graduate program or don't—is going to affect my life. Instead of calculating the length of the hypotenuse in front of me, I am swarmed by more pressing questions that keep buzzing in my head: Will Robert ever be able to see beyond himself and notice that I am failing? Will Sagar yield to his mother and marry one of her Kodak brides, breaking Roxana's heart and probably his own? Will I learn to say *I* instead of *we*?

And most important: What will happen to Robert and me?

8

Our room has a table with two chairs, a fan that creaks from side to side as it sends air swirling across the linoleum up to the window with a view of a fenced patch of brown grass, and a mattress. Robert says he doesn't need a bed; beds are nice but superfluous since one can sleep just as well on the floor. The only time I ever slept on the ground was my summer stay at the Crimean beach. Even in our crumbling dacha with no indoor toilet and no running water, where flies buzzed around the veranda until they got entangled in spiderwebs, everyone had a bed.

My shelf in the closet holds two tops Marina crocheted for me, green and purple, a sundress, and a long skirt she sewed from leftover patches of cotton. Last week, I wore the skirt on Halloween because Robert said it was a perfect Gypsy costume. The rest of my shelf holds a pair of Levi's corduroys, a present from a student in the American class I taught at Leningrad University, the only piece of clothing that was worth lugging across the Atlantic. My wardrobe is completed by a T-shirt with the university logo that Roxana gave me soon after she first came to the house with Sagar. I like the T-shirt's soft, light cotton, so I wear it a lot, sometimes for three days in a row. This morning Robert gave me a questioning look before he left for school. "Can you put on something else?" he asked. "You can't wear the same thing over and over again."

There was no point telling Robert that this was a habit from home: we wore the same shirt several days in a row because we owned only two shirts.

∞

"How did it go at the pizza place today?" asks Robert when I get home after another day at Milto's. From his voice and his posture I know he isn't really interested in hearing the answer. He sits on the sofa cross-legged, watching his foot suspended over the linoleum.

I sit down next to him, the smell of the pizza oven rising from my clothes.

"I think it would be better if you go back to New Jersey and live at my mother's for a while," says Robert and leans forward to rub an imaginary speck of dust off his shoe.

The words hang in the air, refusing to enter my brain. Live at his mother's for a while, I repeat in my mind, making sure that I heard him correctly. What does this mean, living at his mother's, and how long is a while, I want to ask, but the whole statement is so sudden that I don't.

"I don't know what else I can do," he says, his voice thin with lack of promise. "You seem to hate everything here."

I am not sure I hate everything. I don't hate Sagar and Roxana, and even, strangely, I don't hate Sagar's mother, who is probably now already making lists and buying presents for her upcoming transoceanic trip. I don't hate the early morning light that slants through our window and paints straight amber lines on the linoleum. I don't hate our reading Chekhov together, even though there is little hope Robert will ever fully understand the meaning of *toska*.

But what reaches my ears—instead of what he said about my seeming to hate everything here—is that he seems to hate my being here. Something that fits in with Robert's apparent disappointment in me, with his unenthusiastic tone and his immediate fascination with his shoes. Something that I've suspected all along.

"You hate your job, you hate the weather, you even hate my mattress," Robert says. "You never sound happy. All you do is complain that you hate everything around here. Sometimes I even think you hate me."

"I don't hate everything," I say, but the stress falls on the last word, making the statement as wobbly and pathetic as my GRE test strategies or my Milto's pizza-making skills.

"I told you back in Leningrad I'm not ready for this. For living together like this." His voice is higher, unfamiliar, and at the same time resigned, as if he were delivering a lecture to one of his freshman classes. "I'm used to living alone. We talked about this; I never wanted to get married."

I remember the moment in Leningrad: minus twenty-five, three-foot-long icicles hanging off the roof like pointed missiles, the two of us shuffling forward in small, careful steps on the icy sidewalk. I remember his words. I remember Karen's name mentioned: he wanted to continue seeing other women. "I understand," I said back then, although I really didn't. I even added a mousy "thank you" that puffed out of my mouth and hung between us in a little cloud of frost.

"You're right, you did tell me," I say. "I actually like certain things here," I add, but the words come out limp and unconvincing because I know that it's already too late to alter the shape of what's going to happen.

"You'll be better off there, in New Jersey," says Robert. "Just until the end of the semester. You'll stay with Millie; she wants you to come. And then we'll see."

I don't know what there is to see, but I nod. I accept his offer to ship me off to his mother the same way I agreed to his marriage proposal. There isn't much to argue about here, the same way there wasn't much to debate back then. I was stuck inside the boundaries of the Soviet ruin, hermetically sealed from the rest of the world, with my mother ordering me to eat cabbage soup and be home by ten, just as I'm stuck here in Texas, walking to Milto's Pizzeria in sneakers I couldn't pay for, wasting time on the floor in front of a fan, watching horror movies while Robert sits at the university with Karen.

I nod, although going to live with Robert's mother doesn't feel like an offer of help. It feels like a dismissal, and I steel myself against his words—against his razor-sharp solution—so that I don't get unhinged and curl into a ball right here, in front of my first coffee table. I try to be all reason and acceptance, but inside, I crawl into the darkest corner of my soul to hide from my profound failure that doesn't seem to have a cure, the failure that requires my immediate ouster to New Jersey.

"Okay," I say, another new word I learned recently, a convenient word that most of the time means nothing, but once in a while—when pronounced with a frontal "eh" at the end that refuses to hide in the back of the mouth—can break out of its worn-out mold and revert to the meaning of constrained agreement. I agree, but inside me everything is aching and churning with anger. "Okay," I utter, trying to keep my voice steady. I'll go to New Jersey and stay with Millie. And then we'll see.

# *Twelve*

Millie presses me to her cotton T-shirt with the letters ERA stitched in big red capitals across the front. She seems to have grown shorter and wider since August, when I first met her, her graying hair boyish, her eyes smiling out of pleats of skin behind her glasses.

In the evening, we sit in the kitchen and drink a sweet cocktail called a toasted almond. Millie likes sweets as much as I do, as much as any Russian, and she beams with pride when I say that she's Russian at heart. "My grandparents were Russian, you know," she says and toasts me with her glass. The drink is thick and delicious; it is made with heavy cream and two liqueurs I'd only seen once in a foreign-currency store in Leningrad when I worked as a tour guide, Amaretto and Kahlúa.

We don't talk about Robert. Just as with my mother, I don't discuss Robert with my mother-in-law. I tell her about life in Russia. Kahlúa and Amaretto? They are not available. Heavy cream? I saw it once in a café in Moscow. Drinking? Not the way we're sipping a cocktail here. Half a liter of vodka for every two guests; if you open a bottle, you must finish it; pickle marinade in the morning for the hangover—those unwritten rules we all learned from childhood. Marriage? At twenty-four a woman is considered old, a spinster.

Men? On March 8, International Women's Day, men bring flowers, then watch television all night as women whip up holiday dinner in the kitchen between serving them drinks. Children? Most couples don't have more than one; food lines, full-time jobs, and misogynist husbands vaccinate women against motherhood. The only available contraceptive is abortion performed without an anesthetic; you have to bribe the doctor to get one. Millie shakes her head, and I know she thinks I'm making this up to entertain her. Women's rights? she asks, and now I am the one shaking my head because I'm not sure if I don't know the answer or simply don't understand the question.

Sometimes Andy and Donald, two therapists who work for Millie, join us for toasted almonds after they are done with their daily patient load. Andy is handsome and funny, making Millie laugh, his jokes spreading a net of wrinkles over her face. Twice a week he drives to Princeton from northern New Jersey, where he lives, a part I haven't seen yet, a part as mysterious as Andy himself. I don't quite know what makes him mysterious, but I catch myself watching him furtively, trying to conjure up the man behind the ironic smile.

Donald, who lives nearby, is blond and tall and reminds me of passed-out Scandinavian tourists I saw loaded onto hotel luggage carts, on top of suitcases, after a vodka weekend in Leningrad. Only this Donald was born in Wisconsin and never drinks more than one cocktail with us because he is always in a hurry to return to his young wife, Beatrice, whom he married just last year. "Donald and Bea are fighting again," says Millie, rubbing her chin. I don't know how she could have found this out, unless Donald fills her in on his family troubles, but maybe this is a skill she learned in her psychology graduate program, an ability to see through people's façades and go straight to the inner rooms of their minds. I sometimes wonder if she can take one look at me and see that I am not in love with her son, that I feel guilty about leaving Leningrad.

"You know," says Millie, mixing Kahlúa with cream one evening when Andy is not there, "Bea is Don's second wife. He was married to Jill." She pauses as if waiting for me to say something. "Jill is my daughter," she adds when I remain silent.

"I didn't know you had a daughter," I say stupidly, which, of course, means that I don't know Robert has a sister.

"Four years older than Robert, graduated from Wesleyan third in her class," says Millie.

"And where is she now?" I ask, looking around, as if this were Russia, where adult children continue to live with their parents, and Jill would be likely to pop out of the childhood bedroom she'd never left.

"She moved to Cleveland after the divorce," Millie says. "Didn't want to stay here to be reminded of the failed relationship." I notice that Millie switches to more professional, psychological terms, which make her sound defensive, which make the word *failed* ring bottomless with possibilities. Did Donald fail to understand Jill? Did Jill fail to be a good wife? Did Millie fail in giving them professional advice that could have kept them together?

But the gravest realization for me, since I don't know Jill and barely know Donald, is that Robert never told me about his sister. Not when we went to see Marina in a play together during his second visit; not when he met my sister Galya, at whose apartment we had stayed before and after the wedding. He knew that I had six cousins who lived in the provinces; he knew that my mother had three brothers and one sister; he knew I had an Irish setter called Major when I was growing up. All I knew about him was that his parents were divorced. He never told me that he had a sister.

"So Donald is your son-in-law," I say, stating the obvious. "Former son-in-law," Millie adds, almost reluctantly. I want to ask her if she resents Donald's presence in her kitchen, his sipping toasted almond and talking about Bea, his new wife. I want to ask her why she's being so noble and so selfless when lamenting Don's fights with Bea. Do they evoke, in her mind, Don's former fights with Jill? Are these memories the only way Millie can keep her daughter close, the daughter who left to get away from all this? To get away from her?

"He needs structure in his life, and Bea is good with structure," says Millie. "She maps things out; she delineates the boundaries." Her voice is soothing, like honey-flavored cough syrup, as if she wished her daughter were Bea and not the woman Don divorced years ago.

I wonder if anyone gets angry here. Back in Leningrad, you knew how everyone felt about everything: Marina screamed at me, I yelled back, and my mother shouted at us both to stop fighting. Babushkas on the street berated young mothers with strollers if their children were not properly bundled up. Teachers lectured students in front of the entire class for stupidity, lack of patriotic zeal, or a missing comma. School janitors waved their mops at you if you left dirty footprints on the floor. You always knew when you did something other people did not like. They scolded and shamed you to make you feel guilty, to cut you down to size. They were the volunteer eyes of the collective, vigilant and sharp.

Maybe Americans, because they don't have to waste time elbowing their competitors on lines, were able to evolve into a more advanced race of people who do not judge others, at least not openly. Maybe instead of resenting their former sons-in-law's new wives, as Russian mothers would, they analyze their new marital problems and offer professional advice.

Maybe one day I should catch Andy—with his quick movements and kind eyes—while Millie and Donald are still in their offices, and ask him what hides behind all this politeness and calm. Andy seems like someone who has enough insight not to wince at a question like this, who could possibly understand what it feels like to struggle constantly against the undertow of culture shock, to be so different and so unknowing of the most basic things.

The prospect of talking to Andy makes me feel buoyant and at the same time guilty, as if I was planning to reveal to him some innermost secret I've never even dreamed of entrusting to Robert's ears.

∞

At night, I sit in my room in the yellow glow of a table lamp, the sweet taste of toasted almond turning to bitter in my mouth when I think of Robert. His parents divorced when he was fourteen, his father moving to Philadelphia and taking with him the science fiction books Robert had slipped off the shelves of his study, one by one, to savor in his attic room while his braless mother marched for the ERA between the workshops she gave on repairing faulty relationships and connecting to your inner self. Robert spent hours immersed in his father's articles on the laws of physics that governed stars, planets, and black holes—the universe that seemed so much less unruly and more intelligible and constant than the one around him.

I think of Robert teaching math to a freshman class in Austin; I think of him getting into Sagar's Volkswagen to go to the university. I think of the way he moves, the way he speaks. Measured movements, calculated words. A perfect specimen of this new race of people, Americans. I have never heard him raise his voice or swear. I have never seen gooseflesh bump his skin or anger crease his face. As far as I know, his brain has always been the master of his heart.

# *Thirteen*

During the second week of our cocktail sipping, Millie says that I should start looking for a job. This is what Robert said a few weeks ago; these were the words that brought me to the door of Milto's Pizzeria. But maybe New Jersey—only a tunnel away from Ellis Island—is more generous about jobs for recent immigrants than Texas. Maybe Millie will lead me across the lawn to the house hidden behind the rhododendrons and teach me about experiential development or, at least, about keeping her schedule or her books.

I need to occupy my time not to get bored, Millie says. But I'm not bored because I am finally reading all those banned and censored books that lure me openly from the shelves of Millie's study and the local bookstore. I discover that all those dangerous tomes by Solzhenitsyn and anthologies of Brodsky's subversive poems do not cause a stir in those who pass them. If only our steely Soviet leaders had known this, they wouldn't have had to spend sleepless nights banning and policing and confiscating these books at the borders, books that don't force anyone—as it turns out—to become an enemy of the state. Nobody trembles over Bulgakov's *Master and Margarita* here, no one's heart quakes over the line that summarizes the ultimate futility of Soviet censorship—"manuscripts don't burn"—when the Devil produces a novel the Master had earlier tossed into a fire.

Maybe Millie thinks that work will give me structure, the same therapeutic function that Bea provides for Donald. She doesn't know that structure is the last thing I need. I've been structured by jobs since I finished high school at seventeen. I did the first of four daily mail deliveries in Dekabristov Street, when the pavement still echoed with the night emptiness; I copied drafts of classified blueprints at a secret boat factory without ever seeing the slightest trace of a boat; I sliced the spinal cords of rabbits into specimens in my mother's anatomy lab; I occupied a huge desk that guarded access to the director of the House of Friendship and Peace. With everyone else, I chugged along the track laid down at birth: taking classes at the English department of the university; offering private tutoring to earn money for perfume, the only decent thing available in Leningrad department stores; getting a diploma from the hands of an unsmiling dean.

Had I stayed, I would be teaching yawning kids at the end of the metro line to retell Lenin's biography in English or to memorize a vocabulary list from the gray pages of a textbook called *Eternally Alive* so that they could write an essay on the achievements of the latest five-year plan. For thirty years I would walk to the metro station through the gray soup of the morning and after work return to the kitchen chair where my father used to sit when I was in nursery school, my dinner plate with a slice of black bread next to it waiting on the table set by my mother, then by my older sister, then maybe by no one at all. And when I would eventually turn fifty-five, I would no longer have to walk to the metro station to get to work since, like every other female citizen, I would be eligible for a state pension of 120 rubles a month. From the very beginning, there was nothing but structure in our Soviet lives, and nothing but state-approved work.

After the Texas preview of the jobs available to me, I don't fool myself into thinking that I will be teaching grammar anytime soon.

Millie seconds this thought when we are driving back from the supermarket past a sign that says BEEFSTEAK CHARLIE'S, HIRING NOW.
She stops the car and says that we should go in. I don't know who
Beefsteak Charlie is, but next to the restaurant's name is his picture,
almost cartoonish: a pancake face, round and puffy, with a mouth
smiling under a thick mustache.

Inside, Beefsteak Charlie's is a huge, murky space with ladders
and coils of thick wire strewn across the floor. The space is as big
as a ballroom, and as always, when I think of a ballroom, I think
of the first ball of Natasha Rostova from Tolstoy's *War and Peace,*
one of the chapters I didn't skip in the four-volume novel, as I leafed
through the descriptions of military maneuvering and battles. Written
in prose that made my heart flutter, it was all about young, handsome
counts in military uniforms and romantic expectations of first love.
This isn't a Tolstoy ballroom, of course, by any means. I know we are
in New Jersey and not in nineteenth-century Petersburg, but my mind
seems very slow to adapt to my new reality, constantly turning back
and dredging familiar images out of the silty riverbed of memory.
In my head dazzling pairs of dancers have already begun to spin on
the parquet floor, and Natasha's eyes have already caught the stare
of Prince Bolkonsky, setting in motion the passion and betrayal and
Tolstoy's view of redemption that followed.

"Can we have an application?" asks Millie when a woman in
jeans rushes past us, erasing my vision of Natasha waltzing before
the eyes of the whole Petersburg beau monde, setting in motion the
Beefsteak Charlie's chapter of my own destiny.

"Sure," says the woman, without slowing her trot. She disappears behind a door, then reemerges with a paper in her hand. "Give
it back to me when you're done," she says and vanishes again.

I fill out my name and Millie's address. On the previous experience line I write, "Milto's Pizzeria," amazed that there is something
I can write that qualifies for experience. "Position desired," I read.

"What am I applying for?" I ask Millie.

"You're applying to be a server," says Millie, deliberately

using the gender-neutral word, unlike those gender-specific names "waiter" and "waitress."

When I sign my name at the bottom, Millie gives the application to the woman in jeans who keeps running past us, back and forth, with loads of folded linens on her arms. "We'll call you in a couple of days," she says without glancing up at us, taking my paper and stuffing it between the creases of cloth.

છ

Every week Robert calls from Texas. His calls are like the letters he wrote to me in Leningrad: foreign, formal, incomprehensible. With the absence of real life around us, there seems little to talk about. Devoid of the convenient concreteness—the correct pronunciation of characters' names in *The Three Sisters*, the blur of supermarket aisles, the hot tedium of Milto's afternoons, when the place stands empty of sound and life—we stumble and search for topics during the awkward pauses in long-distance airtime.

"How is life in New Jersey?" he asks.

"Good," I say. "We made chicken cutlets for dinner. Millie says I should work so I don't get bored. I'm not bored, not at all. Yesterday I applied to be a waitress at Beefsteak Charlie's." I state the facts in simple, first-grade sentences, for which my university English professor would have given me nothing more than a satisfactory *troika*. For a moment, I think of telling Robert about Andy joining us for dinner, but then I don't.

Robert chuckles on the other end. "That'll be a step up from serving pizza," he says.

"Definitely," I agree. "It'll be a promotion. If I get the job."

There is a pause, one of those uncomfortable silences.

"How is Sagar holding up?" I ask, knowing that his mother's visit is looming close.

"He told me his mother is arriving from India next week. I guess he's happy to see her."

No, he isn't, I want to tell Robert, but I don't. I realize Robert doesn't know anything about his roommate's emotional life, and he probably wouldn't want to know if I told him. What do Robert and Sagar talk about when they drive to the university in the morning? The density of matter in black holes? The laziness and stupidity of freshmen?

"You have to tell me what she's like," I say.

"I probably won't see her much," says Robert, and I know it means he'll be spending even more hours at his office than he was when I lived there. I wonder how often he sees Karen. I wonder if they spend time reading Russian books together, if she corrects his pronunciation and points out new vocabulary. I doubt that she even knows enough new vocabulary to try. And her vowels, I'm certain, are way too clipped and happy—as inauthentic as her soaring intonation at the ends of sentences. But all these linguistic wonderings are tiny mice around the feet of one elephantine question: What happens at the end of their Russian lessons? Do they go to her apartment, where there is a real bed, not just a mattress on the floor? And how frequent are those visits in the book of open marriage? I try to conjure up what happens on the pages of that book; yet I'd rather not imagine. I can only think that Robert must feel relief now—free to see Karen as often as he likes, free to make love to someone who hasn't been damaged by her Motherland, free of a stranger loitering around his house, clueless. Robert is free now to do whatever he wants—whatever Karen wants—since I have been exiled to New Jersey.

# *Fourteen*

Beefsteak Charlie's calls and tells me to report for training on Monday.

"Does this mean I have the job?" I ask Millie.

"Yes," she says and gives me a hug, as if I'd just received an offer to teach at Princeton.

I am not sure how I should prepare myself for server training. The only two waitresses I knew in Russia, Luda and Maya, both worked at the café in the House of Friendship and Peace, where I was the director's secretary. Serving was their profession, just as teaching English was going to be mine as soon as I graduated from the university.

Luda was thick-calved and generous, splashing rice with meat gravy when I didn't have forty-five extra kopeks to pay for the meatballs. Maya, thin and peroxide-blond, wasn't quite as friendly, the object of rumors that my boss spent more time at the café than he had to. She strutted around the dining room carrying bowls of soup, her lips arrogant and red, her lined eyes disdainful, which may have been her way of letting me know that she was able to get closer to my boss than I could ever be.

Among the group of trainees on Monday, no one resembles Luda or Maya. There are twenty-five people, mostly young women, mostly students at Trenton State College. From what I can see, none of them regards waitressing as a career. No one here seems to think—as we all thought back home—that having access to food gives you power, as if a plate of meat loaf were a briefcase with a nuclear code. I think of how everyone in Russia was a guard of what they could access, and everyone used what they guarded to their advantage. Waitresses and grocery store clerks guarded food from customers; department store salespeople guarded imported boots from fashion-starved women; professors on college entrance exam committees guarded university seats from applicants. My provincial aunt Muza was the guard of gynecological services at the clinic where she worked as a doctor, and her grateful patients brought her what they guarded: whole sturgeons and cuts of beef that never made it to store counters, sweaters they knitted for her and her husband, zucchini and cucumbers from their gardens. The only people with nothing to guard, it seemed, were my mother and my sister, who spent all their energy lamenting the absurdity of Soviet life and yelling at each other because they couldn't escape from it. Had I stayed in Russia, I would have become a schoolteacher and joined their sad, unprofitable, guard-free ranks.

છ

Across from me sits Melissa, my fellow trainee. We both stare into menus, pretending we are customers at Beefsteak Charlie's, while the other half of our group are playing servers. The manager, Carol—the woman in a rush who gave me the application—encourages us to order as much as possible to give the servers in training a workout that will make them learn. Tomorrow the roles will reverse, with Melissa and me playing servers. Melissa glances through the appetizer section and orders stuffed clams. I don't know what stuffed clams are, as I don't know half the things that stare at me from the page. What is seafood chowder, for instance, and why in the world is there pasta on the menu? *Pasta*, in Russian, is the word for toothpaste. I ask Melissa for the definition of *pasta*, and she looks at a loss.

"Pasta is . . . pasta," she says, giving me an apologetic smile, letting me know that she would like to help but doesn't know how.

If I had any guts, I would order seafood chowder and pasta marinara, or maybe even something called surf and turf, but I don't want to face a dish I may not know how to approach. I imagine pasta marinara as my sister Marina's toothpaste. Surf and turf makes me think of the footpath leading from our dacha to a small beach on the Gulf of Finland, always muddy, where our feet used to sink to our ankles and make slurping noises when we pulled them up. I cowardly settle for green salad and chicken, but even this seemingly predictable choice turns out to be tricky: the freckled, lanky girl taking my order asks what dressing I would like with my salad. "Dressing?" I ask.

"French, Italian, blue cheese, Thousand Island, Russian," recites the girl, who is obviously more prepared to be a server than I am to be a customer. I have no idea what these words mean—they're apparently adjectives to describe the word *dressing*, the meaning of which I don't know, either. I look at Melissa with what feels like panic.

"Try Russian," she says and gives out a little giggle.

When the freckle-faced server scribbles in her pad and departs, the panic that began in my chest leaks to my arms and legs, to the ends of my fingers and toes, filling every vein with paralyzing fear.

80

I have memorized the entire menu, quizzing Millie about every food I didn't know; I have learned the gradations of steak readiness, from blue rare to burnt; I have committed to memory six types of lettuce that I never knew existed and added so many vegetables to my vocabulary that my head began to spin. Millie explained the meaning of the word *gratuity*. I understood it was a reward, but it still remained murky to me why you would always give someone a bonus for just doing their job.

The three of us—Millie, Andy, and I—were sitting in a booth of a restaurant called Friendly's, finishing our hamburgers and salads, when Millie took the time to explain about vegetables and gratuities to me. "I was a waitress in graduate school, you know," she said. "The job got me through my first year. That's where I met Robert's father when his dissertation adviser took him out to dinner. We met and were living together three months later." She gave me a smile, which made me wonder if this was what she expected me to do at Beefsteak Charlie's, look for my next husband.

I smiled politely, not knowing how to respond to this revelation.

"See?" said Andy, turning to me, his face lit with an energy that made it more handsome and tender: kind hazel eyes, pale complexion, the soft curl of his lips, one of those ironic smiles that showed his teeth. I don't know why I was staring at his lips. "See, America is the land of opportunity," he said. I knew somehow that he was aware of my pause, of my being at a loss for what to utter next. "You can study for your doctorate, learn about broccoli, and meet your next husband, all before you serve the steak."

Millie was the first to laugh, but I couldn't tell if behind her glasses she sincerely found Andy's comment funny. I did and was grateful to him for saving me from an awkward silence.

೮

It is Beefsteak Charlie's grand opening, and I am standing in the ballroom of the dining room, anxious, knowing this is another chance for me to fail. But I tell myself that I'm just like Natasha Rostova from *War and Peace* waiting for her first dance, except that I am dressed in a white shirt and black pants and wearing a red apron with a large white button that says, MY NAME IS ELENA. I'M GONNA SPOIL YOU. In my head the music starts when the doors open and my first customers walk in.

I am as prepared to be a waitress as I would be to teach a class in English grammar, I remind myself, as the ballroom orchestra violins in my head glide to a dizzying high note, as the hostess seats four people at my first table, three at my second, and then four more at my third and fourth. Men wear ironed shirts and expressions of anticipating a good time; women have high heels and the rich hair I envy. I take their orders, remembering to ask for the kind of dressing they want, for the degree of steak readiness they desire. I am ready to direct them to the all-you-can-eat shrimp bar—the pride of Carol and all the management way up to Beefsteak Charlie himself—when my first party decides to order something from the bar.

"I'd like a screwdriver," says a man in a striped shirt, and I'm sure I didn't hear him right because even I know what a screwdriver is. Maybe he really said he was a good driver, but that makes as little sense as ordering a tool. Does he think you have to drive to get to the shrimp bar? I see my fingers shaking, and I clutch them tighter around the pad. The only way out of this embarrassment is to rush to the bar and repeat to the bartender exactly what I think the customer said.

This strategy seems to work, although I don't even want to know what my customers think about my sprinting off to the bar before they can finish ordering their food. Aside from a toasted almond, I realize I know nothing about American drinks. I get orders for blue whales and dirty martinis. For sloe comfortable screws and White Russians. And what is a Black Russian, for heaven's sake? Every time I race across the Beefsteak Charlie's ballroom, the bartender, Samantha—harried and raspy-voiced—listens patiently as she tries to decipher the drink from my mangled pronunciation. "Man, hat, and," I would spit out, the three words I keep twirling in my mind as I rush from table to bar. "Manhattan," Sam would say, with a drop of motherly guidance, as if teaching a parental lesson.

In the next week or two, things don't get any better. I feel sorry for a skinny mother with a ponytail, whose little son never gets his lemonade. I feel like hiding behind the dishwasher when a group of four men in ties send their steaks back because, failing to understand that they were joking, I thought they wanted their meat burnt to a crisp. My orders of baby back ribs sit cold on the kitchen counter, and whole families—complete with grandparents and infants—who come for Sunday dinners get their chicken and baked potatoes before they have a chance to peel the shrimp from the salad bar. I notice that other servers routinely pick up after me, as if I were a slow child who has wandered into a grown-up function. Melissa, a student of photography at Trenton State, who adopted me as her charity case during training, rushes the abandoned orders of ribs to my tables and sets them down with elegance and a disarming smile, making it appear that it has all been planned in advance. Forgotten orders of mussels and minestrone soup inexplicably find their way to my tables. In waitressing, where timing and speed trump the knowledge of linguistics, I am getting consistent Fs. To further my humiliation, the tips are pooled, so every night I leave, unjustly, with thirty or thirty-five dollars—as much as everyone else.

On a Monday evening, when we are both off, Melissa drives me to a department store, and I buy a Levi's shirt that I think Marina would like and a blue dress for my mother, the color of her eyes. While Melissa checks out a display with jeans, I buy her a set with shower gels and creams for the upcoming holiday called Christmas.

# *Fifteen*

A letter arrives in Millie's mailbox: a Russian square envelope with red and blue airmail stripes around the edges framing unfamiliar handwriting. I take out the letter, unfold it, and go straight to the end. It is signed Boris, the name I have never seen penned in his handwriting, the name that sucks the air out of my lungs.

Boris, with his impossibly blue eyes and hair bleached by the Crimean sun, was someone I'd diligently tucked away into my Russian past, and he has no right to cross over the border into my new American life. Besides, he had never written me a letter before. He had never moved a finger to come to Leningrad to see me after we met at the Black Sea beach, aside from his last visit to warn me against the dangers of America a week before I was to marry Robert. I was the one who had concocted plans and counted days; I was the one who borrowed fifty rubles from Nina and hopped on a plane for Moscow two months after we'd met in the Crimea, having lied to my mother that my graduate thesis professor had sent me to an international linguistics conference.

So why is he writing to me now? I said good-bye to him more than eight months ago, on a freezing March night, on a Leningrad sidewalk near Theater Square when the city looked its worst, just beginning to emerge from under five months of winter that, as always, had overstayed its welcome. I was shivering in an unseasonably thin jacket, which I wore because it looked so much better than my padded winter coat, and my feet were wet and frozen as we'd been walking through a porridge of dirty snow. I said good-bye, but I really meant farewell, and everyone knows that a farewell is a good-bye forever. So I stand in the middle of Millie's kitchen, on the other side of the life in which Boris belongs, trying to decide whether I should even turn the page over and read the letter with its words slanted to the right as if they were ready to fall off a cliff.

*Lenochka*, it starts—a diminutive of my name, a dangerous opening.

I skim over the words, searching for those few that would let me know why I am having this ghostly visit from my Russian past.

*I hope your life now is good, better than I said it was going to be . . . I'm sorry if I said things that upset you back in March when I came to Leningrad. . . . You may think that after my trip I went back to Kiev and forgot about you. I was hoping I would. But it didn't happen.*

*I know you may not want to read this.*

Damn right, I don't want to read it, flashes through my head, and I realize that the words that have meteorically risen in my mind have arranged themselves in English.

*If your life in America is not what you hoped, if you ever think of coming back, I'll be here waiting for you.*

I quickly fold the letter and stuff it back into the envelope, as though not seeing these words will make them disappear. I go up to my room and slide the envelope into the inside compartment of my Russian suitcase and zip it up. That's where it will stay: in the dark, devoid of oxygen, slowly withering away. It will share a space with the skirt my sister sewed for me, the one that made a perfect Gypsy costume during Halloween in Texas.

ဆ

Tonight Melissa is studying for a test, so I am on my own. Two of my tables have been pushed together for a family celebration, and I am standing with a pad and pencil in front of eight festively dressed, happy people. Green salad, Italian dressing, onion soup. Two martinis, dry—I now know what a dry martini is. "Another salad, dressing on the side," says a balding man with a heavy face the color of brick.

Dressing on the side? I repeat in my mind, wishing that Melissa would pop out of the kitchen magically but knowing that she won't. On whose side? I wonder frantically, imagining a splash of oil and vinegar dripping down the side of the man's expensive suit. I think of being stripped of my apron and my button, with its impossible "I'm gonna spoil you" promise, and being deported for waitress failure.

"On the side?" I repeat in a feeble voice, hoping I didn't hear it right.

"Where are you from?" asks the man, his voice fringed with impatience.

"Russia," I say. "My husband is a graduate student at the University of Texas." I add this for no reason, hoping, perhaps, that having a husband in pursuit of a PhD would somehow excuse my inadequacy.

As I wait for the two dry martinis by the bar, Samantha explains dressing on the side to me. She demonstrates it by putting the olives on a little plate next to the glass.

I think of the time when I was eleven and kicked out of the district pool for swimming with my head out of the water. I think of the nauseating feeling of shame when my ninth-grade literature teacher tore apart my essay in front of the whole class because I made a noncritical reference to life in the United States.

But what I really think about is the letter I got from Boris, the letter I zipped into the most inner compartment of my suitcase, leaving it to suffocate in the dark. I think of what I don't want to think about—those things that I promised myself would never scar my mind. What if I did go back? What if I packed my suitcase, with the letter from Kiev tucked safely inside, and got on an Aeroflot flight to Moscow, with a quick connection to Leningrad? Back to the city that Robert pointed out was truly mine. *Grad* means city, he said when we first met, and *Lenin*—the possessive form of Lena. This is literally Lena's city, he said, smiling at his own clever manipulation of Russian grammar.

What if I went back to my courtyard, where every grain of dirt is familiar, where children from my nursery school at the end of the quad still crouch on the ledge of the sandbox in the summer? Where in the winter, which has already started there, they coast down the iced surface of the tall wooden slide standing up, just as I did, with arms stretched out, like awkward airplanes, their faces whipped by freezing air? What if I could stand on my apartment's balcony again, with waves of roofs rolling toward Theater Square and the Kirov, with the gray cupola of the only synagogue rising like a buoy in the restless tide of the city?

Then my mother would be right, once and for all. Dean Maslov, who warned me against America with its lack of pensions, would be right, too, telling everyone at the university about the former graduate student who crawled back home from the mouth of the shark. Back home, from darkness to light, back onto the threshold of our shining future.

I try to think of something promising that would help keep me here, that could counterweigh the slippery gray thoughts of going back, but for some reason I can conjure up nothing except Andy's face. The image makes me feel warm inside, as if I had gulped down one of those martinis I've been balancing on my tray all evening long. It helps me tuck Boris back into the past, where he belongs, along with my mother's kitchen, my university dean, and my Leningrad courtyard with all its poplar trees and grainy memories of childhood.

I bring the check to the festive table when they're done with their all-you-can-eat shrimp and filet mignon and strawberry short-cake. The table is littered with empty dishes and half-eaten desserts I should have taken away a while ago.

"Thank you very much," I say to the man with a gold chain and a brick-colored face, placing the check before him.

"Never been to Russia," he mutters. He is a little tipsy from the martini and the wine I've been bringing, and he motions with his hand for me to lean closer toward him.

"Listen, girl," he says, reaching for his wallet. "My advice to you—go back to your husband in Texas."

# *Sixteen*

I realize I don't want to go back to Texas. It is a dangerous thought, and I try to stow it away in the back of my mind, like Boris's letter. I don't want to sleep on a mattress on the floor; I don't want to stare out of the window at the pitiful patches of grass, all brown and dead. My GRE results just came back, and Robert told me on the phone that my verbal score was below 600. It was a meaningless number to me, but when I pressed him on the interpretation, he added it was one of the lowest scores he'd ever seen. "I've never taken a multiple-choice test before," I said to him, but he didn't answer and simply sighed on the other end of the line, a staticky puff of resignation.

Maybe I should be honest with myself. Maybe it isn't just Texas or multiple-choice failures that make me not want to go back to Robert. Maybe it has something to do with Andy, who now stays for drinks every evening he comes to Millie's to see patients. Andy, who aims his smile where I sit as if the stories he spins were custom-made just for me. Andy, who is the first person not giving me a sidelong glance as if peering at a curiosity.

We sit in Millie's kitchen and talk, pretending that the air hasn't thickened between us, that nothing I see in his eyes makes my heart constrict and stutter. We sit and talk about unimportant things, those harmless things that any two people who met recently might find in common. Andy tells me about New York's energy and the city's arteries clogged with traffic, talking about his city the same way I think about Leningrad, the way you would feel about a person you love. In response, I gush about the pale complexion of Leningrad's summer nights and the salty breath of the Baltic wind. He smiles; I sigh. Sitting in the kitchen makes our urban enthusiasm ring with intimacy that makes me feel guilty, and in an attempt to banish the guilt I try to listen more intently, as if a conversation about cities could mask the real reason we search each other out in Millie's house.

He asks me if I want to go for a ride. Going for a ride sounds so freeing, so American that I can almost hear the wind rushing in my ears. I nod vigorously, too eagerly perhaps, glad that Millie isn't there. I get into his car, the small space we happily share for an hour as we drive to a place with a strange name, Weehawken. We walk out into the grainy light of late afternoon and lean on the parapet overlooking the Hudson River, dwarfed by the stone authority of the Manhattan skyline.

The glow from the New Jersey side, receding with every minute we stand there paralyzed by being next to each other, makes the windows of the skyscrapers sparkle with gold in the rays of the setting sun. The city of the Yellow Devil, as our Bolshevik writer Maxim Gorky called it, is shining its dangerous invitation straight into my eyes.

"We could be in New York in fifteen minutes," says Andy. "The tunnel is right over there, right under the Hudson." He points to the gray, rippled water, although I have trouble imagining a tunnel full of cars carved through all that rock under the immenseness of the river. I think of the breathless thrill of walking in those canyons of streets with Andy, of laughing together about Maxim Gorky, who spent many years of his life on the Italian island of Capri, writing about the lower depths that were so readily available on his native soil.

All this effervescence feels dangerously familiar, taking me back to the Crimea and Boris, to the mobbed Simferopol Airport, where instead of elbowing for a ticket to go back home to Leningrad, in one delirious instant I joined Boris, hopping on the first plane headed for Kiev.

"So do you want to go to New York?" Andy asks, and my blood quickens because his sleeve inadvertently brushes against mine.

⍟

The other day Andy didn't go back home and the two of us ended up talking through the night in the attic room under the rafters. Millie had brought a half liter of Stolichnaya out of the freezer after both she and Andy were done with their patients. All three of us sat in the kitchen—not sipping, like the Russian expert on my Aeroflot flight to Washington, DC, but downing shots, as you're supposed to, as real Russians do. Andy somehow knew the proper way to drink vodka, although my own drinking expertise didn't extend past boiling Bulgarian red wine in a pot with sugar and apple slices to get rid of the acidic taste. Then Millie said she'd had enough but the two of us should go on. Go on, she said, smiling and waving us out of the kitchen and into the attic room, as if giving us her blessing, as if letting us know that up there we would be alone.

In the attic, we drank and talked, until the small window became lit from the outside and we no longer needed electric light. I had no idea how much there was to say to someone who had never been to Russia. I told him about my mother's uncle Volya, arrested in 1937, the busiest year of the Gulag camps, for telling a joke. I told him that my mother was a surgeon at a front-line hospital during World War II, scooping lice out of soldiers' wounds with a teacup and sewing up the flaps of torn tissue, until my sister was born, in 1942. I told him about my sister's acting career, about my envying the way she used to sit in front of a three-way theater mirror, ready to transform herself into someone else, someone who knew nothing about Young Pioneers or collectives or the latest five-year plan. I told him that learning English was my way of searching for magic, deciphering the mysteries of foreign words and foreign grammar, listening to a voice on a British record—so unknown, so entrancing, so rarely heard.

When the bottle was finished, we were in the corner of the couch, intoxicated and kissing, the guilt wiped out by Millie's vodka. We both felt delirious and frightened, knowing that this was only the beginning of something big and glorious and difficult. Then morning pried into the house with its insistent light, which lit up the ruins of our night spent in a space we were not supposed to share, and made us sensible and sober. I walked downstairs to my room and Andy got into his car and headed north. We both went back to our respective lives, the god of temporary transcendence dissipating in the harsh morning sunlight. I had told Andy in those few hours so much more than I had told Robert in four months. Maybe I couldn't stop talking simply because Andy was there, listening.

ಬ

I pull out a box of Russian mascara brought from Leningrad, pour a few drops of water onto the little block of coal inside, and rub it with a tiny plastic brush into what back home used to double for shoe polish and what is supposed to make me glamorous. I desperately want to look desirable and attractive, for one person exclusively, so I streak the plastic brush through my eyelashes three days a week, when Andy arrives to see his patients. I don't simply like Andy: the English word *like* is too shallow to contain the intricacies of the Russian *lyubovat'sya*. This is what's happening—I *lyubyuyus'* with Andy—I look at him with love. And that looking with love infuses me with power and grants me permission, for the first time, not to be an awkward, salad-dressing-dense foreigner. It grants me a hope that I have exhausted my share of failure and may not need to go running back to Russia. This thought is invigorating, and I grin into the mirror when I remember the vinegary Russian professor on the plane.

Looking at Andy with love feels strangely both exhilarating and sane, like drinking champagne without getting drunk. It counteracts the leaden seriousness of leaving everything I knew in Russia and fills me with an unaccustomed lightness because what I see reflected in Andy's eyes is a different me, the me I would like to be. Someone exotic and smart. Someone beautiful and non-Western and a little mysterious, the clumps of shoe polish mascara notwithstanding. I stare into the mirror for any sign of mystery or beauty, but what looks back at me is not as captivating as what I see in Andy's gaze. The person peering back is ordinary when unvalidated by his eyes.

સ

You look good, says Millie. You seem to be in good spirits lately.

I don't know what she notices about Andy and me; I don't know if she notices anything. I don't know if I want her to know. But then I think of the way she waved us up to the attic with more than half a bottle of vodka that night, before she went to bed, almost giving me permission to forget about her son in Texas. Maybe she knows that Robert regrets this marriage and would like it to be over.

When I don't work at Beefsteak Charlie's, Andy and I take a drive to a nearly empty diner that is open late; there we sit in a booth and talk. We drink coffee and eat eggs over easy, a new expression Andy has taught me. It is a freeing feeling, completely un-Russian, to sit at a restaurant at an off-meal hour, to be able to eat breakfast at night. Andy has explained all the items on the menu, telling little stories that make me laugh, so now I can order my own meal, knowing what it will turn out to be. He has also taught me about cars, diners, and fast food, and I have taught him about a Russian movie we all grew up with called *The Irony of Fate*, the charm of which had eluded Robert. I tell Andy the plot, delightful and old-fashioned: on a New Year's Eve three Moscow men go to a sauna. They get so drunk they can't figure out which one of them is going on a trip that night. Of course, the wrong man is packed onto a plane for Leningrad, where he sobers up enough to think that he is home in Moscow. He takes the metro to Builders Street and opens what he thinks is his apartment with a standard Soviet key—650 kilometers away from his real home. The young woman who lives there is dating the wrong man, and the rest is sweet and predictable. We've seen this film on TV for the past four years every New Year's Eve, without fail.

"*The Irony of Fate*?" Andy says. "What a terrific title, so Russian. We should try to find the tape here. I'd love to see it."

"And those songs the main characters sing to an acoustic guitar," I groan, leaning toward him, gushing about the lines every Russian knows by heart. "You should hear those songs! My favorite is 'To Have or Not to Have.' " I know it is futile to sing in a foreign language and then translate the verse, but I can't help myself. "If you don't have a house, it won't burn down," I sing in a low voice, although there is no one else in the diner at this hour. "If you don't have a dog, your neighbor won't poison it." The lyrics rhyme and, emboldened by familiar lines, I sing louder. "If you don't have a wife, she won't leave you for another man. And if you aren't living, you aren't going to die." This is the first time I dare sing at all because my sister, who went through musical and voice training at her drama school, had always told me I had no ear and couldn't carry a tune. But here, in this empty diner, sitting across from Andy, I am not afraid to sound silly or make a mistake. I am happily light-headed, so the song comes out soft and pitch-perfect, just as I remember it in the film.

When I finish the last line, I realize that we are leaning toward each other across the table, and it takes only a second to see that Andy is looking at me the same way I look at him, with love.

What I wonder—as we gaze at each other across the table—is why I launched into the story of *The Irony of Fate* at all. Why, for half an hour, did I gab and prattle and try to hum the songs?

Andy and I are both sitting quietly now, without speaking, without moving, because the outline of that screen romance rings familiar to both of us. The happenings on Leningrad television are just as strange and meteoric as they seem to be, unfolding in real time on this side of the Atlantic in New Jersey.

"What was that line again," says Andy. "'If you don't have a wife she won't leave you for another man'?"

We sit quietly over our empty plates, contemplating the irony of our own fate, afraid to think that the movie's happy ending is too sweet and unbelievable for us, too impractical for a real life.

# *Seventeen*

It all feels dizzying, as if I just got off a ride for kids, one of those attractions at an amusement park where the five of us—Millie; Donald; his wife, Bea; Andy; and I—went the previous Sunday. Andy sat next to me in a little seat, like the sidecar of a motorcycle, and held my hand. We haven't yet gone beyond secretly holding hands, embracing, and kissing, as if we were two teenagers, just like the crowds around us. "What should I do?" I yelled into the wind as the torrent of air swept our faces and churned our adrenaline. It felt like such a romantic thing to do—shouting into the wind and asking stupid questions that no one could hear.

"So what are you two going to do now?" asked Donald, Millie's former son-in-law, when we were back on steady ground. He was tall and bearded, a Viking as I imagined one, smiling his Nordic smile, his arm around Bea. He meant what ride were we going to go on next, but to me what he said sounded profound and existential, a question that clearly had no answer.

Yesterday it snowed, big, heavy clumps slowly melting on rhododendron leaves—the kind of wet snow that falls on Leningrad in
May—and it became obvious I needed a warm jacket. My mother
was right, after all, when she told me to pack warm things. Warm
things—a key to any Russian's survival—as essential as soup for
proper nutrition or fresh air for healthy lungs. As she was pontifi-
cating on the value of hats and scarves while pinning wet laundry
on a rope stretched across the room, I cut her off and declared with
absolute certainty that there was no winter in Texas.

"Would you mind driving Lena to a store tomorrow?" Millie
asked Andy as we were tearing up salad leaves and tossing them into
a bowl. I couldn't believe my fortune—Millie making it so simple—
and I stiffened inside, begging the god of winter to bestow on Andy
a free afternoon.

"Of course," he said and smiled at me as if he heard me hold
my breath, as if he wanted to tell me that he was as excited about
going to a store with me as I was about going there with him. He
was standing in a panel of sun slanting through the window, as
perfect as Prince Bolkonsky from *War and Peace*, his hair the color
of chestnuts Millie had bought for the holidays. We both knew she
had just granted us a legitimate chance to be together, and I turned
away, pretending I was looking for a cucumber peeler to hide a silly
smile I couldn't control.

The glass doors of the department store welcomed us into its
huge, anonymous space perfect for our shopping rendezvous. We
could walk on its granite floors past racks of clothes, talking about
nonsense and holding hands. We could pretend we were together, a
couple enjoying their afternoon, so used to walking side by side that
they don't even notice when their shoulders touch.

"How about a down jacket?" Andy said. "You'd look good in
down."

"Yes," I said and beamed. "I'd love it." I felt thrilled about wearing down, whatever down was, if Andy thought I'd look good in it.

He thumbed through a rack as I stood there and watched him,

grateful that I didn't have to choose one jacket out of the sea of coats that floated in all directions, like waves.

"Do you like this one?" he said, holding up a beige quilted jacket with soft blue lining. It was feathery and warm, and Andy zipped it up on me and tied the sash across my waist. Even through all the padding of down his hands felt tender, or maybe I simply imagined how tender his hands would feel. I straightened my spine and pulled my shoulders back in front of the mirror as my sister had instructed me a woman should stand, like an actor onstage.

"You don't even know how pretty you are," Andy said. He was looking at me as I was looking at him reflected in the mirror looking at me. "I don't think you have a clue."

I didn't, but I told myself I had to believe him. In the mirror stood a confident-looking woman in an elegant down jacket, a drop of vulnerability in her happy eyes, growing taller and poised under an admiring gaze. I wanted to believe him, and I wished for both things to be true: I was pretty and Andy loved me.

∞

In the middle of December, Millie announces that Robert is coming back to Princeton as soon as his semester in Austin is over. "He's arriving next week," she says and peers at me from behind her glasses. "He should know what's going on."

I don't know myself what's going on, and whatever is going on is happening too fast. Way too fast. But maybe I do know. Maybe it is like playing the old Russian game of pretending, except the one doing the lying is not the Soviet government but me. I am pretending that nothing is happening; Millie knows I am lying; I know she knows I am lying; but I keep lying anyway and she pretends to believe me.

I stare at the yellow cone of light from the nightstand lamp, thinking of what I am going to say to Robert when he gets here. I can say that Texas is much too foreign for someone who has just escaped the tight embrace of the collective. I can say that the KGB has ordered every Soviet citizen married to a foreigner to get an immediate divorce. Or I can tell the truth and say that I met a man who has given my life texture and color and who makes me feel that I don't have to depend on the kindness of Milto's Pizzeria, or Beefsteak Charlie's, or even Texas Instruments.

When I get down to the facts, it all sounds pretty pathetic: should I choose someone I've known for four weeks over someone I've known for four months? It sounds worthy of a sitcom I've been watching on television lately, where young actors with impeccable hair in twenty minutes of listless dialogue untangle situations much more complex than mine. And would the person I've known for four weeks even want me to leave my husband for him? It sounds so real—leave my husband—but that's what Robert is, even if our marriage was never a marriage, even if Robert resents it. Maybe if I take a clear look at Andy, a look unclouded by this rosy fog, I'll immediately see how little I know about him, probably as little as I knew about Robert when I agreed to marry him.

And suddenly the most unsettling thought springs at me with the ferocity of the giant bear from the horror film I saw: I am exactly like my mother. It took her two weeks to marry her first husband, a hospital patient with shrapnel in his rear end during the Finnish War of 1939, a marriage that lasted only a few months before they were both drafted to the front and lost contact with each other. It took her one week to marry her second husband during the war in 1942, not enough time to find out that he had tuberculosis, along with a common-law wife and a ten-year-old daughter in a northern town close to the Urals; not nearly long enough to figure out that he was a bingeing alcoholic. I know this because just before I left I found a blue notebook in a drawer of my mother's desk, its pages covered with her perfect square handwriting, detailing her life before she moved to Leningrad. She must have written it for posterity, and that meant for me. So I read it. And now I almost wish I hadn't.

∞

Andy comes to Beefsteak Charlie's and sits at one of my tables. "So your name is Elena and you're gonna spoil me?" he says, grinning, looking at my button.

"I'm a terrible waitress," I say. "I've already warned you."

"You did," he says and orders baby back ribs and a Diet Coke. "And dressing on the side," he adds and we both laugh.

I bring his order, and, since it's a weekday and the place is slow, I sit down at his table. "Robert is coming in three days," I say. "From Texas."

"I know," says Andy, although I have no idea how he can know this. Maybe Millie told him. I also wonder where this knowledge leaves us and, more important, if there is an "us" at all. What do I know about Andy, really? He is thirty-two, seven years older than I am. He was married but is now separated and lives alone. He has a younger brother, Frankie, who lives in upstate New York. He is the most irresistible man I've ever met, including Boris from Kiev, who was completely irresistible.

"Why don't you pack up and move out?" says Andy.

"Move out?" I ask. "Move out to where?" In my life, I've moved out once, from my mother's apartment in Leningrad to America. No one in Russia simply moves out because they want to move out, and it is impossible to explain this to anyone who didn't have to wear a red Pioneer scarf when she was nine.

"Move to my place in North Bergen," says Andy. "I have a one-bedroom apartment. But there are actually two rooms," he says, because I already told him that assigning a function to a room is nothing but a Western luxury.

I want to ask Andy in what capacity I would be moving to his place, but I don't because that was what my mother asked her third husband, my father, who was her ulcer patient in the hospital in the provincial town of Ivanovo shortly after the war. My father got a job as the director of Leningrad Technical School and he asked my mother if she would move to Leningrad with him. "In what capacity?" she asked sternly, making sure to preserve the propriety and order she so cherished, letting him know that he couldn't take advantage of the situation.

I don't even want to imagine what my mother would think of all this turmoil. She hasn't had time to get used to the thought of my not sleeping under a bridge with Robert, so how am I going to inform her that I am on the verge of changing both, the partner and the bridge?

"You can sleep on the couch if you like," says Andy and smiles, but his eyes are so liquid that it's impossible to take him seriously. I think of yesterday, when on the way back from our diner trip we stopped and bought a pear at a little fancy fruit shop in Princeton. It was yellow and almost translucent, and Andy took the first bite and offered the fruit to me, still in his hand. As I sank my teeth into the golden ripeness, the juice, sticky and sweet, ran down his fingers and I was about to lick them—an impulse that rose straight from my gut—when I saw the salesperson, an older man with a gray mustache, looking away, as if he knew our relationship was illicit, as if his turning away was a reminder that what we both wanted was off-limits.

I should probably tell Andy I've already done this once before: I packed my life into a suitcase and went to live with a man who, in some old-fashioned circles, might be called a stranger. And what did it lead to? Nothing good, obviously, or I wouldn't be staring this choice in the face again.

"Excuse me," says someone above my head, and I see Samantha the bartender standing over our table. "Can I have a word?"

"You can't sit down with a customer," she whispers into my ear. "If the manager sees this, she'll fire you."

I jump up, picking up my tray, and quickly look around to establish who else has had a chance to witness this latest failure. But then I glance at Andy, and his eyes let me know he doesn't think it is a failure. He is looking at me with pride, as if I'd won a national linguistics competition by impeccably parsing a page-long sentence.

"Please tell me if I could get you anything else," I say after a few moments of silence—a standard, irrelevant sentence I've learned with other standard phrases—although it doesn't matter what I say to him now. His pride and his trust, which I see suspended and focused in his eyes, have entered me directly, without words, making me realize that Andy has already understood everything about me I want him to know.

෪

I am sitting in Millie's kitchen with Donald, telling him about Andy and Robert, asking him what I should do. I realize I have no one to talk to here but Donald, whom I have known for only several weeks. In a weird way, Donald is related to me, being Millie's former son-in-law. Back home, in addition to my mother, who was invariably there with string bags of unsought advice, I had my sister, always ready to share a lesson from her life, which was the enviable life of an actress, thirteen years longer than mine. In the most critical situations, such as Robert's proposal, I turned to my best friend, Nina, whom I met in my first-year university class. We were in Nina's two-room apartment, where she lived with her new husband, her parents, and her brother. She was pregnant, kneeling in the corner of the smaller room next to an armoire, measuring the space for a crib. "Don't be an idiot," she said. "Do whatever you have to do to get the hell out of here."

"What do *you* want to do?" asks Donald, turning the question around, as, I should've known, a psychotherapist would.

I want to be with Andy, but I don't want to hurt Robert.

I tell Donald what I am thinking, and he says I should do what I consider best for me. I didn't know it was so simple.

"Come and stay with us, if you like," says Donald. "Until you figure out your next step." He looks at me and nods several times, as if to confirm what he just said. "Bea and I would love to have you."

This is the sweetest, kindest thing anyone has done for me since I arrived here, and I am about to start crying. I think of the sun streaming through my Leningrad kitchen window, pouring gold on the oilcloth with a sunflower print, on our cupboard and our old stove and on all those cabbage and egg *pirozhki* my mother baked for my birthday just before I left.

"Thank you, former brother-in-law," I whimper through sniffles and hug Donald. Or rather he hugs me with his huge, Nordic arms.

# *Eighteen*

Robert is back from Texas, and he doesn't seem at all relieved that I left. He isn't behaving like the Robert I know, the cerebral, logical Robert who shipped me off to his mother in New Jersey. He is suddenly someone different, someone who speaks with the high, angry notes of my sister's stage voice. Looking despondent, he paces around the living room, refusing to believe what I am telling him. He is suddenly very human, and this makes me feel guilty and ungrateful.

"I can't believe this," he says, throwing up his arms in bewilderment. "I just can't believe it. When did all this happen?"

A long time ago, I want to tell him, but I don't. I stand by the side of the couch, against the wall of Millie's living room, silent, out of his path.

"So let me get this straight: you're here for six weeks, at my mother's house, and you meet someone else? You jump into someone else's arms? Is that what you're telling me? Someone so"—he pauses, searching for a word—"so ordinary."

Would it have been better if I'd jumped into the arms of someone Robert considers above ordinary? His roommate, Sagar, perhaps, who also solves cosmic problems, or maybe Robert's friend the pianist whose concert we drove to across the endless flatness of Texas?

"You have so much going for you. You're smart. Smarter than Karen," says Robert, groping for reasons to demonstrate why, if I needed to jump into someone's arms, they shouldn't have been Andy's. He pauses after he says this because it's the first time Karen's name has been spoken since last December, when we were walking toward our Leningrad apartment, Robert explaining the concept of open marriage to me.

My being smarter than Karen doesn't make things better. I know Robert means it as a compliment, but it only reminds me of the Karen ghost I used to see in our Texas bedroom, silently peering at us from the corner. And is it really an achievement to trump your husband's girlfriend in intelligence?

"You're speaking from your loins," accuses Robert. "Loins," he repeats, which makes me think of Nabokov's *Lolita*. Light of my life, fire of my loins—lines that were banned in Russia. We are speaking all in English now; Robert has no time or inclination to turn Russian case endings over in his brain. This conversation is all too visceral to be conducted in a foreign language, it occurs to me, which is ironic since I'm speaking in English.

"It's never been a real marriage," I say. "We didn't know each other. We still don't. You married me to help me escape my mother," I say, fumbling for a summary that will usher in some closure. "And I'm grateful for what you did for me. I really am."

"Fuck your gratitude," snarls Robert. "Don't tell me why I fucking married you. I flew to that country of yours three times. My mother thought I was out of my mind. Karen almost left me. Did you know that? I spent five thousand dollars to bring you here. How much did this other guy spend to get you out of Russia?"

It never occurred to me to calculate how much I might owe Robert, but maybe I should have. It was a mystery to me how much a round-trip ticket from New York to Leningrad could cost, in American dollars. I'd never known anyone who left Russia and then came back. I was even naïve enough to dream—after a glance at a map confirmed that the route to America lay over Europe—about stopping in Paris and visiting the Louvre. Could I change planes in Paris? I asked Robert in a letter. It is on the way to the United States. Maybe I could stay there for a day or two instead of spending six hours in the airport at Shannon. Paris, I wrote, as if I had a right to commit the magic word to paper, a word that shared space with Tolstoy's ball gowns and royal fox hunts with packs of borzoi. A city that was clearly unreachable, suspended in air over real life, like a mirage. Now I am glad Robert said no, or I would have cost him even more.

But aside from my gratitude and my cost, aside from my remorse at watching the new, visibly shaken Robert, there is something else bubbling inside me, something I haven't been able to verbalize until now.

"I knew nothing when I came here," I say. "I was clueless. I desperately needed someone to explain all this to me. I'd never seen a hamburger before. When I first went to the supermarket I cried because I had no idea what was in front of me. I felt like a three-year-old. People stared at me like I was a drunk crusted in vomit hobbling down the street. And you never helped me. You worked, you read, you practiced music. You never ever helped me." These words are a surprise as they stream out of my mouth, rising like a vapor from the dark pool on the bottom of my heart. "You were always involved with your teaching, with your violin, with Karen." I say her name for the first time, wrapping my mouth around the sound of it. "You lost interest in me. You were like a child and I was your new toy, and when you saw that your toy was damaged, when you saw I didn't know how to do the simplest thing here, you rejected me. You sent me back to your mother's house."

Robert stops pacing and looks at me with disbelief. "I sent you here because you were unhappy in Texas," he says. "I didn't know what else to do with you."

"You sent me away. You didn't have time for me. You abandoned me," I say, purging the toxic words from the murk inside me.

Their sounds explode in my mouth and make the words swell with power as I release them. It feels good to unlock them, to validate their meaning as they enter the air between us. "You sent me away because you just can't live with another person."

"But we talked about this," says Robert with irritation, only hearing what he wants to, letting the rest stream past his ears. "You agreed, for god's sake."

"How could I not have agreed? You knew where I lived, behind bars. You've been to Russia, you know what it's like. Do you remember what it's like? Not a place of options. I had to agree. I had no choice."

For a few moments, Robert stops pacing and stands there, thinking. "Listen, why don't you come back with me to Texas?" he offers. "I can get you a teaching assistantship at the Slavic Department. I can get you into graduate school, I promise. We'll have time to talk. If this is serious, this . . . thing, you'll feel the same way in June," he says, and I know this insight comes straight from Millie. Millie, who I felt had nudged me toward Andy to help her son and who now, lamenting Robert's anguish, is doing all she can to get us back together.

I can't help but think about Natasha from *War and Peace*. She is sixteen, and her fiancé, whom she meets at that first debutante ball, an older Prince Bolkonsky, asks her to put off their wedding for one year, a requirement erected by his authoritarian father. "Go travel abroad," says the father, peering at his son with a mocking smile, "and then, if this love, this passion, whatever it is, is so great, then you can get married." The old man knows life much better than his son, and during that year, needless to say, terrible things happen and Natasha never marries the prince.

I can't imagine falling into a trap straight out of Tolstoy, waiting a year to seek a miraculous cure for a crippled marriage. I can't imagine losing Andy.

"Look. You told me once you wanted to go to Paris." Robert says this with a clipped, staccato rhythm, a desperation flashing around the edges of his voice. "I'll get tickets in the spring and we'll go. Maybe we just need to get away."

The word *Paris* enters my mind but doesn't settle there. It is no longer about Paris, or graduate school, or even Karen. I know I must leave this marriage the same way I knew I had to leave my mother and my country. The same way I made the choice almost a year ago and left the ledge of my courtyard sandbox. I understand this, but the knowledge doesn't make me feel less guilty. I wish this Robert were the old, rational Robert, immune to anguish and desperation.

"In August I would've been ecstatic about Paris," I say. "But not now."

"Please think about it," Robert insists. "Think about what I'm saying. Things really aren't that bad. Just consider it, that's all I'm asking."

I don't say anything, and he makes an exhaling sound, raking his fingers through his hair. "It's really hard to understand you," he says, anger in his voice. "You wanted to teach. You wanted to go to Paris. I'm offering you everything you wanted."

Robert turns around, takes off his glasses, and starts wiping them with his shirttail, as if everything at this moment depended on the clarity of his vision. "You are a fraud," he says, without looking at me. "An impostor, a person I don't even know. Maybe someone I never knew."

Then he returns to striding back and forth, taking injured, baffled steps, every few moments coming to a wall. Where was this fragile gait before and why didn't I see it? I watch him, flattening myself against a window frame, and guilt curdles my heart. The guilt as dark as my dacha well, as sour as rancid milk.

"I'm sorry," I say, "but it's time for me to leave," as Robert makes a roaring noise and drives his fist into the wall.

# PART 2

## *Andy*

# *Nineteen*

I am staring into a box with things I brought from Russia, things that became irrelevant the moment I disembarked at Washington Dulles Airport less than a year ago: my wedding dress made from sparkly polyester the color of lilac, a scratchy wool shawl with red roses, a pocketbook I bought on Nevsky Prospekt in a store called Hunting and Fishing. It hung on the wall next to rifles and spinning rods, intended to be a hunting bag to hold small game, and I bought it because it was made from real leather and had a fringe on the flap that looked more fashionable at the time than any of the three types of hideous plastic handbags our department stores had to offer.

I never opened the box during my first five months in this country. The contents seemed alien and dated, clearly out of place in the sterile strangeness of Texas. I first dared take off the cardboard lid after unpacking my Russian suitcase in North Bergen, New Jersey, when Andy asked to see what was inside. His curiosity made me happy, even giddier than I'd been the past few weeks since I moved into his apartment, so the reminders of my Leningrad life didn't look as pitiful as they would have back in Austin. Yet when I unfolded my wedding dress, it drooped over my arm, staticky and wrinkled. The roses on the shawl seemed to have faded. But the leather fringe on the hunting bag still swayed in rugged elegance as

I lifted it out of the box and hung it over my shoulder. The mirror on the wall reflected an image I could live with, unlike those reflections in Austin mirrors I generally hated: a bewildered girl dressed in silly clothes. My Leningrad hunting pocketbook oddly fit into the North Bergen interior, matching a sweater Andy had bought for me at a department store called Bamberger's.

I needed clothes to go to work. A couple of weeks earlier, I had found a job in New York, near Times Square, on Forty-Second Street.

"You, on Forty-Second Street?" our next-door neighbor repeated incredulously and laughed a short, uncomfortable laugh.

Five mornings a week I take a bus that stops next to our building and half an hour later arrive at Port Authority, which spews crowds of commuters into the seedy tunnel of Forty-Second Street. Neon girls in first-floor windows point to the eerie darkness behind open doors as I walk past men who stand on the sidewalk and mutter under their breath, trying to entice passersby into the underworld of capitalist ills that *Pravda* has warned us about. I walk past the twenty-five-cent peep shows, past the twinkling promise of live nude girls behind shabby entrances, past the lit XXXs, competing with each other in size, to a sign on the door that reads SCS BUSINESS AND TECHNICAL INSTITUTE. I am a teacher now. I teach English as a second language to immigrants fresh from Soviet Russia, thirty hours a week.

I distribute mimeographed copies of dialogues to my class of twenty-five students, mostly women, mostly from small towns south of Moscow, places I would never have thought of visiting when I lived in Russia, places where Soviet citizens were supposed to be happily building a bright communist future instead of emigrating to the West. They come to class on the *subvey* all the way from Far Rockaway, trying to learn enough English to find employment when they graduate six months later. SCS Business and Technical Institute offers English classes complete with phone labs, promising office jobs to all its graduates.

Phone lab sessions make me nervous. Once a week we all go to a big room with a black phone proudly sitting on every desk as if this were a KGB listening center where we are supposed to play agents. I know I have to train my students to be receptionists, but what right do I have to head this effort if this is the job I failed to get in Texas? "IBM. May I help you?" reads the mimeographed page of my script. "IBM. May I help you" is what my students memorize, what Valya from Pinsk and Klava from Chernovtsy diligently recite into the telephones that look completely real. They do well on this part: they answer the phone without the sheepishness I would bring to the task. They confidently hold the receiver and enunciate the question into the nonexisting line.

It is the rest of the conversation that gets convoluted: What do you say to the callers who foolishly take you up on the offer of helping them? What do you do when you cannot decipher their words distorted by static, when you know you wouldn't be able to make out what they say even if the lines were perfectly clear? It occurs to me that this phone lab is another instance of *vranyo*, where we all pretend that if we ask the May I help you question with the assertiveness required in the manual, the subsequent words from the other end of the line will miraculously flow into our ears, as transparent and accessible as water from the tap.

"Make up scenarios for professional office dialogues," said the program director, who showed me the lab, and I wrack my brain in a futile search for possible business conversations, trying to imagine what would compel these textbook customers to call an imaginary IBM office manned by ex-Soviets from the end of the *subvey* line.

I am as afraid of the director as I am terrified of answering the phones. Her name is Bonita Binder, and her straight spine and thin frame convey the same inflexibility that is locked in the repeating consonants of her name. She brandishes work sheets and mimeographed exercises as she strides down the halls, the most recent one about the weather. *Hot, humid, freezing, windy* are the adjectives leading the vocabulary list for the students to memorize, followed by the Celsius to Fahrenheit conversion formula, which I commit to memory before distributing the copies. The last page contains a list of idiomatic expressions I've never heard before. "A woman is as changeable as the weather," read my students, a sentence followed by an instruction to create situations that would illustrate the point. The women in my class giggle and oblige with little misogynistic stories from their fresh Soviet past. Valya from Pinsk, who was an engineer in her Russian life, tells us how her office, eighty percent female, could never fulfill their quarterly plan because her colleagues spent hefty chunks of their workday queuing up for groceries, constantly changing their minds about which line to join. "First she want to stand for bologna," says Valya, slicing the air with the heel of her palm, "then she decide she need butter. More changeable than weather, that girl." Valya pauses and looks at my handout with Bonita's idioms. "Though weather in Pinsk was bad," she concludes.

During her class visits and phone lab demonstrations, Bonita stands erect on her sturdy feet tucked into black flats, refusing to give me a smile of reassurance, remaining as serious and stern as she thinks the SCS Business and Technical Institute ought to be. She would fit well, I think, into the cheerless offices of the Leningrad Young Communist League, where I had to surrender my membership card to be entombed into the safe in case I ever decided to return.

At home I march around the kitchen in my slippers, impersonating the SCS director, driving the May-I-help-you offer into our phone receiver with as much authority as I can muster. Andy laughs and scoops me into his arms, saying that Bonita Binder is nothing but a control freak. I don't know what that means, but his embrace feels tight and warm, giving me hope that the threat of being a receptionist no longer looms over my head, that teaching at SCS is only the first step in the direction of the path to college teaching and my impersonation of Bonita Binder will soon become as irrelevant as the wrinkled lilac wedding dress I pulled out of my Leningrad box.

&

I get a letter from home, four pages of my mother's worried handwriting, urging me to snap out of this love delusion, think hard, and go back to Robert, my marriage to whom was decreed by the Leningrad Bureau of Civil Acts and stamped into my passport, with my whole family as witnesses. I can see her and Marina whispering late at night, after my sister comes home from her evening performance, the television glowing with the late *News from the Fields* and then going blank when all the programs end at midnight. They are alone in the apartment, so why are they whispering?—yet this is the picture I hold in my mind, the two of them huddled on my mother's bed, muttering and sighing.

I write back—two pages about Andy and our apartment overlooking a park—words that I know will not persuade my mother. I enclose a photograph of Andy and his Datsun. I also put in a picture of me grinning on the couch with a glass of Amaretto, on a tasting spree of all the liqueurs behind the glass in our living room cabinet. I know my mother's logic: if I didn't have enough food, she will reason, I wouldn't be lounging on a divan with a silly smile, happily downing drinks. I write about my first professional job teaching English to Russians—just as I did in Leningrad!— and about my lunches at Popeyes on Forty-Second Street across from my school. Almost every afternoon, I walk through the inviting smell of hot grease and order chicken legs and wings, all extra-crispy, all fried in deep vats of oil no one in my country has ever seen.

"If you tasted this chicken," I write, "you'd swallow your tongues," a Russian idiom my mother likes to use when her *kot-*

*lety* turn out especially succulent, another brick of evidence in support of my absent deprivation. "We're going to send out a résumé and look for a college teaching position for me," I write, translating what Andy said recently. There is no word—or concept—of a résumé in Russian, so I replace it with the word *letter*. "We," I write—the same pronoun widely used back home—although this American *we* is altogether different. It is a trim, individual *we* with space for two people only, Andy and me, as opposed to the bulky Soviet *we*, big enough for our apartment neighbors, our work collectives, Aunt Polya from our nursery school kitchen and Aunt Lusya with our middle school mop, and other unspecified aunts and uncles who yelled, pontificated, and harangued, all melding into one noisy crowd that passed under our windows on May Day with banners, balloons, and fake carnations swaying on wire stems.

∞

Every few weeks or so our phone rings in the middle of the night. When Andy wakes and fumbles for the receiver, there is silence on the other end, nothing but faint static in the ether. I can imagine Robert crouched over the phone on his Texas mattress, with darkness behind the windows buttressing his resolve, egging him on in his resentment.

The glowing hands of the clock on our bedside table show 2:15. I imagine Robert on the other end of the line, reaching out to me through the blackness, trying to connect, all too late. My mother's saying pops into my head, one of those slivers of wisdom that always rhyme in Russian, that I always failed to learn: "We don't value what we have, then cry when we lose it."

Or maybe these early morning calls are about something completely different and Robert isn't trying to connect. Maybe he simply wants to shame me for what I've done, to make sure my moral plunge to the lower depths—worthy of Maxim Gorky's sharp proletarian pen—stares me in the face. Or maybe it isn't Robert at all.

Andy's breathing is even and calm again, the breathing of a sleeping man. The clock ticks, nudging its hands toward 3:00. Warm in my new bed, I lie awake in the dark, happy to be next to Andy, awash in my thanklessness and guilt.

# *Twenty*

Andy shows me how to write a résumé, and we re-create my Russian life—my university English classes and my desk duty at the House of Friendship and Peace—using phrases such as "educational background" and "work experience." Committed to paper and arranged in columns under headings, my Russian past looks unfamiliar and impressive, having acquired unexpected solidity and heft. It looks as if it were the past of someone else, some other Elena Gorokhova, self-confident and successful, who welcomed foreign delegations visiting her city, then at night dove into the depths of philological research at the university. I didn't know I had a master's degree in English and linguistics; I didn't know what a master's degree was until Andy told me. It feels satisfying to be called a master, even though I still have trouble mastering which article to put before which noun.

"If you want to get a college teaching job, you have to go to graduate school and get a doctorate," says Andy, and I think of the Russian doctoral degree I never even dreamed of, which marked the top spot on the Olympus of Russian academia, accessible only to heads of major university departments, professors whose office doors were never opened to reveal a live human being inside.

"With the amount of credits you took," Andy adds, "you may already have a doctorate." The other day he pored over the translated copy of my university diploma, five typed pages of courses I took for six years after work, four times a week, two classes a night. "I can't believe the amount of hours you studied English," he says. "No wonder you can speak it." I am not always sure I can speak or write it, but Andy's voice is so tender and sincere that I decide to believe him.

I tell Andy of walking along the Neva embankment with my university friend Nina when classes ended at ten, of the dark contours of the Admiralty and the Hermitage on the other side, grim and unglamorous at that hour of the night. We walked over the Palace Bridge—the river strapped under the armor of ice for five months—leaning into the wind, talking about banned books, Tarkovsky's films, and those who had already left the country. "I'd go anywhere to get out of here," Nina said. "Anywhere. Even to Patagonia." In our tight friendship, she was the one with a Jewish husband and hopes for immigrating to the West. I had no such far-reaching plans: my biggest wish was to reunite with Boris from Kiev, whom I'd met in the Crimea. Four times a week, Nina and I walked and talked, trying to glimpse into the future—not the bright future that glared from the pages of *Pravda* but the real life lurking ahead of us, as impenetrable as a winter night in Leningrad.

છ

We walk into our apartment as the phone is ringing, and I sprint to the receiver on the kitchen wall. A man from Hudson College is asking for me. I straighten up, as if ordered to stand at attention, as if afraid that he can see me all the way from his office on Kennedy Boulevard, stooping and clutching the phone in my sweaty palm. He is looking at my résumé, he says, wondering if I could come in for an interview tomorrow. They have a summer position, teaching English as a second language, starting next week. The person who was going to teach the class quit this morning without notice, he says, exasperation in his voice.

"What did I tell you?" says Andy, triumphant that his plan is working. "Out of the hundred résumés we sent out, we may have just found you a job."

I am proud of such an un-Soviet initiative on our part, even though I am not sure if I have received a job offer yet. All I think about is the ominous word *interview*, which takes me back to the half an hour of sweating under the incinerating gaze of Bonita Binder of SCS Business and Technical Institute, who made it clear she almost never hired nonnative speakers of English to teach immigrant students. I sat on a folding metal chair across from her desk, rehearsing every phrase out of my mouth, summoning up every phonetic rule I ever learned at the university in a desperate attempt to demonstrate that I could sound like a native. Of course, I knew I couldn't, and I knew that she knew, the obvious travesty sitting between us like a foul monster, making me muddle up verb tenses.

∞

In my navy dress from Bamberger's, I am sitting across from the dean of Hudson College, Steven Cromer. He is wearing a white shirt with a red tie, his suit jacket hanging on the back of his chair, and I am relieved that I decided to wear the stern navy dress to look as businesslike as he does. The dean sounds much more friendly than Bonita Binder, telling me about the ESL classes and asking when I moved here from the Soviet Union. He is the first person I have met in this country who doesn't call it Russia, who knows about the fifteen republics that constitute my country. He is a sociologist, he says, who applies statistical methods to locate and count the references to his articles in an ocean of world research. I admit that the scientific significance of his quest eludes me, but these references must excite him because he gets up and starts pacing back and forth on his long legs, covering the length of his office in four steps.

"I was referenced in the Soviet journal *Family and School* last October," he says, and I nod vigorously, acknowledging that I am aware of the publication and assuring him that it has a wide audience of Soviet parents and teachers. Talking about the Soviet Union brings a faint smile to the dean's lips, as if it were a fantasyland he'd always dreamed about visiting.

"I saw from your résumé that you're from Leningrad," says Steven Cromer.

"The real capital, much more beautiful than Moscow," I gush, watching the dean half-close his eyes as if he had the image of the Hermitage imprinted on the insides of his eyelids. "Moscow is eclectic, nothing but a big village," I go on, trying to say what I think will please his ears. "Leningrad has a soul."

"All those free universities and free health care," says the dean dreamily, and I don't know if I should say something to qualify the adjective *free* or keep quiet. I don't want to tell him about hospital wards without water and sheets, or abortions without anesthesia, or university admissions boards with lists of party bosses' children in their desks, so I remain silent. "We have a lot of students from Cuba here," says Steven Cromer. "The Soviet and Cuban governments seem to have figured out some things." For a moment, I think of asking what students from Cuba are doing in New Jersey instead of attending free local universities, but I don't. The possibility of waving farewell to Bonita Binder's expressionless face and the KGB-style phone labs at SCS Business and Technical Institute makes me want to jump up and down, although I know perfectly well I can't do it in the serious office of a college dean.

"Congratulations," says the dean and shakes my hand. "Welcome to Hudson College."

For a moment, I am stunned. Was that the entire interview? What about checking if I know the participial constructions or the proper use of the perfect progressive tenses? Or pointing out that I've missed an article or two, something no Russian will ever learn? Or asking me for the most effective way to facilitate group work in a multilingual classroom? Instead, the dean stands up and says he hopes I will be happy as part of the Hudson College family.

I am already happy. Steven Cromer walks to an open box sitting on a chair and lifts out a booklet with a spiral spine. "You should read this report," he says.

"Steven Cromer," the front page reads. *Contributions of a Comprehensive Faculty and Staff Development Program to a Comprehensive Community College.* I think the title is unnecessarily redundant, but I nod enthusiastically, letting the author know that I am eager to find out more about him and the college where I am going to teach for the next six weeks.

A column of sun slants through the window and lights up the silver G on the dean's belt buckle, a symbol I recently saw on the cover of *Gentlemen's Quarterly* in a kiosk as I was walking to work. I say good-bye, and Steven Cromer probably thinks I am smiling because I have enjoyed his musings on all those free perks I foolishly left behind, but the truth is I can already imagine Andy's laughter when he hears about my new boss, the socialist with a Gucci belt.

# *Twenty-One*

It is August and we are in the Catskills—Kastilsky Mountains, as my former SCS students used to call them. Kastilsky sounds so familiar, so nostalgic. It is as if the name belonged to a railway station where electric trains from Leningrad slowed down by a grove of birches and balding firs that hid your old dacha with a caved-in roof and a wavy fence.

We are visiting Andy's younger brother, Frankie, who lives in a sprawling house with sloping floors and a pond near the fringe of the forest. Swarms of gnats do their evening dance over the brown surface of the water, just as they did near my dacha in Leningrad. Frankie's given name is Fred, but he recast it in the sixth grade because his friends from Queens were all Italian. He could possibly pass for an Italian, I think, with waves of dark hair and a tall, slim build. But there is a drop of sadness in his light green eyes that can only be traced to a tiny Jewish town in prerevolutionary Russia, which his grandparents fled around the time my mother was born, three years before the Bolsheviks seized power in 1917.

Taking turns, we climb up a wobbly ladder helping Frankie paint the house as his three-year-old daughter, Heather, pedals her tricycle on a grassy path between the driveway and the shed, making a breakneck U-turn by the compost pile around a rhubarb patch. This could be my Russian dacha if the dacha had magically expanded, growing water and sewer pipes inside its walls and sprouting a chimney reaching all the way down to a furnace that could work on a fuel other than wood. We would be the envy of our whole village near Leningrad and especially of our truck driver neighbor, Fyodor, who—in his two years working for a state lumber factory—delivered enough materials to his own backyard to build a two-story structure that towered over our fence. Frankie's house even smells like our dacha at the end of summer: of burned wood, dust, and slices of sinewy rhubarb stems on the kitchen table, hard and sour, waiting to be dropped into a pot of boiling water for compote.

But I know this isn't our dacha, and even the old familiar smells cannot fool me. I know this is America, where I don't have to weed or water or harvest anything since there is nothing growing around the house except robust bushes and patches of tall grass. I know this sliver of country life in the Kastilsky Mountains is as un-Russian as the Austin supermarket. The house is too grand to be a dacha, the land around it too spacious and wasted. And the lilac bush by the back door is full of withered clumps of flowers, rust-colored and parched, because no one had cut them off in June and put them on the kitchen table in a vase to usher in the humid, fragrant breath of summer. Despite the gnats, the pile of compost squirming with worms, and two skinny birches trembling on the forest fringe, this isn't Russia. Despite the lilac bush with common, heart-shaped leaves, this isn't home. The trees are thin, and many look as if they haven't yet recovered from the winter, their branches tentative and slender. This is a teenage forest that has grown too fast and now boasts the height but not yet the maturity or breadth of bone.

Yet what I find under the leaves is viscerally Russian: a mushroom on a tall stem, its red cap and black specks near the root placing it, undeniably, into the category of noble mushrooms. It doesn't belong to the army of skimpy peasants we had to pick in

Leningrad—hollow stems and silly umbrella heads that were only good for salting—because of the dozens of mushroom hunters who had arrived by sunrise and who also knew the spots. As I wiggle the red cap out of the ground, I see another one, just as big and splendid, and then a smaller one, and then a real giant you would never find in our dacha woods because it would've been picked a long time before it could reach this size.

I take them all, as many as I can carry in my arms, a glorious harvest that would humble any mushroom-picking rival around my dacha, an armful that would make my sister weep. Proudly, I walk into the house, smiling at the lucky chance that has allowed me to accomplish the impossible. I carefully put the mushrooms on the kitchen counter to sort and clean and get them ready for the skillet.

Heather is by the sink, watching me wash the mushrooms, asking if she can dry them. Of course she can, I say, and she carefully runs pieces of paper towel over the sponge underneath the caps. I chop the mushrooms up and they begin to sizzle in the biggest frying pan I can find, infused with melting butter, releasing the familiar forest smell of dacha and home.

My timing is perfect. Out of the kitchen window I see a car pulling up in front of the house: Andy's parents, Doris and Artie, who live fifteen minutes away from our apartment, have just arrived to join us for an August weekend in the Kastilsky Mountains. I watch his mother, with carefully styled blond hair and lipstick, bustling to get her jacket out of the backseat—a mother unlike any I remember in my Leningrad courtyard. Every morning, my mother and the mothers of my friends brushed their hair into donutlike updos held by hairpins, their faces never marred by makeup. Like everyone else, they owned one good dress, a house robe, and a few skirts and blouses they wore to work that fit on a couple of hangers in the family's armoire. Doris wears silky jackets and high heels, which lift her up to the height where her sons can embrace her without bending down.

The mushrooms are ready. I slather them with sour cream because I want everyone—Frankie and his parents and Heather and Andy and Frankie's wife, Jen, who should be back from her babysitting job any minute—to experience the pure forest taste.

The whole family is in the kitchen now, kissing and embracing, unable to ignore the thick, woody smell that has permeated the air. The dish rack is full of clean plates, and I pick one up and spoon the first portion of the fragrant stew.

"What is this yummy-smelling thing?" asks Doris, taking a step toward the stove.

"Wild mushrooms," I say proudly. "Fresh out of the forest. I just picked them twenty minutes ago."

Back home the reaction would be a joyful racket and a clamorous struggle to get the first taste. But what is happening in Frankie's kitchen looks more like the final scene from Gogol's *Inspector General*, the most famous silent scene in the history of theater. Doris stands frozen in the middle of the floor, halfway to the stove. Artie is by the kitchen door, his mouth open as if he were going to say something but suddenly discovered that he'd lost the gift of speech. Frankie's arms are stretched toward Heather, who is by the stove, looking up at the plate in my hands, anxious to try the mysterious dish. Because everyone is still, I freeze, too, not knowing what to do next, trying to decipher this awkwardly strange reaction to a simple offering of food.

"They're really good," I say to break the silence, picking up and chewing on a forkful of the mushroom stew to demonstrate what I think should be obvious.

"I don't know, dear," says Doris, breaking out of her trance. She shakes her head and steps closer to the stove to take a better look. Her hands are on her hips as she leans forward to examine the contents of the frying pan. "Wild mushrooms . . ." she mutters, stepping away as though the smell alone could poison her. "I just don't know."

"I want to try them," whines Heather. "Please, Daddy, please!"

I stand by the stove, feeling like an idiot for having desecrated a healthy American kitchen with a wild menace from the nearby woods. They must all think I am trying to poison them. I suddenly see myself with American eyes, eyes that never spotted a wild mushroom growing out of the forest loam. As far as they know, I may have cooked the most venomous mushroom called *muhomor*, the one my mother used to chop up in a saucer with a little sugar—and the next morning the windowsills of our dacha were black with dead flies. But worst of all is that I now see myself with the eyes of Andy's parents: it was bad enough that their American son opened his house and his soul to a recent arrival from the land of collective farms and five-year plans, but now she is trying to impose her fungal, foreign ways on their entire family, starting with an innocent three-year-old.

"I want the mushrooooooms," Heather keeps whining, tugging on Frankie's arm.

"No," says Andy, and she stops, taken aback by the determination in his voice. "The first person allowed to try this is me."

"Not fair!" yells Heather as Andy approaches the stove and heaps a mushroom ladleful onto a plate. For a minute, he stares at the dark stew, then takes a breath and sends a forkful into his mouth.

"You're right," he says. "They're delicious."

We stand side by side near the stove, working on our plates of mushrooms, finishing every last bit, a certainty congealing in my mind, the first rational thought commemorating the six months' anniversary of our mindless bliss. A certainty as permanent as the ancient oak near my dacha, as solid as my mother herself with her ingrained demand for stability and order. Maybe it is the flavor of wild mushrooms that makes me see what's happening, but one thing suddenly becomes perfectly clear. I realize that my mother no longer needs to whisper to Marina her fears that I will be stranded and lost in an alien land, ending up alone, with no one to lean on.

# *Twenty-Two*

My ESL students are from Ecuador, Peru, Venezuela, and Colombia. They are from Puerto Rico and the Dominican Republic. They come from countries whose names I have heard only on a TV travel show in Leningrad, exotic names that our Cyrillic alphabet twists and mangles, trying to tame them to a Slavic pronunciation. For me, these names evoke the humid jungle we only knew from Kipling's books, with panthers and pythons and parrots the colors of nursery school crayons. Many students are from Cuba, the only country name our Russian language has no problem with, phonetically. Cuba is simple, a name we've all heard in the news since childhood, two syllables requiring a single breath.

Before my first class at Hudson College the only Cuban I had met was Roxana, the unauthorized, un-Indian girlfriend of our Austin roommate. Thinking of Roxana takes me back to Texas, which instantly resurrects Robert and the sense of guilt scratching in the back of my head, like an ungrateful cat. I try to carve him out of my mind, the way I used to cut white circles of fat out of *kolbasa* slices back home, but my mental knife lacks sharpness and precision, botching up the boundaries, jolting and lurching in my uncertain hand. I wonder if Robert is in Austin, or in Princeton; I wonder what happened to Roxana and Sagar and the suitcase full of Kodak brides my former roommate's mother lugged across the ocean.

"I'm sorry I'm not going to meet your mother," I told Sagar when I said good-bye to him in Austin.

"Can I please come to New Jersey with you?" he asked with a sad chuckle. "Maybe I'll be able to escape, too."

I look at the strange names on my ESL class roster: Ascanio, Irlanda, Leidy, Jafet. But the oddest name is also the most familiar, a first name that belongs to a skinny twenty-one-year-old man from Cuba. My tongue freezes for a moment before wrapping around its sound—so melodic because it intones the name of the great Siberian river the founder of our Soviet state adopted for his pseudonym while hiding from the tsarist police, so close to the sound of my own name.

Lenin Rodriguez does not like to speak. He sits in the last row, his head down, the hood of his sweatshirt hovering over his eyes. When I call on him, he answers reluctantly, as if each word were a boulder he had to push up the slope of his throat.

"Come on, Lenin," I nudge him. "If you don't speak in English, you'll never learn it." In addition to teaching grammar and vocabulary, I do a bit of cheerleading. In my own English classes we had to sit with our arms folded on the desk as the teachers towered over us, erect as statues of the real Lenin, denouncing our stupidity and lack of diligence, threatening everyone with *dvoika,* a failing grade, in both behavior and English verb tenses. Only the Cuban Lenin doesn't respond to my motivational attempts, not showing a sliver of appreciation for my total lack of Soviet severity and discipline.

I wish Lenin would open his mouth today of all days because in the back row of my classroom sits Marlin Tomkins, the director of the ESL Program, dressed in a navy suit and tie as formal as his title. He is writing up my first evaluation to be filed in my Hudson College personnel dossier, which will be available to every director and dean curious about the level of my teaching skill. Between the vigorous scribblings on his yellow legal pad, Marlin turns his head right and left, his watery eyes behind thick lenses examining my students as if through fish tank glass. I should concentrate on my class's second language acquisition by teaching the simple present tense in a meaningful context, but my eyes keep returning to the director, to his expressionless eyes and his upper lip protruding over a receding chin. Instead of thinking about grammatical rules and pedagogical strategies, I wonder if Marlin knows how well he fits his name.

"He no like speak," says Altagracia, who always sits in the front and who likes to speak for herself and everyone else. She is Colombian, short and sturdy as a fireplug, the age Lenin's mother would be. About once a week she passes out sweet *pasteles* with guava jam during break time, making sure that there are enough left when the tray gets to the last row. "He come here two month ago, in boat," she says, volunteering bits of Lenin's story. "Three days in ocean. Very bad."

"No, no boat. *Balsa*," interrupts Marisol, an Ecuadorian girl from the second row, who draws a gaze from every male in our college hallways. "Golden Latina," they whisper, as she sashays past them on her long legs. Marisol's amber eyes are expertly lined to make them look even bigger, and her skin is the color of the café con leche I get during the break at a little grocery store across the street from our school. "Like what car has," she says, drawing a circle in the air with her hands, as the rest of the students chime in with half-English-half-Spanish versions of what mode of transportation Lenin used to travel from Cuba to the United States. Marisol turns in a calculated motion that makes her blond curls fall across her face, graciously accepting vocabulary help from her classmates. "Tires," she repeats, looking at me, providing an explanation. "Car tires together like a raft. Three days in ocean on car tires."

I wonder what Lenin thinks about Altagracia and Marisol and everyone else in the room volunteering the story of his escape from Cuba on a tire raft. All the eyes in the room are on Lenin now except the director's. He is staring at Marisol, at her café con leche shoulders bared by a sundress, and there is a little human curve in his fish mouth, a smile of admiration for such preternatural beauty.

I can't see Lenin's eyes from under the hood, but I discern a new softness in his posture, as if the boulders have lightened in his throat. His body is half-turned toward Marisol—toward the golden luminosity of her face—in an almost fragile, unprotected way. Maybe he feels relieved that the students have released the story that has been caged up for two months in the darkness under his hood. Maybe he is grateful that the most beautiful woman in Hudson College has molded her cinnamon lips around the words that explain his harsh arrival in this country. I am glad that Marlin is here to listen to this emerging story, to witness its coming out.

I try to imagine the stormy ocean at night, with blasts of wind and waves and pounding rain—which makes me think of Aivazovsky's sea paintings in the Leningrad Russian Museum, huge canvases full of furious white foam and tiny ships perched on walls of swollen water. I try to imagine a raft made of car tires lashed together by ropes, Lenin and the others clutching the black rubber rims not to be swept into the angry sea. Are they sitting shoulder to shoulder, holding on to one another? Are they lying facedown, their backs to the salty deluge, fused to the rubber surface like leeches to skin, sensing with an animal acuity that one of them has just been washed away into the roaring blackness? How many people piled onto that raft in the humid darkness of a Cuban night, I wonder, and how many stepped onto the beach in Florida three days later?

I know I should stop looking at Marlin staring at Marisol or imagining the stormy ocean between Cuba and Florida and instead present the ESL director with a well-planned and professionally executed lesson based on the latest theories of second language ac- quisition. But I know it will be impossible to extract a word out of Lenin in front of all the students, especially with a stranger looming in the back row, so I decide to break my class up and have them work in small groups. It is a daring move since I have never tried this technique before, but the ultimate goal of teaching is to engage every single student, even those who recently arrived here on a raft made of nothing but tires.

I match weaker students with stronger ones, reticent tongues with those more fluid. I ask Marisol and Altagracia to move to the back row to work with Lenin as I distribute to my class a picture to discuss and describe in writing. It is a picture of an airport terminal I copied from an ESL dictionary this morning—such an absurdly fast and riskless way to travel.

"Would you like to join one of the groups?" I ask Marlin, hoping that he accepts my bold offer, that this audacity does not demolish my future at Hudson College. For a second Marlin hesitates, but this is the precise moment when Marisol lifts her eyes and parts her lips in a smile aimed directly at him, the moment that certifies he is still a human being, despite his stern director's suit and his fish tank gaze.

I walk around the class, helping my students with the words they don't know, correcting their grammar. But my eyes and ears are attuned to the group in the back, where Altagracia points to something in the picture and Marlin adjusts his glasses and explains. The four of them are sitting in a small circle, Marlin between Altagracia and Lenin, his eyes bright behind the lenses, his face animated by the proximity to Marisol but also, I'd like to think, to so many unimaginable stories.

When I look at them again, after another walk around the room, I hear Marisol saying something to Lenin in rapid but soft Spanish, her gold earrings swaying with her speech cadence. I am just about to chide her for not speaking English in an ESL class when she gently touches the hood of Lenin's sweatshirt and lifts it off his forehead. Lenin's eyes are big and surprised, the color of a midday sea lit by the sun. He doesn't resist or pull his hood back down, but then who could protest the touch of this glowing Latina?

I glance at the clock on the wall. Only two minutes are left until the end of the class, and I hastily collect the papers with the students' airport terminal descriptions, hoping that in his evaluation Marlin won't take points off for my inadequate time management. He shakes the hands of all three students in his group, his face serious and cold, back to the director's face again. Then he collects his briefcase and his legal pad and walks over to the teacher's desk, where I am standing, having just realized that I've forgotten to assign the homework.

"I'll write it up within a day or two," he says, nodding at the legal pad under his arm. "I have a couple of suggestions, but on the whole, it was an exhilarating class."

I don't know the word *exhilarating*, but it can't be too negative, I think. It bursts with the energy of an *x* and an *r*, and the *t* at the end pops into the air with one bold, vigorous jolt.

ഔ

On the way home, after the class, I think that the next time I see Lenin, in two days, I will ask him to write about his experience on the tire raft in English. I will ask Altagracia and Marisol to help him. I think of my own trip here, exactly a year ago: an Aeroflot stewardess in a fur hat moving down the aisle with trays of roasted chicken and rice, a dish I had seen only at the faculty cafeteria when I taught Russian to American students the summer I met Robert. I think of the ten hours in the sky, gawking from my seat at the frozen vastness of Greenland, instead of three hellish days and nights on a tire raft tossed in the black ocean like a shred of debris from a passing cruise ship. I don't know what people clinging to old tires think about when it becomes clear that in this dark gamble the ocean is going to claim its share, that some who started the trip will never see their destination. Did this realization daunt Lenin and his raft mates? Or had their fear already reached the human limit, leaving them only to hold tight and try to breathe and clutch at something, anything, no matter what it was?

એ

One week after Marlin's observation of my class, on my one-year anniversary of living in this country, Andy takes me to a Spanish restaurant in North Bergen, where the menu bristles with new words: *mariscada, paella, frittata, sangria*. Twenty minutes later, half the unfamiliar dishes, it seems, are placed in front of me, mussels and clams in a cast-iron pot steaming with briny aroma, mounds of yellow rice studded with smoked sausage spilling over the lip of a huge plate. It's Spanish from Spain, Andy lets me know so that I don't run and ask my Colombian student Altagracia for a recipe, although I have a sense that she could make a formidable *mariscada*. Altagracia, I think, would know how to make a culinary masterpiece out of almost anything. Andy has ordered a pitcher of sangria, which turns out to be a drink, red and sweet and full of drunken apple slices.

I think of the American sitting next to me, sipping Stolichnaya vodka, on the Aeroflot plane that brought me to this country. We raise our glasses and offer a toast over the pots of new, aromatic foods—Andy to me and I to Lenin, who managed to escape his bright Cuban future on a raft made of tires.

# Twenty-Three

B y the end of the summer I am officially divorced and hired to
teach the next academic year at Hudson College. Every two
weeks the secretary of the Basic Skills department hands me a pay-
roll check, an amount greater than I used to make at SCS, for less
than half the time. I don't mind working less and making more. It
allows me to send extra parcels of clothes to my mother and sister
and books to Nina, although I am not at all sure if the American
novels I pick up at library sales ever slip past the sharp eye of Soviet
customs.

Some do, it turns out from Nina's letter, while others do not.
Doctorow's *Ragtime* makes it, together with Saul Bellow's *Herzog*
and *The Chosen* by Chaim Potok, but two James Bond novels
get tangled in the customs net and never reach Nina's address. In
my mind, I see a gray-suited KGB official, a graduate of my university's English department—possibly someone I used to know
personally—surrounded by stacks of confiscated paperbacks and
magazines in English, their spines cracked by the hands of those
zealous bureaucrats toiling in his office. I think of these guards
who are privy to the latest offerings from the West they seize at the
border, hard at work protecting ordinary Soviet citizens from the
contagion of capitalism.

*Thank you for the jacket for me and shoes for Mitya,* writes Nina, whose son is now almost one and a half.

> *How did you know that I've been longing for a jacket like this, driving everyone around me crazy with my insanity? With the hundred rubles I'd saved I spent all winter and spring riffling through consignment stores, predictably finding nothing—and suddenly this! You, old girl, with your regular parcels, are an exception from everyone who has left, and now, for the first time in my life, I walk around with my head held high because my clothes are not worse than those of my students. And for Mitya—you know how absolutely impossible it is to buy shoes here—the stuff our factory Skorokhod produces isn't simply ugly, it is completely unsuitable for the one function it's made for, walking.*

*Rudik sends his most profound thanks for the medicine,* Nina writes. Recently her husband had been diagnosed with a stomach ulcer, and Andy suggested that we send them the new ulcer pill, Tagamet.

> *First we didn't know anything about it and Rudik wanted to gobble it up right away. Then we asked around and found out that it was something completely unique, something no one here has ever seen. So this is our dilemma: should he take it now and hope the ulcer goes away, or keep it for a rainy day? Rudik has made an appointment to see a decent specialist, someone who knows about Western medicine, so we'll do what the doctor recommends.*
>
> *So glad (and so envious) that you enjoy teaching. As far as England goes . . .*

I wrote to Nina earlier that Andy and I were planning to go to London—the city both Nina and I know by heart from our school lectures—as soon as we could scrape together the price of two airfares and a hotel.

*I won't make any comments about England since we've decided that it simply doesn't exist. It isn't there, along with France, Switzerland, and everything else to the west of us. The only place that is real is our indestructible Union of Soviet free republics.*

*And one last thing: it made me a little sad to read that you don't have real friends there . . .*

I know I have one real friend, at least—the friend who is four thousand miles away, and the thought of it makes me a little sad, too.

∞

We need to look for a house, Andy says. I don't quite understand why we need a whole house for ourselves, but he talks convincingly about owning versus renting, supporting his argument with examples of higher property values and bigger deductions that fly past my ears. I haven't yet mastered the system of taxes here, but if Andy says we will be better off living in a house, I happily agree.

It is fun driving around new towns and gawking at the interiors of different houses, imagining that we could be the owners of eight rooms, two bathrooms, and a garage, but the idea of such enormous debt is foreign and forbidding. We had no concept of mortgage back home. Whatever we could find to buy we almost always bought with cash, and that direct method of exchange made things simple and quick. There were no lawyers and no banks, and the notion of interest ranked high among capitalist vices, along with violence, sex, and unemployment.

Every Sunday we park at a real estate office, get into the broker's Chevy, and drive around towns that blend into one another along their amorphous boundaries. I think of the Leningrad suburb where our dacha stood, of a field dotted with squatting wood structures surrounded by fences called Old Peterhof, where the next town was on the other side of the woods, a stop away on the electric train. Here, the house we see first is in Bloomfield; its next-door neighbor, our real estate agent points out, lives in Glen Ridge. The broker is in her fifties, with dry hands and graying hair pulled up in a bun, probably a grandmother since the ledge behind the backseat is littered with half-used sheets of ladybug stickers. She reminds me of my Leningrad high school teacher Irina Ivanovna, an English grammarian with a patient smile and a quiet passion for verb tenses.

"What are you looking for in a house?" she asks, a question that bewilders me. What do I want in a house? I think. A sturdy roof, solid walls, and wooden floors, for sure, as well as running water and indoor plumbing—but I know this is not what she means. The agent sees my puzzled face and helps me with more questions. "Are you looking for high ceilings, for instance? Some people won't look at anything with ceilings below nine feet. Or parquet floors?"

I quickly do the feet to meters calculations in my mind. In our apartment in Leningrad—and every apartment I'd ever been in, with the exception of my sister Galya's place, built in the 1960s and called a Khrushchev slum—the ceilings were a minimum of eleven feet high and the floors were all parquet. I nod enthusiastically, confirming to the agent that I would indeed like high ceilings and parquet floors.

"And how about a fireplace?" says Andy, looking at me for approval. "Do we want a fireplace?"

The word *fireplace* elicits images of the Hermitage: tsarist thrones and baldachin beds, rococo carvings and complicated chandeliers, fine mosaics and rare inlaid woods. This is an unwelcome distraction, and I promptly force my mind to pedal back and focus on the room we are standing in. It is an entranceway to a house that was built in 1903. It has a massive oak door with leaded windows, and across from it there is a fireplace. I look up: the ceilings are over nine feet high.

I wish my mother could see me, marching through all these houses, declaring my preferences for parquet and fireplaces. What would she think? Has she ever sat in front of a fireplace—not a museum piece we have all seen a hundred times when provincial relatives came to town and we had to take them to the royal places Leningrad was famous for, not a wood-burning stove she used to heat the house in Ivanovo and at our dacha, but the real thing, a decadently open alcove with enough room for a fire to show off to an audience, to dance and twist and lick the logs with orange tongues of flame? She would be too practical for this, my mother. She would want to restrict the fire to the gut of the stove, close it off with a lid so it was restrained, efficient, and docile. A fireplace, in my mother's mind, would be, without doubt, too wasteful, too disorderly, too free.

"We must have a fireplace," I say, and Andy nods, confirming our new requirement to the agent.

"All right," she says eagerly. "Then let me tell you more about this house. The owner died recently and left the house to a charity, which may suit you because they say they'll hold the mortgage for the buyers."

There is no word for mortgage in contemporary Russian, so there is no way I can describe to my mother what the broker has just told us. The best word I can come up with is *credit,* the word my mother used when we bought our television fifteen years ago. "We bought it with credit," she proudly announced when two men delivered a huge square box with the price tag of 575 rubles, three times my mother's monthly wages. Every month for five years she went to a local savings union to pay down the credit, even as the television set started heading for premature death with spasms of crackling noise and lines jumping across the screen.

At home, Andy and I sit on the couch and talk about the houses we have seen. One had a porch caving in to the right, an unfortunate reminder of my dacha. In another, the first floor smelled of yesterday's soup, and pots of aloe sat on peeling windowsills, just like the nursery school in the courtyard of my Leningrad apartment building.

"Look, they all need a lot of work," Andy says, "but they're the only houses in our price range." *Fixer-upper* is a new word I add to my growing vocabulary of contemporary American, and it makes me marvel once again at the plasticity of the English language, at the ease with which it marries stems and suffixes to create names for novel concepts.

We sit on the couch and talk, not discussing the house with a fireplace until every other place gets its share of pros and cons and is predictably rejected. We leave that house for the end, like a dessert.

# *Twenty-Four*

In a letter to my mother I write about our plans to buy a house, knowing that in her mind this will solidify my claim to a normal life. The idea of buying a house, I know, will calm her fears and stop the flow of inquiries about when I am going to return to Robert. I describe the house we put a bid on from memory: three floors, three bedrooms, floor-to-ceiling built-in bookshelves in the living room, chestnut banisters and moldings, two stained-glass windows, turn-of-the-century chandeliers downstairs. I neglect to say it is a fixer-upper. On paper, it sounds like the palace of Peter the Great that adorns the front of the Summer Garden in Leningrad. In reality, it boasts sooty walls that seem tired of the old wallpaper hanging down in strips over bloated linoleum floors, cracked and uneven as Leningrad sidewalks.

ജ

The real estate agent calls us and says that our bid has been accepted, with one condition. In order to qualify for the mortgage the foundation has offered to hold for us, we must be married.

"Can they do that?" Andy asks, annoyance in his voice. He is leaning on the kitchen wall, the receiver propped by his shoulder. "Can they make our being married a condition to buying the house?"

"No, legally they can't," the agent says. "But they're doing it. Their interest rate is seven points lower than what any bank will give you. So I guess, this means they can."

I listen to the conversation and cannot help but wonder if Andy is like Robert, willing to get married but not wanting to get married. Is this aversion to marriage something typically American, something that has eluded me since I arrived here, like so many other things I still don't understand?

"Of course, we're going to get married," I hear Andy say. "We just haven't talked about it."

We haven't talked about many things. We have simply lived, a year of oblivion and happiness, a year without pointed questions my mother is too far away to ask. Andy hangs up the phone and sits on the couch where I am marking students' essays. "Will you marry me?" he asks, looking at me and waiting for a response, as if he believed there were a chance that I could possibly say no.

&#8450;

I write a letter home that Andy and I are getting married next month, imagining the reaction this announcement is going to receive in Leningrad. I think of my mother on her way back from work unlocking our mailbox, a wooden rectangle with our apartment number, 117, painted in black. She is in a hurry because she has already glimpsed a foreign airmail envelope through the holes cut out at the bottom of the box, and she fumbles for the key with quick, impatient fingers. The elevator may be working—or not—and she may have to walk all the way up to the sixth floor, slowly and methodically, step by step, heaving her weight made heavier by a string bag full of groceries from one floor to the next, resting on the landings by the windows facing the courtyard. She will not open the letter until she gets into the apartment, takes off her coat, hat, and scarf, and puts the eggs, cheese, and butter in the refrigerator that towers in the corner next to the coatrack. She is deliberate and disciplined, my mother; she has always believed in proper regimen and order.

Strangely, I can feel the rough brown wool of her coat, which she carefully hangs on the hook, and the softness of her scarf Marina has knitted. The hallway smells of onions she keeps on the shelf between the outer and inner entrance doors, but also of the melting snow that has already turned to gray slush on the bottoms of her boots. In house slippers, she walks into her room, sits down at the desk, and carefully opens my letter, cutting through the top seam with a letter knife, a part of a desk set including two inkwells and a blotter left from my father.

What does she do when she reads that I am getting married, for the second time in two years, to another American? I see her grasp her hands around my grandma's picture, which stands, framed, next to the family photo album, as if she were telling my story to her own mother. Does she sigh with relief that I won't end up alone in an alien country? Does she sigh with sadness, knowing that this new marriage means I will never come back to live in Leningrad again?

In two weeks, on February 13, she will be sixty-eight, and we are going to call her, booking a call hours in advance, through two international operators. Her face shows the new folds of wrinkles my departure for America has carved into the skin around her eyes. She wants to tell Marina about my getting married again, but my sister's play has opened tonight, and that means no one knows when and in what state Marina is going to come home.

I knew when Marina was drunk before she even opened the front door: I heard the elevator door bang shut and for a few minutes a key would scratch around the keyhole, in slow, unfocused stirs. Then, once she managed to get the key in, it would jiggle tentatively, as if trying to figure out the right way to turn in the lock.

Those were the nights when my mother and I would stand by the door, waiting for Marina to slump into the hallway, her eyes half closed, words tangled in her mouth like wet laundry. We would pull off her coat, lifting her arms as if she were a rag doll, then drag her into her room, heave her on the divan, and throw a blanket at her, like a stone.

"Again! Drunk as a plumber!" my mother wailed the familiar refrain. "What did I do to deserve this?" She stumbled through a series of predictable scenes—pulling off Marina's boots and coat—alternating spasms of anger and despair. After hauling my sister inside, I usually abandoned the scene for the room where my mother and I slept, and turned on the television's grainy images as Mama sobbed and helped Marina undress, invoking a lengthy list of relatives who would have dropped dead at the sight of this shame. When the wailing stopped, there was a sharp smell of valerian drops, the plant-based tranquilizer we all turned to in moments of crisis. Then I heard my mother rumbling through the shelf with medicines, pulling out a package of sweet, white, over-the-counter tablets that were supposed to pacify her heart.

The next day Marina would be all sweetness, her bloodshot eyes bovine, seeking forgiveness. In a short-lived fit of postdrunken humility, she would scrub the laundry on the washboard in the bathtub, or concoct a complicated soup, or simply fail to fight with us over something irrelevant and small.

I think of my mother holding my letter in her hand, wishing that no one in Marina's theater would have a birthday, or a play opening, or another happy event that needs to be celebrated. I hope she can tell Marina about my impending marriage as soon as my sister gets home, so they can sigh with relief together, or sigh with regret. I feel sorry for my mother, who is left to dread theater premieres and anniversaries, who has to listen for the tentative scratches of the key all by herself now. I feel guilty that she has no one to help her shoulder my sister to bed, no one to complain to about her curse.

But I also feel relieved that I am on the other side of the ocean from my mother and my sister, out of their reach.

૪૭

Andy and I sit in our apartment and make a list of what we need to do: get a marriage license, make an appointment at the city hall, ask my friends at the college if anyone can lend me a cream-colored dress. We have decided it will be a small affair, just the two of us, with Andy's parents as witnesses.

I think of my first wedding, at the Acts of Marriage Palace on the Neva embankment, where I had to invite my Leningrad family, my aunt from the provinces, and my friends—about twenty people in all—the smallest wedding that place had ever seen. I hated the high-ceilinged room where we stood in front of an official with a red ribbon across her chest so out of place in this formerly splendid, prerevolutionary space; I hated her speech about the creation of a new society cell; I hated being the center of attention, the polyester dress clinging to my legs.

After we sign the papers and exchange rings in the office of a Jersey City judge, Andy and I go to the movies. We sink into the dusty seats of a small theater in the East Village in Manhattan and watch a double feature of Agatha Christie's Miss Marple, its old black-and-whiteness as sweet and comforting as the day itself.

My new in-laws have invited us to an expensive restaurant in Greenwich Village, where we sit near a fireplace over small plates with a lettuce called endive and then bigger plates of meat called beef Wellington. We pour champagne and drink to our wedding day. I don't know if Andy's parents are as pleased with our hasty marriage as they say they are. They smile reserved American smiles and wish us happiness.

Back in our apartment in North Bergen, I take off my dress borrowed from a fellow teacher and the gold necklace lent to me by a counselor who works with Andy. Nothing has changed, not even my Russian last name. I think of how cold my actions would sound to a stranger: I married Andy to be able to buy a house just as I married Robert to get away from my family. Two marriages, two years apart. Exactly what my mother did: she married her first husband in 1940 and her second, Marina's father, during the war in 1942. Am I my mother's daughter, after all?

# Twenty-Five

We borrow five hundred dollars from a friend and book two tickets to Leningrad from London in July, 1982. Two birds with one stone, says Andy, who knows I've wanted to see London since the fifth grade, when I first learned about its history and its landmarks in the English class of my new school. Two birds? I ask, perplexed. In Russian, traveling to both England and Russia kills two rabbits with one stone, but whether it is birds or rabbits, the thought of seeing both London and my native city makes me exhilarated.

I buy several pairs of blue jeans, orders from actresses at my sister's theater who are thrilled at the prospect of a direct merchandise connection. A pair of American jeans costs an actor a month's salary of 120 rubles on the Leningrad black market, where deals are made in the murk of underground metro passages and where products are difficult to authenticate before the money changes hands. I am not sure if I feel perfectly comfortable with the prospect of selling jeans at such exorbitant prices to my sister's friends, but Marina insists that I'll be doing them a favor.

*Where else can they get a guaranteed pair of Levi's?* she writes in a letter.

*In Gostiny Dvor, next to vinyl shoes? They can't wait, these girls, and the talentless Mashka Blinova is the worst. Every morning, as if she had no memory, she sidles up to me to ask how many more days until you arrive. You're deranged, I tell her.*

Marina's words fly across the page, and I can almost taste her irritation. *Stop pestering me,* she tells Mashka. *Stop pissing boiling water.* I can hear her voice ringing in the greenroom, admonishing the jean-starved actress for her dogged questions.

After I reread my sister's letter, I convince myself that selling jeans to her actor friends is a noble obligation I can't possibly refuse. Besides, Andy reminds me, it is the only way we can afford this trip.

&#8450;

London rises from the dusty pages of Soviet textbooks like a daydream: Westminster Abbey with its Gothic soaring flight of pointed windows; jolly and robust Beefeaters at the Tower who pretend to guard me as if I were a prisoner while Andy clicks the camera; a clothing store called Laura Ashley, whose flowery dresses in the magazine *England* I used to ogle for hours instead of opening mail and answering phones at the House of Friendship and Peace.

I think of my seventh-grade English teacher, Zinaida Petrovna, lecturing the class about the Norman Invasion of 1066, the Great Fire of London, the construction of Big Ben. She wore a crow's nest of graying hair and a moth-eaten cardigan carefully mended with brown thread, but London—the London she could never see—was her passion, her unrequited love. She paced between the rows of desks, speaking ardently about the wars, the plagues, the royal weddings and betrayals—pausing in midsentence as if those foreign cataclysms had been part of her own life and she needed a moment to fumble through her memory for what happened next—as we sat there, inattentive, steeped in our adolescent dramas, clueless about what was being offered to us. I let the names of kings and queens fly past my ears, dreaming about some boy from the senior grade, concocting plans to rope my sister into taking me backstage after her performance to get close to her actor friends. So now I stand in front of massive gravestones, not recognizing the clusters of gold letters carved into the marble, unable to weave the threads of individual lives into a comprehensible tapestry of royal history. And where is Zinaida Petrovna now? A lawful pensioner, probably, sitting on a bench in the Summer Garden where Pushkin used to go for a stroll, bending over a small bed of dirt to water cucumbers and dill at her crumbling dacha. Instead, she should be the one inhaling the briny air from the Thames, as damp as on the embankments of the Neva. She should be the one walking in her brown cardigan toward Westminster Abbey, where she would, undoubtedly, have no trouble figuring out instantly who is related to whom underneath these hefty marble angels. She, who should be here, is locked in Leningrad, while I am sauntering around London, ignorant of its history and undeserving of all its royal grandeur.

∞

After a week of guilty sightseeing, we get up early and, loaded with two heavy suitcases, take the tube to Heathrow Airport. Our bags are packed with blue jeans for the actresses from my sister's theater and presents for everyone I could think of since I began planning the trip. I thought of my mother hurrying from her medical institute to the district visa office to apply for the documents necessary to invite us to stay at my old Leningrad apartment, of her joining the line forever snaking out of the waiting room along the wall of the narrow corridor with a blinking fluorescent light. I thought of Marina hoarding bottles of Bulgarian ketchup and cans with cod liver and sprats. Where does she get all those cans with fish and jars with mayonnaise, and coffee beans that disappeared from stores when I was still a senior at the university? Where does she get beef for my mother's sour cabbage soup and lamb for the shish kebabs she is so good at marinating for summer cookouts at the dacha?

I thought of my university friend Nina and her son, Mitya, who is now two, living in a place that has never heard of disposable diapers. I thought of Nadia the *refusenik*, whose family has been refused a visa to leave the Soviet Union to go to Israel, of her mangled right breast, which she showed me after she got home from the maternity hospital, where a female doctor with small, surly eyes gouged out a few inches of infected flesh before scolding her for having developed mastitis after giving birth. I thought of all of them while filling our suitcases with panty hose and baby pacifiers, mascara and eye pencils, lipstick, powder, and T-shirts we bought at a wholesale store on Thirtieth Street in Manhattan. I thought of all of them while packing blouses, pants, skirts, and jackets from the clearance rack at a store called Mandee.

It is already noon in Leningrad, and I know my mother has been looking at her watch since she got up—earlier than usual—because she couldn't sleep. I know she has calculated every step of our trip, giving Marina updates of where we are at any given moment. "They must be on their way to the airport," she says, glancing at her wrist. "They're probably going through customs right now," she offers, not knowing that the only place that requires you to go through customs control when leaving the country is our Motherland.

Mama is probably wearing her best dress, the one I sent her with my first paycheck from Beefsteak Charlie's. Her eyes are smiling, which makes them even bluer, as she moves around my sister's room, which is for the next three weeks going to be mine and Andy's. She walks with a light step, humming an old war song, barely recognizable to anyone who can hear her because—like me—she has no ear for music.

෴

"Are you excited?" Andy asks, and from his face I can see that he is. I nod, but there is a dark fear lodged inside me, the old dread of facing Soviet customs agents, the old panic at being powerless and guilty before the stone-faced guards of my country's borders. I don't want to admit to Andy that I am scared, but he can see it from my stooped shoulders and my bitten lips. I stare at my boarding pass, questioning my sanity when I suggested to him a few months earlier that we spend July in Leningrad. It sounded so exciting then, when the trip was hypothetical and airy as a cotton cloud. We were thrilled to find inexpensive tickets: People Express to London, Aeroflot to Leningrad, and the thought of seeing everyone, of walking on the streets of my city again, almost made me breathless. But now, looking at the Aeroflot plane, I feel as I did in the waiting room of the Leningrad dental clinic when our first-grade teacher took the whole class for an annual visit of drilling cavities and filling root canals.

There is nothing to be afraid of, I tell myself. My Soviet passport says "resides abroad" stamped in official purple ink, and our marriage license is safely packed in my handbag. I may still be a Soviet citizen, but I am married to an American who is right here, next to me, monitoring my every step. No border guard would dare prohibit me from stepping onto Soviet soil, or leaving it once I am there, I tell myself. Why then are my palms so clammy? Why can't I be as nonchalant as all these Western tourists?

In London it is still morning when we join a group of British passengers waiting for our flight to Russia. They leaf through their guidebooks with maps of Leningrad, all except a woman in her fifties, whose face, beneath a layer of Western creams and cosmetics, carries faint marks of her Slavic heritage. She is talking to a man who may be her English husband as she glances in my direction because from my tensed mouth and slumped back she knows I am Russian. Maybe she recognizes herself in this same airport thirty years earlier, terrified before her first visit back home.

Once we strap ourselves into the polka-dotted Aeroflot seats, the engines start without warning, and, with the speed of a military jet, the plane roars down the runway and up into the low sky. The sudden thrust of the engine presses my back into the seat, and my ears pop. The stewardess, wearing an orange life vest to demonstrate the emergency procedures, stumbles and almost falls, her fur hat rolling down the aisle.

Andy takes my hand and squeezes his fingers around it.

"Welcome to Russia," I say, although I don't know if he can hear me over the thunder of the engines.

න

I have heard different explanations of why Aeroflot planes suddenly become silent in midair, hovering noiselessly as if their engines were turned off, or why they descend almost vertically, in a mad dive that makes the passengers gasp as their lives flash before their eyes. One theory suggests that Russian military pilots rotate flying civilian planes, bringing their cavalier style to Aeroflot takeoffs and landings. Another attributes the insane descent to the Soviet prohibition against taking pictures from the plane, as if those patches of woods we are able to glimpse on the way down were full of rocket-launching facilities and secret military installations. I don't care about the reason. I simply lace my fingers with Andy's and we both exhale when the plane touches down and we taxi for what seems like twenty minutes past a wall of evergreen forest and fields of unmowed grass, toward a small structure with the word LENINGRAD and a red flag on the roof beating in the wind.

Two soldiers with machine guns watch as we leave the plane and climb into the waiting bus. Inside the terminal, our British group is locked in a room where we must fill out customs declarations: our wedding bands, my silver chain, three hundred dollars in cash. Foreign media, none. No gifts, either (I carefully removed the tags from every piece of clothing I brought: presents are subject to a tax equal to the item's price). In our suitcases, the Soviet customs agents find stacks of jeans, jackets, and shirts that could last us for several months if we don't bother washing any of them. But they don't seem to be interested in clothes, looking, probably, for a tome of Solzhenitsyn or a copy of *The New York Times*.

Next to us the Russian woman in her fifties is helping her British husband to navigate the customs form. She looks up and gives me a little smile. "You look so scared. Like a bomb has exploded on your face," she says in Russian.

I am scared, and I feel the fear spreading its tendrils all the way to my fingers, making them tremble. I know this fear courses in the veins of every Russian, like a disease. "Is it your first time back?" asks the woman, already knowing the answer. Is it possible, I wonder, that in thirty years I will be like her, straight-shouldered and dignified, not afraid of Soviet border guards, not intimidated by their stone faces and their guns?

We are eventually herded through the narrow corridor to passport control. Andy goes first. I see him stand before a woman in a military shirt with epaulets, who is perched on a chair two feet above him. Expressionless, she stares at him, then at his passport, then at Andy's reflections in the mirrors in her fluorescent booth. After five minutes of silence, she stamps his passport and pushes it under the glass. A turnstile opens and Andy crosses over onto Soviet territory, where my mother and sister are trying to push to the front of the waiting crowd to greet us.

I am next.

# Twenty-Six

My mother's hair is thin and snow white, covering her head like the fuzz of a baby bird. "Like during the war," she says and pats her head with her palm. "I look like a typhus victim." After I left, Marina tells me, Mama's hair, long and brown, began to fall out in clumps, and for a year or so she had to wear a wig. Then it started growing back, white and fluffy as the Leningrad January snow.

I kiss my mother and Marina three times on the cheeks, the Russian custom. I press into Mama's breasts and stand still for a few moments, enveloped by her softness. I stroke Mama's hair, the white down around her head, like a halo. She opens her arms to Andy, and in her eyes I read approval.

For the next two days, we are corralled at home in my old apartment, sitting in the kitchen in front of endless plates of *pirozhki* filled with cabbage and egg my mother baked, chunks of beef slathered with mayonnaise and roasted under a crust of grated cheese. We feast on Marina's famous potato *kotlety* swimming in a sauce of wild mushrooms they picked the year before in our dacha woods. I know that this cornucopia of tastes required weeks of hoarding and standing on lines, things I used to do with my mother and sister before my provincial aunt came to visit for the summer, her three sons in tow, or when my mother's Kiev cousin, Aunt Mila, rode on a train for two days to bathe in the translucent air of white nights. It is our family's tradition to secure enough food to impress our guests, especially those from far away. Yet, after two days of eating, I can see that Andy has become restless, and, from the glances he throws me across the table, I know he is dying to escape the kitchen.

I try to take the dishes to the kitchen sink, but Mama stops me. Guests aren't allowed to do any work. "Go rest," she orders and walks to the bathroom to turn the water heater on.

There is nothing to rest from. We open the door to the balcony and look down onto the street. A few people are waiting at the bus stop, where every morning I used to take bus number 22 to my English school. It crawls out from behind the corner, a double yellow Hungarian-made Ikarus, its two cars connected with an accordion of black rubber. Behind the bus stop is a kiosk where we returned our empty bottles: fifteen kopeks for a half liter of milk, sunflower oil, or vodka. I tell Andy an old joke: *Two friends meet on the street. —What are you up to? asks Kolya. —Working, saving up to buy a car, replies Sergei. And you? —Drinking, Kolya says. Five years later, they meet again. —How are you? Kolya asks. —Working, still saving up for a car, says Sergei. And you? —I brought back all the empty bottles, says Kolya, and bought myself a car.*

Shards of conversations reach my ears, but their rhythm seems wrong, as though a tune previously known but now forgotten. Only two years have passed, but a strange feeling floods me when these familiar scenes unfold below, like frames of a film I know well, only dubbed in a foreign tongue.

As I stand on the balcony awash in sentimental thoughts, Andy thinks of more practical things. He looks down and sees a truck parked in front of a corner liquor store, a line forming behind it. I have already taught him the first lesson of Russian shopping. When you see a line, join it, and only then find out what is on the other end.

This seems like a perfect opportunity for us to escape the four walls of my apartment, if only for a little while. "Let's see what they've delivered," Andy says. "And bring some money," he shouts as I follow. He runs out the apartment door and down six floors of stairs because he hasn't yet figured out our Soviet elevator system: to go downstairs you must press the up button to get the cabin to the top floor.

Three minutes later, we are at the end of the line, behind men in construction gear checking their pockets for change. It turns out, the line is for cheap port called *chernila*, or ink—just as noxious and purple as the name—one ruble twenty-three kopeks a bottle. But the truck has also delivered cases of vodka called Golden Ring, too expensive for getting drunk at work, the best Stolichnaya made for export. Since no slicing or wrapping of this scarce commodity is involved, the line moves fast, and fifteen minutes later we are inside the basement store, hugging four bottles of Golden Ring, the most we can buy because there is a limit of two per person.

&#8365;

Mama wants to keep us in the kitchen, all to herself, plying us with borsch and *pelmeni* and racking up the guilt just in case we decided to leave this culinary paradise. Nothing has changed in the two years of my absence. I am still leashed to this table with an oilcloth whose sunflower pattern is smudged from wear; I am tethered to the bathtub faucet that dribbles water in a capricious trickle and to the gas heater that doesn't light; I am enslaved by the pot of mushroom soup, by a casserole of meatballs on the stove. But on the third day, watching Andy pace Marina's bedroom like an animal in a cage, I revolt. I act as an *egoistka*, to use Mama's word, and selfishly choose my husband's sanity over my family's control.

"I haven't shown him the city yet," I plead, as if I were twelve and had to ask for permission. "We'll be back by evening," I quickly add, letting her know we'd rather not be chaperoned.

"Well, do as you like." Mama pouts and rattles the dishes into the sink.

A wave of resentment rises in my throat like vomit—the memory of every past quarrel we ever had, the anger at being a child again—but I swallow it and say nothing in response.

We take a bus to the center of the city and walk under the poplars along the Boulevard of Trade Unions toward the Admiralty and the Neva. It is a cool, drizzly day in July, a typical Baltic summer day, and Leningrad looks just as it did when I left. The red banners of the Communist Party hoisted on yellow and light green façades clash with the classic lines of Palace Square and the baroque stateliness of the Winter Palace. It isn't simply the incompatibility of the old and the new, it occurs to me, that has always been an odd idiosyncrasy of Leningrad; it is the dissonance between the artistic truth and the monstrous Soviet lie it has been forced to accommodate.

We cross the street to walk toward the Hermitage when a babushka, who has been sweeping the pavement with a bunch of twigs tied to a pole, stops, props up her hip with her fist, and begins to yell. *"Besstydniki!"* she shouts after us.

"What does she want?" Andy asks, regarding her in slight bewilderment, bemused by the sight.

It takes me a few seconds to figure out that she is outraged because we didn't use a crosswalk to get to the other side of the street.

"All of you foreigners," she shouts in Russian, brandishing her broom. "You have no shame. You come here from all over—and you don't have the decency to go by our rules!"

A few people have stopped to look and consider if they should take part in this scandal spawned by a couple of disrespectful foreigners.

"We have neither shame nor conscience," I say to Andy, repeating my mother's words, as we hurry away under the babushka's smoldering gaze.

"They come here from God knows where and they behave as

they wish!" she continues screaming, now louder because she has acquired a small audience.

**∞**

Maybe because I feel guilty, or maybe because I am curious to re-visit places that I know will always be tucked into the corners of my memory, I yield to Mama's pressure that we should all spend a couple of days at our dacha. "It's only a bus ride from Peterhof," she says, trotting out another reason why we should go. "You'll get to see the fountains and the Summer Palace of Peter the Great. How can you be in Leningrad and not visit the fountains?" she asks, producing an ace that she knows I wouldn't dare challenge.

The next day we pack our bags and take an electric train to Peterhof. We wake up to an overcast sky, but by the time we step onto the platform in the town Peter the Great ordered his architects to copy after Versailles, the wind has ripped holes in the sheets of clouds, and the sunlit gold spire rising above the roofs points us in the right direction. We trudge along the spectacular cascade of fountains: the golden statue of Samson tearing a lion's jaws open, nymphs pouring water down from their eternal jugs. It is difficult to do much sightseeing with the heavy bags we have packed, so my mother volunteers to sit on a bench and guard our things. Freed from our load, we stroll around the lawns of the park—signs in the grass prohibiting us from stepping off the path—all the way to the coast of the Gulf of Finland, from where we can glimpse the golden dot of St. Isaac's Cathedral dome gleaming in the sun.

Andy is impressed by all this royal splendor, but I am already thinking of our next stop, the dacha, with trepidation and unease. There are no fountains there, not even running water. I conjure up an image of my dacha, and pictures readily float to the surface of my memory: cranking up a rusty well chain in our yard and filling two watering cans so Mama can lug them to the beds with tomatoes and dill; hauling buckets with drinking water from a pump a quarter mile away. Andy already knows this, but he was raised in a garden apartment in Queens, so all I've told him about our outhouse and our well is stored in a part of his brain with such other improbable things about my country as getting drunk on paint thinner or rolling naked in the snow.

The bus takes us to the end of the road, and from there we walk, just as we did for over twenty years when I lived here. We walk past the Gypsy house open to every gust of wind and every hooligan because it has no fence, past the Gypsy bull tethered to the same flimsy stick in the middle of the field covered with little suns of dandelions. My heart sinks when the dacha comes into view: it is even more dilapidated than I remember, with peeling window frames and whole patches of walls bereft of paint, with tall weeds drowning frail bushes of strawberries and squash. The structure is visibly leaning to the right, as if tired of standing straight for so many years, as if it has finally decided to give up.

"We didn't have time to come here and do much work," Mama says apologetically. "We had so much to do in the city to get ready for your visit."

"It's really nice here," Andy says when I translate my mother's words, but I can see he is just being polite.

Marina turns the key in the lock, and it takes her a few vigorous pulls to force the front door open. Inside it is airless and stale; it smells of dead flies and moldy sheets. I have never loved the dacha because of all the gardening work it required, but this is the first time I have felt embarrassed being here. My eye is quick to notice the little things I have never paid attention to: bloated floorboards, kitchen walls papered with yellowed copies of *Pravda*, mouse droppings on the faded oilcloth of the table. I feel embarrassed by my own embarrassment, as I awkwardly walk on creaky floors from the kitchen back to the veranda, breathing in the stifling air of my former life.

Having spent every summer of my childhood here, didn't I see the ruin of this place? Or is it possible that it has only deteriorated in the two years of my absence? Deep down I already know the answer: in these two years, my eyes have become accustomed to a different reality—that of painted walls, flush toilets, and level floors.

"We're going to have dinner soon," says Mama, sending my sister to the garden to pick some lettuce and dill, hurrying to unpack the bread and *kotlety* she brought from the city. I know she senses what I am thinking, and I help her rinse the dishes in a bowl of warm water as she unwraps bologna and cheese and puts away the sheets of newspaper so she can reuse them to bring back the leftovers.

After we eat, Marina soaks the dishes in a bowl of warm water, the same bowl I remember we used to make jams, while Mama takes us around the garden. We walk between the bushes of black currants and gooseberries, under the branches of apple trees full of little green apples that won't be ready to eat for six more weeks, past beds of onions, radishes, and carrots, but mostly weeds.

"Since Dedusya's death, it hasn't been the same," Mama says. My grandfather's image readily comes into focus: he is standing among all the fruit bushes he planted, a mane of snow-white hair, legs growing out of the earth, his body as solid and unyielding as a tree. I know Mama has the same picture in her mind—Dedusya commanding us to water or to weed—but how can I explain any of this to Andy? How can I make him see my grandmother's round face in our kitchen window watching me play in the sandbox, or smell the raspberries sighing in a pot on top of the wood-burning stove, or feel bare feet sloshing through the marsh on the way to the hard, windy beach on the Gulf of Finland?

Mama moves to the vegetable bed to show us tiny cucumbers hanging under the umbrellas of leaves, and we obediently follow. I know I can't begin to explain a Leningrad dacha to someone from New York, so I don't even try. What I don't know anymore is where I belong. Which end of the ocean that divides the continents, the ways of life, should I now call home?

# *Twenty-Seven*

Andy wants to take us all to a restaurant, and Mama is bewildered. She doesn't understand how getting on a bus and sitting in an empty room, at the mercy of surly waiters and questionable cooks, can be better than eating what she and Marina have prepared in our own kitchen.

"They're all so spoiled over there," I hear her grumble to Marina when she doesn't think I am within earshot, standing under the coatrack in the hallway, as I used to do when I was a child. "They live all the way on the other side of the ocean. They never knew what we saw here. It's easy to go to restaurants when you didn't see the war."

My mother saw the war, up close, from the operating room of a train parked on an auxiliary track and turned into a mobile hospital, a mile away from the front.

"Here you go again, using the war as an excuse for our present mess," snaps Marina. *"Tol'ko by ne bylo voiny,"* she mocks. "We will withstand anything if only there will be no more war." This is what my grandparents used to say, this is what my aunt from Kineshma, and my uncle from Ryazan', and even my erudite aunt Mila from Kiev said. This is the refrain I was brought up with, the statement I used to hear from every Russian over fifty.

"When did the war end?" Marina says, and from the sharp intake of her breath I know she is not really asking a question. "Almost forty years ago. I don't see life being better now than it was after the war, or when Khrushchev ran this country, or in the nineteen sixties, when I was in drama school." Marina's voice now seems to project into an audience, deep and appropriately dramatic.

"Don't boil over," Mama says. "You always exaggerate, you're always too negative."

"I'm too negative?" Marina's voice rises another tone. "I am not negative enough! If you stopped waving flags for a minute, you'd see what I'm talking about. We live in a country full of hypocrites and bandits. And of people like you, the true believers, those who survived Stalin only because he was too busy murdering the other twenty million."

There is silence, and I know my mother has tightened her mouth, thinking about whether she should respond. She has heard all this before, my sister's degree of bullishness in inverse proportion to the recent number of times her key has scratched around the lock, not finding the keyhole.

"It's time to stop blaming the war and start living like normal people," says Marina, back to a whisper. "Like they live in other countries."

"And how exactly do you know about life in other countries?" asks my mother.

There is a short silence, and I know my sister has paused to give Mama one of her big-eyed gazes of contempt. "Just look at them!" she hisses, probably pointing to our room. "In two years you haven't learned anything. Haven't you seen enough pictures of normal life?"

"Pictures are pictures," says Mama, her voice metallic after my sister's tirade. "We don't know what life there is really like."

There is another pause, and I can hear Marina snort. "You don't *want* to know." I hear clanging of pans, Marina bending over the lower shelf of the kitchen cupboard in search of a pot big enough for her famous soup made from a Georgian recipe. "It's so much easier to shut your eyes on this disgrace and talk about the war."

∞

Two days before our planned outing Andy and I go to Kavkazsky restaurant on Nevsky Prospekt to test the food and reserve a table for six. Besides my mother and Marina, we have invited my sister Galya, whose small apartment is close to the end of the metro line, and my best university friend, Nina, whom I haven't seen since last week, when Andy and I, to my mother's displeasure, chugged for an hour on a tram to visit her at home.

My mother has never liked Nina, and this may have been one reason I have always stayed so close to her as a friend. To Mama, anyone not belonging to our family is a *chuzhoi*, not one of us, and thus is subject to a stricter set of judgments. With only so many jars of mayonnaise and cans of sprats to go around, we can only feed our own, she has always believed, just as we can only help and feel sorry for our own. I used to resent my mother for her narrow-eyed glances toward my friends who came to the apartment when I lived here. They heaped their coats on top of the refrigerator, she would complain, or for hours occupied the kitchen drinking endless cups of tea and arguing about useless, impractical things.

I used to sulk at my sister for her lack of manners when Nina, who didn't have a phone at home, would ask to make a call when she visited. As my friend was dialing the second number, Marina would stomp out of her room, her eyes burning with anger as if Nina had crossed some obvious hospitality line, and announce in her stage voice that she suddenly needed to call her theater. I wished my mother and my sister had come from Leningrad, like Nina's parents, and not from a provincial town on the Volga.

I am surprised at this resentment, its edges still raw; at how easily I snap at Mama when she complains that Nina has called her only twice in the last two years. And why would she call you more often? I wonder. To hear reproach in my mother's voice because deep in her heart she believes that it was somehow my friend who induced my departure; that, if it hadn't been for Nina, I might have never left?

We walk from the Hermitage toward Kavkazsky restaurant on the Nevsky Prospekt I remember as the magnificent parade of lights, a celebration of resplendence, and a sensory feast, the city's main artery lined with palaces adorned with stately columns, complicated moldings, and bas reliefs of stone nymphs. But where is that Nevsky now? If there were no street signs, I would think we were still back in the industrial district near my apartment. Is this drab street the same avenue I've so carefully cherished and stored in my memory? In two years, has Leningrad's relentless Baltic rain washed off all the paint from the buildings, leaving only dirty streaks on crumbling walls and a sense of desperation in the air?

We pass a small crowd of people getting ready to storm an approaching bus amid the clatter of trolleys and trucks and the ferocious whistling from a militiaman trying to prevent two girls from jaywalking. In front of the Kavkazsky restaurant, a doorman dressed in what looks like a silly pretend military uniform stands guarding the door, instead of doing what he has been put there to do, opening it. I have already explained to Andy the absurdity of Soviet restaurants, although he hadn't fully grasped the concept until we sat down at a café a couple of days ago.

After I spent fifteen minutes translating every item on the ten-page menu and after Andy made his choices for appetizers and main courses, a waitress materialized by our table, announcing in a voice simultaneously fierce and exhausted, "We only have beef Stroganoff."

"Okay," Andy agreed, "but I'd also like some caviar and a bowl of mushroom soup."

"We only have beef Stroganoff," the waitress repeated, fierceness in her voice now taking the upper hand.

"They only have beef Stroganoff," I said in English, stressing the word *only*, letting the waitress know that she was not dealing with a simple case of a dense out-of-towner.

But what about all these delicacies typed onto the ten-page menu? Andy's eyes seemed to be asking. What about the caviar and mushroom soup? With the annoyed waitress rolling her eyes by our table, I could see Andy attempting to process another case of my country's make-believe, trying to reconcile the fiction of a ten-page menu full of various choices with the typical Soviet reality of having none.

Now, standing before the human turnstile to the front door of Kavkazsky restaurant, Andy has a pack of Marlboros clutched in his hand and two more stuffed into the pockets of his jacket, just in case. The doorman's eyes freeze on the pack in Andy's hand, and he shifts his weight from one foot to the other, his posture losing some of its ferocity. From two steps away, I watch the silent exchange: Andy nods toward the door, the doorman steps aside, Andy hands him the pack, the pack vanishes into the pocket of the man's overcoat, the door opens.

"The universal language," Andy whispers as we walk in. He has a childish smile on his face, ecstatic that he has succeeded at what looked like a small black-market operation. Inside, the place is predictably empty, and we choose a table by the wall, away from the only other party, a Russian couple sitting in the corner.

"So how did they manage to get in?" asks Andy with a mock frown. "In the absence of American cigarettes?"

"*Blat*," I say, referring to the pervasive method of barter and exchange, the ubiquitous Russian word for personal connections. I can see that Andy doesn't understand, so I try to think of some specific examples of *blat*. "That man may be a manager at a department store that recently received a shipment of Finnish shearling coats," I say. "And now the doorman's wife has one of those coats hanging in her armoire." I probably use a sheepskin coat as an example because it was my own pathetic dream when I lived here, a dark envy of every shearling-clad woman that had for years curdled my heart. As Andy knows, it was all academic: I had no *blat* and no money to afford a fur coat even if I did.

"And what about the woman?" he asks, playing along.

"She may be on the university admissions board, one of the professors who has the roster of the students to be admitted in her drawer even before the entrance exams begin. She may also be the head of the university party cell. So the waiter's daughter is now guaranteed a seat at the School of Journalism despite the fact that she couldn't write one good sentence in high school." I pause, looking at the woman, considering a new identity for her. "Or maybe she is a gynecologist." I think of my provincial aunt Muza, who usually lumbers home from work with a string bag full of *blat* provisions, her personal connections weaving through the fabric of the town's female population. "If she is a gynecologist, she is a regular at this restaurant, no doubt about it."

"Okay," Andy says. "I think I get the picture."

Kavkazsky also has a ten-page menu, but there is more than one real dish to choose from. We try Georgian red beans with spices and chicken in walnut sauce, then skewers of marinated lamb and flattened chicken *tabaka*, all flavorful and spicy. We try as many dishes as we can eat, but the bill doesn't seem to be able to climb over five dollars, at the blue jean exchange rate, no matter what we order. A saucer of black caviar finally tips the scale and adds a hefty fifty cents to our bill.

"I feel like a millionaire here," Andy says, counting out the rainbow of ruble notes, his eyes shining with excitement. "I love this place."

It is ironic, I think, that you can like my country only from far away, armed with Western cigarettes and dollar bills illegal to own for anyone who lives here.

After we finish our exploratory lunch, a second pack of Marlboros makes its entrance into the doorman's pocket and we make a reservation for my family and friends two days from now, a party with caviar, shish kebabs, and vodka, and a price tag of about thirty dollars.

# *Twenty-Eight*

After days of gliding on parquet museum floors past the Hermitage paintings and icons at the Russian Museum, Andy says he wants to be immersed in real life. For the next week or so, we stand on various lines. We buy a log of bologna and wrap it in newspaper to carry home; we bring back four bottles of Bulgarian ketchup that put a smile on Mama's face. We bake in the sun in front of a vegetable store, under a red banner stretched across the building, and leave an hour later with a string bag full of ripe tomatoes from Azerbaijan. "What does the banner say?" asks Andy as we inch toward the door. I translate the slogan, mundane and predictable—"We thank the party for the people's welfare"—one of many crimson fragments of Soviet wisdom spread across the most impressive structures of the city.

When lines for food are no longer exciting, we go to houseware shops in search of Soviet treasures: cut-crystal shot glasses I remember from my childhood, a small metal pot with a long wood handle and a narrow neck for making coffee. We buy an iron padlock with a heavy key that Andy calls an antique. Antique? I repeat because I am not sure I heard him correctly. I think of my mother locking our dacha barn with a contraption just like this one only two years earlier, the key the size of her palm she always carefully put away under a brick near the fence. I think of the curious time warp we are caught in, of my city hermetically sealed from the rest of the world, fossilized in time like a fly in Baltic amber.

&

I wake up at night, when pencil-thin beams of sun paint stripes on the floor, streaking through the drawn curtains. In June, night is nothing but a few hours of translucent dusk when the sun barely touches the horizon, and even a month later the light still persists, making people sleepless. Who would choose to sleep when the twilight so quickly dissipates, when the buildings come into focus and their eyes of windows begin to shine by four in the morning?

Shreds of conversations float up to our open balcony, students returning from all-night walks on the Neva to watch the lowering of the bridges. What is the language they are speaking? The words are disjointed, made faint by laughter and the distance they have to travel, their cadences indecipherable to my new English-immersed ears.

The first streetcar clangs under our windows and screeches on the turn, waking up Andy. "How did you ever sleep here?" he asks, squinting at the light.

I walk to the balcony and draw the curtains open, letting in another morning. "I don't even hear them," I say. "I never did." To me, the clatter of streetcars has always been soothing, like the sound of trains. From the balcony, I look at the tide of roofs rolling toward the gray cupola of Leningrad's only synagogue, at the wrought-iron canal banisters, whose unique design is visible at this early hour. I know Andy and I have the same thought in our minds. It is time for us to go back.

"We're leaving in five days," says Andy, trying to cheer us both, looking up from the yellowed copy of *A Farewell to Arms* he found on the bookshelf.

ഇ

For our farewell party we stay at home and invite my friends. We all crowd into Marina's room, talking and drinking, and for a couple of hours it feels like being back in time. It feels like any of a dozen parties we have had in this room, with Nadia the *refusenik* making dissident jokes and Tania, who lives with her husband and son in a communal apartment separated from her mother by a curtain, complaining about the neighbors and her insipid engineering job. I haven't noticed Nadia's pale cheeks or the dark half-moons under her eyes before, but Tania looks the same as I remember. She is broad-boned and stately, with rich blond hair I've always envied, a hefty ponytail that hasn't lost its thickness or luster despite her washing it for years in the communal kitchen sink.

With Nadia and Tania chatting by the piano and with Nina next to me on the balcony from where we can see the smooth skin of the Griboedova Canal, it feels like the old days. But this surface semblance can't fool anyone here. We all know that nothing is the same, and that realization is as palpable in the air as the low clouds of humidity seeping between buildings, promising rain. I can gab with my friends about life here, down to its most delicate nuances, but I am no longer a part of it. I live across the ocean in an American house, the pictures of which I feel uneasy about passing around.

No one needs any pictures, though, to see the distance that divides us. All they need to do is glance at Andy, at his straight spine and unencumbered shoulders, at his Western look—which comes not from leather shoes or Levi's jeans but from the way he moves without apprehension, the way his eyes are not afraid to see into the future.

I don't yet know many things that did—or will—happen to my friends. Nina hasn't had a chance to tell me yet that she lost her teaching job at the university after I left because she kept my upcoming capitalist marriage a secret, thus failing to save the dean of the department from a big embarrassment before his party bosses. "If you'd told us," the dean said, "we would've fired her, not you."

We won't know for several more years that Nadia's father will die of a heart attack and her grandmother will die of grief before they finally get a visa to leave the country. They will have to pack up in one week, leaving behind most of the things that have surrounded them for decades, including the apartment the family has lived in since before the siege of Leningrad.

I won't know until 1990 that Tania, her husband, and their two young sons will get on the plane to New York, stay in our house until we can find them an apartment, and file the papers asking for political asylum. It is 1982, the murk of Soviet times, and the word *perestroika* is still completely alien to our ears. None of us—my friends, Andy, or I—can even think of being able to meet again, especially on the other side of the Atlantic.

∞

The next morning we take a taxi to the airport, the same wing cordoned off for international departures where I'd said farewell to Mama and Marina two years earlier. I fill out the required declaration form to let customs know that I haven't sold my wedding band or my silver necklace, that I am not attempting to smuggle out rubles, worthless anywhere beyond the borders of this country.

I kiss my sister and say good-bye, but it is not the bitter farewell of two years ago, when we all thought that I might not be able to return.

Again, Mama surreptitiously wipes her eyes; again, they are like broken glass. "*Pishi,*" she says, "Write often."

"Listen." I take her by the shoulders. "We're sending you an invitation to visit us the moment we get back. I've already found out all the details at the embassy in Washington. You'll need to take it to the visa department of Oktyabrsky District and follow their stupid steps."

She nods and tries to smile, a handkerchief clutched in her hand.

"We'll see you very soon," I say. "We have a house now; you won't have to live under a bridge."

She turns away and shakes her head, embarrassed by her fears.

Mama and I have never talked about love, in Leningrad or later all the way across the world. Maybe we have simply taken love for granted, the first rule of survival that binds most Russian families together, the glue that has helped us all withstand the war, and senseless bureaucrats, and Soviet lies.

At the glass door that separates my country from the rest of the world we put our arms around each other and for a few moments stand still. There is an earthy smell on her soft skin: apples, still unripe; damp dacha linens that survived the winter; the bitter, sticky milk of dandelions.

# Twenty-Nine

When my mother first came to visit us, in 1983, Aeroflot planes were not allowed to land in New York. Instead, we bought her a ticket from Leningrad to Montreal, where she changed airports without speaking a word of English, and several hours later came out of the passport control at LaGuardia, smiling.

Now, in 1988, she has taken a direct flight and landed at Kennedy. The word *perestroika* has entered the vocabulary on both sides of the Atlantic, and Mama emerged from a small crowd of dazed Russians who came to visit for the first time since their families had left the Soviet Union twenty years earlier.

On the way home, as our Datsun rolled across Manhattan toward the Lincoln Tunnel, a young woman in skintight shorts approached Andy's open window at a red light on Forty-Second Street, where I started my ESL career. Maybe she couldn't see that there were two passengers in the car, or maybe it didn't matter to her, but what happened next made my mother wince and stiffen. The woman lifted her tank top above her chest, and I immediately knew what flashed through my mother's mind. She had been right all along. America was indeed the mouth of the shark, with all its vices and ills on display, just as *Pravda* had warned her.

ॐ

I am seven months pregnant, and Mama's eyes are radiating happiness. For years she has been asking probing questions, having given up on the idea that my sister would ever get married or produce a grandchild, realizing that I was her only hope. We know it is going to be a girl. A few months earlier, I sent the results of the amniocentesis to Mama and Marina in Leningrad—a picture of paired chromosomes, the photocopied blurry combination of the two Xs that must have surprised them since there is no prenatal testing available in Russia.

Mama and I take a tour of the hospital where the baby is going to be delivered. This is the first American hospital either of us has ever seen, and we walk around gawking at carpeted waiting areas and patient rooms with only one bed, as if we were tourists admiring the landmarks of an unfamiliar civilization. I am happy to know that the health plan my college provides will eliminate at least one anxiety—worrying about medical bills—in the realm of childbirth stresses. But for my mother this tour is more visceral. She realizes, maybe for the first time, that for the seventy-four years of her life in Russia, every Soviet official and every newspaper and every television announcer has lied to her. They have always told her that the West was rotting, along with its hospitals and doctors and its retrograde obstetrics incapable of delivering the new inhabitants of the world's bright future. They have assured her that Soviet medicine was the best in the world— free, progressive, and equal to none—and now, as our nurse guide shows us the baby monitor and the anesthesiologist's station at each delivery bed, my mother realizes that it was never so. I know Mama is happy to see that her granddaughter will be born in what she can only perceive as medical luxury, but there is a slight ambivalence in her face, the shadow of betrayal that dulls the joy in her eyes.

I think of the maternity hospital in Leningrad where I was

born, of women leaning out of open windows, shouting details about their delivery to their husbands below, who were not allowed past the reception desk. When I was growing up, it was common knowledge that visitors from the outside presented a sanitary hazard, although in my mind the absence of clean sheets, medicine, and running water had always trumped the possible dangers dragged in by fathers wanting to see their newborns. They arrived in the evening, after work, to stand on the streetcar tracks in front of the hospital and shout questions to their wives who were hanging out of the open windows. The men cupped their hands around their mouths so their voices could reach to the third and fourth floors, shouting questions about the color of their children's eyes and hair as streetcars jingled a warning for them to get off the tracks.

"This is a very good hospital," says Mama quietly when the tour is over, and I know she is thinking of all the hospitals she has seen in her life, those places she was told were the best in the world. I know she is thinking of her sister, Muza, an obstetrician in the provinces, who will never know about baby monitors or epidurals, who would be bewildered if she found out that an American father-to-be can sit by the delivery bed and hold his wife's hand.

∽

When I go into labor, my obstetrician is on vacation and I am assigned to the covering doctor. Andy drives me to the hospital, with my mother in the backseat. As soon as I am hooked up to a baby monitor, regular contractions stop. Then they start, then they fade again. Hours pass as I lie in bed, waiting, wishing I could whip the time as if it were a lazy horse.

I don't know what Mama is doing in the waiting room; she has probably brought one of her Russian books with her, having prepared everything in advance, as usual. I shouldn't think about my mother, anyway; I should concentrate on the breathing I learned in

Lamaze class. For six weeks Andy and I drove to a nurse's house where four pregnant women lay on a living room rug and pretended to deliver babies. The nurse, practical and peppy, taught us all kinds of exercises and techniques that made me feel confident and prepared.

An anesthesiologist comes to my bedside and asks if I want an epidural. No, I say emphatically, and shake my head to make sure he understands that I am not a weak American reaching for medication at the slightest twinge of pain. I am sure I can have a natural childbirth, just like my mother, my aunt, and every Russian woman within the borders of the Soviet Union, who are not privy to the medical equipment and care this hospital has to offer. The anesthesiologist leaves, then pops his head inside again to say he will be just outside my door.

More hours pass. I write a note to my mother with an update, and Andy takes it to the waiting room. There isn't much to report except stronger contractions that seem to have become longer and more frequent, just as the enthusiastic Lamaze nurse has taught us. Andy is by my bed with slivers of ice he slides into my mouth, one of many things my obstetrician aunt Muza wouldn't fathom.

Another contraction rumbles in like a train, and, when it ends, I notice that my fingernails have left little purple crescents in the flesh of my palms. A silly memory comes to mind, Nina's description of when her son, Mitya, was born. It felt like someone stuck an umbrella in, she said, and then opened it up inside you. It makes me wonder, as I lick my lips and swallow sweat, where this helpful image was hiding when the anesthesiologist was here.

In the interval between contractions I think of my co-worker Zoe, who teaches yoga in addition to ESL, of the description of her daughter's birth a year earlier, obviously a more enlightened and refined experience than I already know mine is going to be. Zoe had a doula in the hospital room, who instructed her to deliver her baby in a squatting position in order to achieve what she called an orgasmic birth.

The next contraction wipes the word *orgasmic* out of my mind, and I know Zoe and her doula would be very disappointed if they could see me. When I catch my breath, I yell for the anesthesiologist. By now, the Lamaze class is a distant memory, and it is obvious that I am a failure. "Where is the anesthesiologist?" I shout, as the next freight train detonates inside me. "He said he was right there!" I shriek. He lulled me into believing he was just outside the door, and now he's vanished, that bastard.

The epidural is in, a few hours of respite. How did my grandmother give birth to six and my aunt Muza to three without epidurals? Why was my mother so desperate to have another baby after she gave birth to Marina during the war, undoubtedly not under the most desirable conditions? And what about my friends Nina, Nadia, and Tania, a younger generation who chose to risk the same birthing indignities in the hands of indifferent staff and inferior hospitals?

The epidural bliss is wearing off now; no more anesthesia is allowed. It is time to start pushing, says the doctor. I push. Harder, he says. I push harder. I don't know how to push, let alone push harder, but I do what I'm told. It all feels unreal, as if I am onstage, acting in a play. The nurse is my director, orchestrating the visceral performance where we are all pressing forward to bring on the final scene. Push, push, she chants. Harder, harder, she sings. I claw at Andy's hand, belching nonhuman grunts. But no matter how hard everyone tries, we get stuck somewhere in the middle of act three.

"It's a breech," says the doctor. "I'll try to turn the baby, but we may need to do a C-section."

The C-word makes me think of a vertical scar from chest to crotch Aunt Muza talked about on one of her summer visits to our dacha when she described a surgery she had performed. From here to here, she said, enclosing a foot of her round stomach between her palms. I don't remember how old I was when I heard this, but the image has stayed with me ever since: an entire belly open, skin pulled apart with clamps, then sewn up with wide stitches of my aunt's resolute hand. I imagine myself on the operating table, my insides exposed, like one of those papier-mâché torsos in Mama's anatomy museum with coils of intestines and chunks of major organs I used to stare at when I was in elementary school.

"Ask him how big the scar will be," I say to Andy. I am not sure this is the right thing to worry about right now, but for some reason, this is the only thing that surfaces in my mind.

I write a note to my mother with the news about the breech, and Andy takes it to the waiting room. Ten minutes later, a page with her squared handwriting comes back, describing a maneuver she performed once before the war when she was the chief and only physician of a provincial hospital near a peat mine that mostly employed women. She was twenty-four, just out of medical school, and had never delivered a baby before, but there was a woman in the last stage of labor right there in front of her, already nine centimeters dilated, and what Mama saw was not the baby's crown but its butt. Although she didn't know what to do, my mother didn't panic. She raced to her office and returned with a textbook she had wisely brought from Ivanovo, where she went to medical school. She was orderly and practical, even at that age, and she calmly ran her finger down the contents pages. The chapter on childbirth included two paragraphs on how to treat a breech. She propped the book open on a chair and followed the instructions she still remembers half a century later.

I translate the note for the doctor. He says he has never heard of this but will give it a try. I feel some churning, some major rearrangement in my gut. It doesn't work.

I can no longer see the nurse because she is behind me, wheeling my bed out of delivery and into the operating room. Andy and the doctor are already there, wearing gowns and caps the color of newborn chicks, but I can see only their heads from behind a screen the nurse installs around my waist. The screen cuts me in two: one half of me is conscious, with a working mind, a beating heart, and moving arms, and the other half is numb, no longer mine. It now belongs to the operating nurses, whose capped heads bob above the screen, and to the doctor, whom I can't see now because he is bending down. I think of his scalpel slicing me open from the rib cage to the bottom of my belly, of the strange reality in which I am able to understand what he is doing but not feel it. I think of the diagram of blood vessels Mama asked me to copy from a textbook when I was twelve, a tangle of red arteries and blue veins running from the heart to the lungs and down to the liver, uterus, and kidneys—everything in primary colors—what the doctor is probably now staring at as the old image bobs to the surface of my memory.

I see Andy crossing from the numb side of me to the working side, cradling an infant in his arms, holding it clumsily, away from his body, as if it were made of glass. He sits down on the side of the bed for me to see her, plump and pink, wrapped in a baby blanket, with a cap over her head. There is not a single blotch or blemish on her skin: she didn't have to struggle to get out. She was simply lifted out of my open belly and into her father's waiting arms.

We stare at our daughter's eyes struggling to stay open, at her blond hairs sticking out from under the cap like corn silk.

"Ten fingers, ten toes," says Andy. His face has a fragile, unprotected look, an expression of unguarded openness I've never seen before. "She's perfect."

I carefully touch the baby's face, and she wiggles her lips as though she were smiling.

"The doctor did a bikini cut," Andy says. "I insisted."

"Bikini cut?" I say. A bikini is the last thing that comes to mind right now.

"He cut below the hairline. You'll never see the scar."

I've forgotten all about the scar, with the nine-pound infant trying to squirm out of her blanket in the crook of my arm.

"Willful, isn't she?" says a nurse, who is doing something behind my head.

Stubborn as a goat, as my mother would say, words that in Leningrad were always aimed at me.

# *Thirty*

From the day Sasha was born, Mama never again spoke of returning to Leningrad. It was understood that she would stay where her only granddaughter was. Did we even discuss it? I had filled out a three-page immigration form, a daughter requesting reunification with her mother. She simply stayed with us, reading chapter books in Russian by the crib, embroidering kitchen towels we never dared use, making buckwheat with onions and pots of sour cabbage soup.

She never looked back, it seemed. She left her life of seventy-four years and stayed with me and Sasha. I couldn't understand why she never expressed any regret or nostalgia for her Russian life. It had already been eight years since I moved here, and I still missed my friends, the brown serpentine of Leningrad canals, the low cotton clouds steaming over the city from the Gulf of Finland. I could still smell the salty wind that sent cigarette stubs into the courtyards and in June whipped clouds of poplar seeds into a whirlwind of summer snow.

Mama never uttered a word about wanting to go back. She had left her apartment, the city where she lived a major chunk of her life, and her colleagues from medical school who remained her friends until the end. She left her native tongue, the only language she ever knew how to speak. She left her sister, Muza, with her sprawling brood of grand- and great-grandchildren and her only remaining brother, Vova, her cousins and aunts and her six nephews. She left Marina.

For the next few years, Mama made it her goal to bring Marina to this country. She focused her energy on filling out applications for my sister to participate in the green card lottery, learning about it from a Russian newspaper published in Brooklyn, her only source of information about what life was like outside our Nutley house.

8>

Andy finds a carpenter to frame a bathroom on the third floor of our house, and my mother moves upstairs. Every day we collide in the kitchen, where she gives me advice on grocery shopping and the benefits of soup.

"You must eat soup for the first course," she admonishes, citing the Soviet wisdom I have heard so many times before in our Leningrad kitchen. "Soup is essential for digestion and a healthy stomach. And you must eat it with bread. Bread is necessary for proper peristalsis." She deliberately uses a physiological term, calculating that I will not be willing to argue with science.

"People don't eat soup in America," I snarl back. "Not like we ate soup in Russia, every day." I have lived eight years here without my mother policing my menu, and my peristalsis is working just fine, I want to tell her. Instead, I feel like striking back at her bread argument and her praise for soup, as if they were the true culprits. I feel like telling her that the food we choose to eat needs no criticism, especially from someone who only recently arrived from the land of string bags and lines. "And why did we stuff ourselves with bread?" I ask. "Because there was nothing else to eat. Because there were six *kotlety* for the three of us that had to last for at least two days."

My mother purses her lips, and I can see she is offended. I know it wasn't her fault that we were allowed only one *kotleta* each, but her soup and bread tirades, her incessant advice about everything I do propels me back in time. I feel like a child again, stuck in our Leningrad kitchen, the place I thought I had escaped.

&

Andy and I are at a new Italian restaurant that just opened a few blocks from our house. We brought a bottle of Chianti because the restaurant does not have a liquor license—the main reason we chose to go there. It is a Friday night, and Mama is at home with Sasha. Our friends with small children are envious because we have a live-in babysitter. No, I say, what we have is a live-in babushka, with all the good and the bad that it entails.

*Babusya*, she calls herself, the diminutive for *babushka* we all used to call my grandmother. *Babusya*, says Sasha, who is just beginning to speak.

I know that without my mother's help I wouldn't be able to finish my doctoral dissertation about how nonnative speakers acquire English articles, all those silly *a*'s and *the*'s—which I haven't completely acquired myself. I couldn't go back to teaching full-time at Hudson College. I know we are very fortunate to have a live-in grandmother, but the price for being so lucky is to have my mother back, mothering.

Andy is a psychotherapist, and he seems to understand these things better than I do. "We all wish we could choose our parents," he says. "But it's all really just the luck of the draw. You're dealt a hand of cards when you're born and that's the hand you play. You cannot change that."

"But I did change it!" I say, a bit too loudly, because a woman at the next table stops poking at her salad and lifts her eyes to look at me. "I left," I mutter in Marina's dramatic whisper. "And I was fine, for nine years. Now she's here, back to monitoring my every step. Wear a hat or you'll catch a cold. Swaddle the baby or she'll get sick," I mock. "My mother is back to controlling my life."

Andy is patient and calm, sipping his wine, used to hysterical outbursts in his office. "She doesn't really control anything here," he says. "She lives with us, and she doesn't even speak English."

"But she's learning!" I cry in desperation. "And I am the one teaching her!" A few months ago I brought an ESL textbook home from work when Mama told me she wanted to start learning English. Now we go over a unit each week, and she diligently hands me the homework exercises I assign. She writes them in her careful, dogged letters, often phonetically, not noticing that she has misspelled a word. I review her pages, writing patient comments in Russian, pointing out the errors she couldn't notice. "Do you know the joke about bringing your own rope?" I ask Andy.

I don't feel like telling jokes right now, but this one seems very topical, so I oblige.

*An American entrepreneur comes to a Soviet factory where the foreman boasts that Soviet workers never go on strike. Just give me a few days, says the American, and I guarantee you a revolt. The next morning, he tells the workers that they'll all be working twice as many hours for the same pay. There's not so much as a grumble in response. The following day he tells them they'll be working twice as many hours for half the pay. Still no one says a word. Finally, in desperation, the American tells the workers that the next morning everyone is going to be hanged. Timidly, one man raises his hand. Good, thinks the businessman—finally, a protest! Will you be supplying the ropes, asks the worker, or should we bring our own?*

"Bring your own rope," Andy says, laughing. "I like that."

We empty our glasses of wine, grateful that we brought a whole bottle.

I know I should start figuring out how to play the game with the cards that have been dealt to me, but I can't help feeling resentment. Before we left for the evening, I couldn't ignore Mama's slant-eyed look of disapproval. "Why do you need to go to a restaurant?" she grumbled. "You have a refrigerator full of perfectly good food!" Complete with a pot of soup she made three days earlier that needs to be eaten, preferably today, I thought. "You're always running somewhere out of the house; you never sit still. Just as you did in Leningrad." Only now you have a baby, and you leave me here to take care of her, is what she probably meant.

I feel angry at my mother for chiding me about going out on a Friday night.

I feel guilty when I think of her reading a chapter book to Sasha on the second floor of our darkened house, of her switching off the light when my daughter falls asleep and quietly climbing the stairs to her room on the third floor.

In addition to feeling angry and guilty, I also feel stupid when we leave the restaurant because I am freezing cold walking the few blocks back home. I feel like an idiot shivering in the wind that blasts into my face, reluctantly yielding to a thought that my mother may have been right about the hat.

# *Thirty-One*

**M**ama and I have just returned from our pediatrician's office. For the first time in her two-year-old life, Sasha is running a fever. Take her home and give her Tylenol, says Dr. Marcus. In a couple of days she'll be fine.

At home, I take Sasha upstairs to her room and hold her in my arms. She is a bundle of burning flesh, a hot, tiny body that depends entirely on me. I think of the time when I was little and had a bad flu. I still remember that illness as a fever dream, as being drawn into a whirlpool under the oilskin of a black river so full of silent dangers no one had warned me about. I remember the sense of coming up for air when the cool weight of Mama's hand rested on my forehead before the wet pressure of a compress lifted my face above the surface of the water. Did she sit by my bed during the whole time I slipped in and out of delirium? Did she know from the beginning, enlightened by her physician's wisdom, that my body would win the battle and recover, that the whirlpool in the black river would not be able to claim me?

I rock my daughter, hoping she'll fall asleep, but she insists on playing with her stuffed toy Puffy, a little plush dog with floppy ears and a smile my ESL students gave me when I returned from maternity leave. She wraps her arms around Puffy the way I wrap my arms around her, and I look at the three *matryoshka* nesting dolls my mother brought when she arrived from Leningrad, the smallest only an inch tall, rising up like a tiny staircase on the chest of drawers next to the crib. I think of mothers and daughters stacked up inside one another and of the three of us living under one roof, like these *matryoshka* dolls—something unimaginable to me only a few years ago, something so natural and indisputable back home.

I hear the clanging of pots in the kitchen—Mama probably beginning her predinner leftover-evaluation ritual—when Sasha's body suddenly tenses and shudders in my arms, as if from an electric shock. Puffy falls on the floor, and I stare at my daughter, motionless and still. Her eyes are closed, and her head hangs back from my elbow, no longer supported by the muscle of life. I yell her name; I shake her. She doesn't open her eyes. She doesn't move.

I shout for Mama because I don't know what else to do, rush to the kitchen phone and dial 911. The man on the other end sounds calm. How can he be speaking in such a dispassionate voice as I'm telling him my two-year-old daughter has stopped moving? The truth is I don't even know what I'm saying to him. Without any effort on my part, it seems, my mouth does its work, wrapping around screams and howls, the only sounds it is capable of making.

The operator interrupts. "Is she breathing?" he asks.

I look at Sasha's motionless body in my arms, her closed eyes. I don't know if she's breathing. How can I know if she's breathing? She isn't moving. She isn't responsive. I hear myself shouting into the phone again. I don't know what I'm saying, but it feels like action. It's all I can do.

"Put a spoon in her mouth," says the man on the other end, "so she doesn't bite her tongue," and I am not sure I heard him right because this sounds like such a bizarre instruction.

I hear the doorbell ring. I hand the unmoving body of my daughter to Mama, whose face seems as white as the sink behind her, and race to the front door. A man in his twenties, our local travel agent's son, who helps his parents in the office two blocks down the street, is standing on the porch, panting. What is he doing here? Why is there a travel agent at my door?

We don't need any tickets right now, I think, ready to sprint back.

"I am an emergency volunteer," says the man. "I ran straight from the office, to be here before the ambulance arrives."

I hear him speak, but the only words that reach my brain are *emergency* and *ambulance*. This is an emergency, and an ambulance is on its way. The emergency involves my daughter. The 911 operator asked if she was breathing. I didn't know if she was.

The travel agent neighbor follows me into the living room, where Sasha is stretched out on the couch. Mama is next to her, with her hand on Sasha's wrist. This is the first sensory image my body processes since my daughter shuddered and froze. The picture imprints in my mind: Sasha's blue dress on the tan leather of the couch, her tiny wrist cupped in Mama's hand.

We lean over her as she opens her eyes. She is alive.

∞

The paramedics say she had a febrile seizure. I don't know the word *febrile*, either because I've never heard it or because my mind is short-circuited and can't connect words to their meanings. Most likely, there is no permanent damage, they say. I would prefer they didn't preface their statement with "most likely." After we see our pediatrician, we will need to schedule an encephalogram.

It is my fault, clearly, that I didn't detect Sasha's fever earlier, that I took her and Mama to my in-laws' swimming pool this morning, allowing her to roast in the sun. There is no doubt this outing pushed her fever even higher, bringing us to paramedics in our living room and an ambulance flashing its lights outside our house. How can such complete responsibility for another life be placed on any one person's shoulders? How did Mama withstand the burden of raising my sister during the war and later me in Leningrad, practically single-handedly?

I see Andy, who should be in his office seeing patients, walk through the front door. I should be surprised by his sudden appearance in the middle of his workday, but strangely I am not.

How did you know? I ask.

He says he didn't know. He just felt he had to come home.

The paramedics tell me they are going to take Sasha to the emergency room to lower her fever. We get into Andy's car and follow the ambulance along familiar streets I don't recognize in the red and blue glow of flashing lights in front of us.

The nurse in the emergency room greets us as if we were her long-lost friends. She is someone we do know, it turns out, Andy's former colleague from Jersey City Medical Center, Ann. For some reason, I am not surprised to see her, miraculously transplanted to this hospital tonight of all nights. This coincidence is simply another bend in the zigzag line of today's warped reality.

Andy tells her about the febrile seizure, or maybe she already knows what has happened from the paramedics' report. Ann is reserved and efficient, her careful hands undressing Sasha, her eyes letting us know we are going to be all right.

The next image burned onto my brain is Sasha naked, sitting in the sink of the emergency room, seemingly dazed in her lukewarm bath. She is unusually quiet, bouncing her palms over the surface of the water, as if discovering for the first time how resilient it is, yet how yielding. If Mama could see this, she would think we were insane, bathing the child in cool water, making her sick.

I call home and tell Mama that everything is all right. The seizure was the result of high fever, I say, and now Sasha is back to normal. Mama exhales and I hear wet, sniffly sounds before she quickly hangs up.

As we wait for the fever to subside, I tell Andy what had happened before he got home. I tell him about the passionless 911 operator and his bizarre instruction, about trying to stick a teaspoon between Sasha's teeth and failing because my hands refused to stop shaking. I allow myself to utter a sentence that has been stuck in my brain like a splinter, a statement that until now I was afraid to release into the air because it seemed to have the power to jinx the outcome.

"I thought she had died in my arms," I say, daring to validate the dark gravity of this afternoon with words. "She was there and I was holding her. She was playing with Puffy. I held her, thinking she would be there forever, and then she wasn't. She was full of life one moment and then gone from life the next."

The words come out hard and heavy, weighted down by the memory of those endless minutes that I sense will stay with me. I hear the sounds leave my mouth, and as they emerge between us, it is clear how insignificant and small everything else has become. It is also clear how unprotective I am as a mother, how vulnerable and underprepared. I have always taken my own mother for granted, shrugging away the offered lessons. I have failed to learn the parenting rules and blithely disregarded the homework.

# Thirty-Two

It is August 1991, and we place a call to Marina in Leningrad. She has already made two trips to visit us in Nutley: one in the mid-1980s and the other soon after Sasha was born, both immortalized by sets of pictures Mama has installed in her new photo album. Every now and then we look at my sister wearing New York City T-shirts in front of Manhattan landmarks; we turn the pages to see her on the deck of our house—raising a glass of wine, bending over the baby carriage, setting down a plate next to my mother, whose face is shining because both her daughters are again together, if only temporarily, on the same side of the Atlantic Ocean.

There are photos of Marina at the Concord Hotel in the Catskills, where we all went for Christmas at the invitation of Andy's younger brother, Frankie, who is the dining room manager there. Mama's album unfolds a series of images of my sister happy to be in America: Marina circling the Concord skating rink on rented skates; my sister showing Frankie's wife, Jen, how to season a turkey; Frankie introducing Marina to the Russian celebrity performer for that night, someone my sister, a celebrity actress herself, has never heard of.

But now Marina is back in Leningrad, and we place a call to her once a week, a complicated and expensive affair. First, we must reach an American international operator, who then, often unsuccessfully, attempts to connect to the Soviet operator handling overseas calls. My mother always takes her watch off her wrist and stretches it on the kitchen table under the wall phone to keep track of the time we spend talking to Marina. At three dollars a minute, we must be quick and concise.

Andy dials the American operator, but there is a delay and he leans against the wall with the receiver pressed to his ear. I give him a quizzical glance, and he shrugs. We wait, my mother shaking her head to demonstrate her irritation. "At these prices, it would be faster to fly there," she grumbles.

Then Andy straightens up and separates his shoulder from the wall. "Really?" he says into the phone and listens intently, his face scrunched. Then he is put on hold again. "The operator says he thinks something has happened in Russia," Andy tells me, and I immediately translate it to Mama. "They may have overthrown Gorbachev." Mama and I simultaneously look at each other because we know that no Russian government has been overthrown since 1917. "The operator doesn't know what it is," says Andy, "but it is something big."

∽

That evening and the next day we are glued to CNN, watching people building barricades on the streets of Moscow and Leningrad, the same streets where only a couple of months earlier these same people marched under red banners to celebrate International Workers' Day. I peer into the faces gathering in front of the Parliament in Moscow they now call the White House: fathers with their school-age children getting a hands-on lesson in history, women with faces wrinkled by worry for their sons who have rushed to protect the building from encroaching tanks, pensioners who have seen cataclysms before, waiting on the sidelines, leaning on their canes. Are these the same people who over seventy years have patiently been bringing their own ropes?

"I told you this couldn't go on forever!" says Andy, whose words, when we visited Leningrad, I dismissed as the naïveté of a Westerner who had never had to face the enormity and might of the Soviet state. This is a machine, I told him, that incarcerated and murdered tens of millions of its own people; a state that defeated Nazi Germany, at the price of tens of millions of more deaths. This, I reminded him, is a place with eleven time zones and seventy nationalities; a place with nuclear weapons, fifteen independent republics, and three major television channels.

I was so certain I knew my country—its past and its future—better than an American ever could. Is it possible that Andy, precisely because he was an outsider, was able to see through the veneer of all that Soviet prowess, which I simultaneously used to ridicule and fear, and catch a glimpse of the system's crumbling core?

I think of those in Leningrad I know so well, wishing I could see what they are doing at this very moment, trying to imagine this day through their eyes. Is my sister scared, shivering at the thought that this new state of emergency will keep her forever caged within the confines of our Motherland? Is she sitting behind a locked door to our apartment—the music of Tchaikovsky's *Swan Lake* flowing from every television channel as an absurd accompaniment to something none of us has ever seen—watching from our balcony as the crowds beneath bustle toward Isaac's Square, the seat of the city government? Or maybe she is among the crowd, among those shouting men and sharp-elbowed women climbing into cabs because today all taxis are giving free rides to anyone heading to the square?

I know Marina has a visceral abhorrence of crowds, which she has harbored since her first visit to Moscow, when she was eight, an experience that may have shaped her cynicism about our Soviet life. My sister told me the story when I still lived in Russia, and this is what I am thinking about now as CNN is showing us Moscow: Mama and Marina chugging on an overnight train from Ivanovo to see the May Day parade in Red Square, to see Stalin himself standing by the Kremlin wall.

It is early morning of May 1, 1950, and Marina, Mama, and Mama's cousin Katya, whose couch they're sleeping on, are walking toward the Moskva River, where Katya's group from the telephone center is assembling before the demonstration. Katya is a *telefonistka*, an impressive title, a word that rolls off Marina's eight-year-old tongue like a whistle. It is sunny and warm, the perfect weather for International Workers' Day, and the streets have been washed by blue trucks that she saw earlier spraying water in heavy, blazing arches. Marina is between Mama and Katya decked out in their best dresses, holding their hands, jumping over the puddles left by the trucks.

They wait in the crowd before the entrance to Red Square, and then everyone starts walking: people with banners and portraits of the politburo members and red carnations made from paper swaying on long wire stems. At the entrance to the square they stop, jerk forward, then stop again, and Katya explains that this is where they are going to be divided into six columns. They inch past a row of men in military uniforms, their gold epaulets touching, so that no one from one column can slip into the column closer to the Kremlin, where the politburo watches them from above the square.

Mama hoists Marina onto her shoulders so she can see. Now my sister is in the midst of a forest of swaying sticks with flags, banners, and portraits, in the midst of balloons and red carnations. She squints and peers to her left, where everyone else is peering. There, five columns of people away, a group of men stand on granite platforms against the Kremlin wall. In the center is a separate dark figure in what looks like a military uniform. Marina knows it is Stalin, the country's conscience and revolutionary glory, the people's father, as the radio reminds them every morning. He is the father to all who march in this square and all those gathered around radios from here to the Kamchatka Peninsula. Only he is so far away Marina can barely make him out. He looks tiny and ant-like, not at all like the man they all know from paintings, grand and immortalized in oil, and there is nothing glorious about him that she can see.

Then the ant called Stalin raises his hand, and the square explodes. Every mouth opens in one uniform roar, and the forest of banners and portraits shudders and sways, as if struck by a blast of wind. It is so terrifying that Marina starts screaming. She screams and screams as hard as she can. But the May Day demonstrators are all safely below, and she is the one trapped in the eye of the storm. Poles on her left rattle by her ear; sticks with portraits seem to aim at her head from the right; flags shake with crimson furor and hiss like flames. The roar peals over the square like thunder, mouths fusing into one howling throat, one hungry set of jaws with rows of sticks for teeth, ready to crunch and chew and spit her out.

Marina shrieks and sobs, all in vain, because her voice doesn't stand a chance against the roar of the whole square. She hunches over and rubs the tears around her face. With her arms over her head, cowering and bawling, she rides on Mama's shoulders to the side street, where Katya finally hears her cries.

Staring at our television, I wonder if Mama is thinking about that trip to Moscow, too. "I'm so worried about Marina," she says, her eyebrows mashed together. "I hope she isn't foolish enough to go outside. Maybe they will cancel the theater because of all this," she says, wistfully. I know how much Mama wants Marina to be with us; how much she would give to have her right here, watching these barricades on television.

"They will cancel everything, for sure," I say. One look at the barricades and the tanks makes it clear that no curtain is going to rise today, no movie screen will spring to life, and no school bell will summon students to their desks. No matter how it ends, I know what we are watching today on our television screen will be a chapter in future history books. It all feels like Sasha's febrile seizure, I think: For decades, Russia has been ill and it is now burning with fever. The overloaded system shudders and goes into shock.

We sit in front of the TV all day. People mill around the barricades, pass thermoses of hot tea to soldiers sitting on top of tanks, and I know that Mama, like I am, is thinking one thing: how is this all going to end? We both know that Russian revolutions do not usually boast peaceful finales. In a grave voice, an announcer speaks about an elite division of special troops approaching Moscow's center, and I don't have to translate anything because the screen is now filled with images of steel rumbling along the streets. Mama sighs and shakes her head. She is the only one of us who has seen real tanks.

The scene switches to a Russian woman, tears in her eyes, standing in a small crowd on a Moscow sidewalk. "What does this all mean?" she laments into the camera, which pans over a line of armored vehicles parked on the side of the street. "Our own sons must shoot at us now?"

We all hope no one shoots as we look at the people on the street, their faces not stained with familiar cynicism and resignation. A young, bearded man directs a small crane lowering a block of cement to form a barrier; a group of students wave the driver of a trolley bus to join the line of cars barricading the entrance to the square; a soldier whose face is splattered with freckles smokes on top of a tank hatch. The camera follows an elderly woman, wearing a dark coat and with a kerchief around her head, carrying a string bag full of bricks. She stops, lifts out the bricks one by one, slowly, and places them on the barricade.

I wonder what Mama thinks of the barricades and the tanks. Whose side is she on, my enthusiastic, communism-building, wartime surgeon mother? After three years in America, does she still believe in the bright dawn and the necessity of marching in step with the collective? I wonder what she thinks of the tricolor Russian flag, beating in the Moscow wind, instead of the bloody red Soviet banner that branded her entire life.

It is now very quiet in the room, so quiet we can hear one another breathe. Two synchronous visual moments align themselves and freeze before my eyes: a division of tanks in the center of Moscow set against a sea of people, and the three of us—across the world—watching the confrontation on the screen. This is how I will remember the day: the sultry silence of a New Jersey summer; Mama's frozen profile with anxious crinkles at the corners of her eyes; a kerchiefed Moscow babushka helping build a barricade from a string bag full of bricks.

# *Thirty-Three*

For a couple of years, we don't hear anything about Marina's green card lottery, but my mother is persistent. She fills out an application once a year as the rules allow. Each time, she makes sure I buy a money order for a hundred dollars, the price of the petition, and write the name of the U.S. State Department on the front. Then she walks to the post office and gives the envelope to the clerk in person, to witness that it is stamped and sent on its way.

In 1993 a phone call comes from Leningrad: Marina, choking on her own words, announces that she has just received a postcard from the U.S. Embassy in Russia.

"What postcard?" I shout into the phone because I can hardly hear her across the static of international ether.

My mother is standing next to me, craning her neck, trying to hear what my sister says, prompting me what to ask her. "I can't hear anything," I whisper, waving at Mama to be quiet.

"A postcard!" Marina yells. "About the green card lottery. I won."

My mother throws up her arms, then presses them to her chest, as if her lungs had suddenly emptied of air.

I tell myself I also feel ecstatic, but maybe not quite as excited as my mother. A doubt creeps into my mind, a toxic thought of utter selfishness. I am ashamed to reveal it to anyone, so for days, I wallow alone in the tar of its sordidness.

Thirteen years ago I left Russia, primarily to escape my family. Now, my family has followed me here, one by one. My mother came for a visit and never left; my older sister is soon to arrive, a newly issued green card in hand. I'm lucky my aunt Muza, with her three married sons, her five grandchildren, and a dog, is too provincial to consider relocating to the lair of rotting capitalism, five thousand miles away.

Unwelcome images float to the surface, and I try to push them back down. I imagine a key scratching around the keyhole, unable to find the opening. I hear Mama yelling at my sister; I see Marina slumped in our Leningrad kitchen chair, an unlit cigarette hanging from her lip. I want to banish these pictures, but they keep rising up in my memory, like bile.

"You have to learn to play the hand you've been dealt," Andy reminds me in his therapist voice. "Stop wishing for another hand."

ॐ

Since it is getting more and more difficult for Mama to climb steep stairs to the third floor of our house, we decide to rent her an apartment within walking distance of where we live in Nutley. Or maybe this decision is less noble and more selfish than it appears on the surface. Maybe this offer, so pure and admirable at first sight, is nothing more than a defensive move before Marina's imminent arrival.

With the help of a friend who is a paralegal, I fill out the forms and collect the necessary papers. I must guarantee that Marina won't end up on welfare, that she is educated and healthy and stable. The pages are filled with little squares of moral excellence, and I check them all. Has never been arrested, check. Has never been associated with the Communist Party. Has never taken drugs. Has never carried a weapon. Check, check, check. On the U.S. immigration form, my sister is a paragon of constancy and integrity, a perfect immigrant any country would be happy to embrace.

When I call the real Marina, she sounds anxious and brash.

"You have no idea what life is like here," she yells into the phone, her voice carrying across the ocean in the full scale of its outrage. "You can't imagine the hopelessness, the desperation. It's *bespredel*," she says, using the Russian word that in three short syllables encapsulates the idea of being placed beyond all possible limits, the word we have all overused in our Soviet kitchens for so many years.

"But what happened to the putsch of August 1991?" I ask, knowing instantly how naïve it sounds, how simpleminded and silly. "That was only two years ago. There was euphoria on people's faces. I saw it with my own eyes. We all saw it."

"Euphoria?" Marina mocks. "Don't make me laugh." Her voice is familiar and taunting, but it is edged with new gloom. "We are all on the *Titanic* here, and it is sinking. I get up at seven in the morning to save a place in line for milk. For milk! Yesterday a woman recognized me in the store, from a play or television, I don't know. You? she asked, wide-eyed. You have to stand on line, too?"

I look around as I listen, at a carton of strawberries I just brought from ShopRite, at my neighbor's pool just behind the fence. I try to imagine Marina standing in the hallway of our Leningrad apartment by the phone, in front of a refrigerator empty of everything except milk, alone and afraid.

৪০

Two big things happen almost simultaneously. On the phone, Marina tells us that she has just received her green card. On this side of the ocean, Dr. Klughaupt peers at the picture of my mother's mammogram and points to a white spot in her left breast.

"It's most likely cancer," he says.

In my mind, the word *cancer* immediately conjures up my father. I see him sitting in bed in his long underwear as Mama turns the knobs on our television set, summoning a figure-skating couple gliding over a rink, a woman pirouetting on one foot, her back almost touching the ice in a movement called the death loop. I see him hanging on the shoulders of Mama and Marina, who carry him to a waiting taxi that will take him to the hospital. The sound emerging from the doctor's mouth hisses through the air and lacerates my ears, like a curse.

I wonder if Mama has a similar reaction to the Russian word *raak* when I translate to her what Dr. Klughaupt said. *Raak*—with its all-reaching claws capable of cutting off oxygen and squeezing out life—a word no one wants to hear at a doctor's office, on either side of the world.

"But at her age, it is probably fully curable," the doctor adds quickly, and I immediately translate that, too.

My mother accepts the diagnosis calmly, with the unflappability of a survivor. The same stoicism she used when she knocked on the door of every party boss in Leningrad to get my father into a hospital, when she operated on a nine-year-old wounded boy in a military hospital during the war despite the order not to treat civilians, when she kissed me good-bye at Leningrad International Airport thirteen years ago, accepting our separation, which she thought would last forever.

∞

Marina arrives on the day following Mama's outpatient lumpectomy. It went well, said the surgeon: she removed ten lymph nodes, and only one turned out to be cancerous. The doctor is the same age as I am, but this is where our likeness ends—she is blond, self-confident, and optimistic. She enthusiastically recites the instructions to me: Change the dressing tomorrow. Call if she develops a fever. We'll follow this with six months of radiation and five years of tamoxifen. She will be fine.

"You'll be fine," I say to Mama, but I am not sure she believes me. She smiles anyway because she knows that tomorrow Marina will be here, because of her tenacity. Tomorrow the three of us will reunite and be together again, just as we were in Leningrad, the thought that makes me simultaneously ebullient and nauseous.

&

Mama's new apartment looks onto the tops of trees and has almost as much light as our old place in Leningrad. The ceilings are lower, but the parquet floors are newer, and, unlike in our old apartment, the faucet in the bathroom gurgles with hot water at any time of day or night.

Marina, no longer dazed and jet-lagged, keeps it unbearably clean. She also changes Mama's dressings and whips up complicated meals for both households, the two of them and the three of us. "It's so easy here," she says, "when you don't have to spend half your time searching for ingredients."

A week after her arrival, she walks to a local deli and gets a job making sandwiches and salads. Several days later, the deli's counter blooms with containers full of Marina's borsch and bowls of salad Olivier she whips up as effortlessly as she did back home. She invents a recipe for roasted chicken breast, the best-selling item at lunchtime, followed by my sister's baked *pirozhki* stuffed with scallions and chopped hard-boiled eggs.

Every day, as I drive to work past the deli and the apartment building where my mother and Marina now live, I feel guilty for my fetid doubts, for underestimating the talents of my older sister.

&

A month after Marina's arrival, my mother and sister invite me to bring Sasha for an early dinner after her kindergarten day is over. I am a little uneasy because this is our first dinner together since I left our Leningrad kitchen. It feels like the first rehearsal of a play, with three of us performing new roles: my mother as the hostess in her own apartment albeit not in her own country, my sister as caretaker and newcomer trying to find her footing, and I—a guest, a translator, and a cultural adviser to both of them. To add to the pressure, I am also the procreator, the parent of the family's only offspring.

We sit around the table in Mama's living room, our former kitchen table we recently replaced with an antique Andy pulled out of our basement. The armchair and the reading lamp are from our house, too, next to a glass side table with a wrought-iron frame Mama found on a Nutley sidewalk. I think of how the three of us used to sit in our Leningrad kitchen, the smudged oilcloth under our teacups and little saucers with dacha strawberry jam, the smell of yesterday's soup and fried onions permeating the walls. Here it smells of the lilacs I cut from a bush in our backyard and of the freshly made culinary concoction still simmering on the stove, the pot Marina stirs with her resolute hand.

I know my sister has spent time and thought preparing this meal: borsch with shiitake mushrooms, homemade eggplant caviar, cucumber salad with sour cream and dill, chunks of salmon steeped in butter sauce. When I compliment her on every course, she waves her wrist and praises the ingredients. "With ShopRite around the corner, I could make dinners like this for a battalion," she says, dismissing her indisputable cooking talent.

I envy Marina's creativity of pairing shiitake mushrooms with beets, her moxie for figuring out the recipe for the proverbial eggplant caviar everyone back in Leningrad used to extract from cans. Why didn't we ever dare replicate it at home? I wonder, and, with my sister presiding over this feast procured at ShopRite, the answer instantly becomes obvious: because we lacked the ingredients the recipe required.

Sasha eyes the eggplant caviar suspiciously; she eats one spoonful of borsch and licks a dollop of sour cream, leaving the cucumbers untouched.

"What's the matter?" my mother asks her.

"I don't like mushrooms," Sasha whines and makes a face. I know what comes next: she hates the taste of dill, too.

"Aunt Marina made this especially for you," says my mother in Russian, in her teaching voice. "You must eat it all." I know Mama thinks that American schools are too accommodating and permissive, and now this back talk is obvious proof that they allow too much disobedience and provide too little order. Or maybe she thinks that the failure to teach a child proper behavior is not the result of schools at all but rather my own lack of discipline and will. She takes Sasha's spoon and picks out a mushroom. "Here you go: one, two, three."

Sasha sucks in her lips and flattens herself against the back of her chair. I think of the story Mama has so often told us, the story I would remind her about were she not so intensely focused on the inward search for a culprit of this scandalous revolt. When Marina was little, my mother used to feed her spoonfuls of gooey farina my sister hated and refused to swallow. All day Marina wouldn't yield, banning the glue-like mush from entering her body, so Mama had no choice but to put her to bed with her mouth full and her cheeks swollen like two balloons.

I glance at Marina, wondering if this is also what she is thinking, if scenes with our own grandma in their wooden Ivanovo house are reeling in her head. But we are all playing different roles today—perhaps with the exception of my commandeering mother—so I cannot tell what is on my sister's mind.

"Sashenka, this isn't very nice," my mother fumes. "We're trying to do what's best for you." My daughter may not understand what is best for her—and neither may I—but my mother always knows. "Open your mouth, quickly, one, two, three."

Sasha slides down from the chair and crouches under the table. My mother's orders must have hypnotized me with their familiar controlling cadences: almost automatically, without thinking, I get up and sharpen my voice.

"Come out at once," I say, a command directed to the floor. "And take your seat at the table."

I see my mother frowning, just as she did decades ago, when instead of quietly playing in the sandbox with the rest of my nursery school collective, I took off on my own to explore the archways and vaulted hollows under the buildings of our courtyard. Aunt Polya, the food and punishment authority of the nursery school, shouted at me in her kitchen voice and put me in the corner, where I stood upset but not remorseful.

"Sasha, come out of there," I insist, intentionally speaking English, erecting a linguistic wall to separate myself from my mother.

It is completely quiet in the room, and we hear pedestrians' voices from the street: two brazen children fighting over something with their mother. I don't know what I resent more: my senseless irritation at my daughter or Mama standing witness to my parental helplessness. Crouched under the table, Sasha keeps silent, and I can feel the anger creeping up my chest: the anger at my stubborn American daughter, the anger at my overbearing Russian mother.

# PART 3

## *Sasha*

# *Thirty-Four*

Whenhen Sasha is five, she first notices graffiti scrawled on the overpass over the FDR.

"Look!" she calls from the backseat, an expression of bewilderment and glee spreading over her face. "Who did that?" she wants to know, her eyes focused on the letters she can now read.

"Bad boys," Andy says. "Only bad boys write on walls."

She leans out of her car seat to hold the graffiti in her gaze as long as she can. "I want to be a bad boy, too," she says, and it sounds so precious from the lips of a preschooler that we both giggle foolishly.

By five, she can read in both English and Russian, and I am prematurely happy, content to see that our hours of reading aloud to her have sprouted such enviable results. Her kindergarten teacher tells us that her classmates routinely ask Sasha to read the signs on the school walls and book titles on the shelves. When she obliges, they run over to the teacher to make sure her answers are correct. This, sadly, seems to be the extent of her interactions with other children.

One day when the teacher is sick, the class is taught by a teacher's aide. They are talking about dinosaurs, and the aide writes the word *Jurasic* on the blackboard.

Sasha raises her hand. "Mrs. Cowan," she calls out. "*Jurassic* has two *s*'s."

"No, it doesn't," replies the teacher's aide. "Now please sit down and pay attention," she admonishes and goes on with her dinosaur story.

For a few minutes, Sasha pretends to listen. Then, when Mrs. Cowan has turned her back to the class to write on the blackboard, she gets up and tiptoes to where she knows there is a fat dictionary standing on the shelf in the adjacent room. She has seen its hard red cover and the word WEBSTER embossed in gold on the front. She climbs onto a chair, reaches up, and pulls the tome off the shelf. Holding it pressed to her chest like a favorite doll, she carries it to the other room and opens the pages to "J."

Mrs. Cowan is not pleased. "Why do we even have a dictionary in kindergarten?" she complains to the director.

That evening Sasha and I drive home in the golden light of the evening, past the newly constructed buildings of a big pharmaceutical company, its eight stories of glass sparkling in the glow of an early sunset.

"Look at all those windows," Sasha says wistfully. "Do you think the bad boys want to break them?"

"What bad boys?" I ask.

"You know, the ones who write graffiti on the walls," she says, and in my rearview mirror I can see a glint in Sasha's eyes.

Inwardly I can't help but respect this bold, rebellious statement from my five-year-old. But I am almost thirty-nine, and I have learned the uninspiring wisdom about the futility of breaking windows. Should I nod in agreement, in the hope that she will learn to stand up to authority? Or is it my job to teach my daughter an early lesson—the lesson I failed to learn from my own mother, the one about the necessity of *poryadok*, order?

 George

Andy and I are in Toys"R"Us looking for Sasha's Christmas present, but I quickly realize that the singular of this noun—*present* as opposed to *presents*—does not fit with the sense of grandiosity fueling this outing.

"One present?" Andy says in disbelief. "When I was her age, I got a dozen presents. All I remember is a sea of gift-wrapped packages, never just one. We have a small family, so we need to make sure she gets plenty of presents."

I am not at all convinced that it is wise to pile up the whole inventory of Toys"R"Us at the feet of a first-grader who didn't ask for a magic Santa, or a dollhouse with tiny furniture inside, or even a game of Chutes and Ladders. The presents I received in Russia were few, coveted, and treasured. A suede jacket my sister brought back from her theater tour in Latvia, where factories had never abandoned making clothes people would want to wear, or a special edition of collected fairy tales my aunt from Kiev sent me for my birthday. One long-desired present, in my mind, is worth a whole sack of the unrequested toys that Andy has deposited in our cart. But I know I can't persuade him to restock the shelves with all these games and dolls Sasha will not appreciate. This is America, after all, a country of unnecessary abundance and unintended waste. Maybe I still don't understand how it works. So I am willing to defer to Andy in what to me seems like a worthy undertaking clearly bent out of shape. I am willing to believe that we can earn good parenting points with a bunch of gifts from a chain store.

 co

It has been a year since Marina's arrival, and she has announced she is moving to New Orleans to get married. I am impressed by my sister's boldness, but my mother is simply ecstatic. She has been waiting for her older daughter to get married her whole life, always blaming theater and acting for my sister's single state. Who would want an actress for a wife, my mother always lamented, who would voluntarily entwine his destiny with the theatrical lack of order, with the frivolity and chaos of the stage?

My mother has already met Marina's fiancé, Tom, who flew to Nutley a few months ago to introduce himself. Mama says that he looks and sounds decent, and, knowing her critical eye, I decide to believe her.

The story is bizarre and appropriately dramatic. On a wintry day in March, during the six months Marina was waiting for the green card papers to be processed, she was walking along Nevsky Prospekt, wrapping a scarf around her face, trying not to notice begging babushkas and alcoholic amputees, trying not to hear the pleas from Gypsy children and accordions being squeezed by demented Afghan veterans—all the desperate and the grotesque, the detritus that has floated to the surface after the wreckage of a seventy-four-year communist delusion. The wind has swept cigarette butts and ice cream wrappers, whirled them across the sidewalk over patches of dirty ice, and tossed them into people's faces. Another gust of wind, and a page of newspaper flew into Marina's hands, folding a headline in front of her eyes. The Lonely Heart marriage service will connect you to an eligible man in the U.S. Contact us and we will send you up to ten addresses to write to. Photograph required.

Marina had many photographs to choose from: head shots from films and copies of the pictures that hung in her theater's lobby. From the list the agency sent her, she chose six names that sounded good to her ear. Every address ended with the magical letters USA, so she didn't even try to decipher the irrelevant codes of the individual states her prospective husbands lived in. I have a suspicion that—just as my ESL students who tell me they live in the city of New Jersey—my sister didn't know where she was sending her inquiries. She wrote a letter and copied it by hand, five times. Tom from New Orleans, Louisiana, was the only one who wrote back.

"That's what I've always wanted," Marina says, "to have my own house with a garden where I can grow tomatoes. To have my own life, away from all the insanity of the world, behind a ten-foot fence."

I know Marina likes to be dramatic, so I try to focus her attention with a practical question.

"Won't you miss the theater?" I ask. "After all, you've been an actress for almost thirty years."

My sister is absolute, not needing to think for even a moment.

"There is no theater left to be missed," she quips. "It all collapsed, together with communism. It all went to pieces, just like the country."

I am as skeptical of my sister's assessment of the arts in Russia as I was when we lived there. For her, theater was always work, while for me it never ceased to be anything but magic. I would have given anything back in Leningrad to be like her—to sit before a three-way mirror and watch my face transform to that of someone completely different, someone you wouldn't find in our school textbooks. I would have given anything to be part of the real make-believe, exciting and meaningful, not the everyday official make-believe we all had to live by. I envied my sister's acting gift as viscerally as I abhorred her taking the magic of Theater for granted.

But it is irrelevant now whether Marina is or isn't exaggerating about the demise of Russian Theater. She is in America "for permanent residence," as the stamp in her passport announces, and it seems she will be residing in Louisiana, where theater is as nonexistent as green grass in July.

"But you're an honorary actor," I insist, referring to the national title she was awarded a few years after I left. "Are you really just going to give up acting altogether?"

Marina drives her fists into her hips. "Let me tell you the story of this honorary title," she says. "The bastards at the Ministry of Culture said I was the sister of a traitor. Of someone who sold out to capitalism." Marina makes big, serious eyes, impersonating the censors. "We don't honor siblings of deserters who betray the Motherland."

So here it is, the truth of what I have accomplished: in addition to costing Nina her teaching job at the university, I almost cost my sister a national promotion.

"Our chief director was the one who stood up for me," says Marina. "It isn't the sister we're nominating for this award, he said to those idiots. It is our own actress who has been with this theater for over a quarter century."

"The point today is this: everyone has left." Marina lands the last phrase with a dramatic thump, demonstrating again that her seasoned acting skills have remained intact.

There may be some exaggeration here, but Marina's statement about theater in Petersburg is closer to the truth about all of Petersburg than I would like to believe. After all, my high school friend Tania is in New Jersey now, working in an export company staffed by immigrants from Russia. My *refusenik* friend Nadia is in California, having reunited with half of her college class from Leningrad. My university English professor is teaching Russian in New York, where several of my former students now write computer programs or give private piano lessons.

The only person who has not left is Nina, still my closest friend. All these years I have been waiting for her to come here, thinking that next year would certainly be the one marking her arrival. I have been saving old sets of dishes and silverware she would surely need to start her life here; I have stashed a coffee table in the basement; I have even refused to part with my old car. But Nina's life is complicated, stitched to our common country with the strongest thread. First she couldn't emigrate because she was taking care of her parents: her mother suffered from severe diabetes and rapidly progressing dementia, and, a year after her death, Nina's father succumbed to an aggressive cancer. Then Nina went through a different kind of turmoil, divorcing and getting married again. And now it is her mother-in-law, with a sick heart, who needs her care. Yet, despite everything, I stubbornly hoard all the usable things into a basement corner, hoping that one day she will come and claim every piece of junk I've saved for her.

Thinking of Nina, who lost her job after I left, and of Marina's hard-earned honorary title highlights an uncomfortable truth: my action fourteen years ago was never mine alone. Like the wake from a careless boat, it rippled through the lives of those who stayed behind.

It also, to my consternation and chagrin, has failed to make me into a different person beyond the confines of my Motherland, someone more confident and optimistic. I was naïve to hope, it turns out, that once I crossed the Soviet border I would find myself miraculously free, weighed down only by the one twenty-kilogram suitcase Aeroflot allowed. When I said good-bye to everyone who came to see me off at Pulkovo Airport, when for the last time I glanced back at my family and friends through the horseshoe of the international metal detector, I was silly to think I was hovering on the brink of a brand-new life. I didn't know yet that Russia, like a virus, had settled in my blood and hitched a ride across the ocean.

# Thirty-Five

I continue to teach Sasha to read and write in Russian because I want her to be perfectly bilingual. I want her to melt when she reads the poems of Akhmatova, just as I do. When she is six and seven and eight, she complies, which fuels my fantasies. I imagine her swooning over the simplicity of Pushkin's verse; I picture her with a flashlight under a blanket, turning the pages of *Dead Souls*, deciphering the weird wit of Gogol. Closing my eyes, I visualize her engrossed in *War and Peace*—all four volumes—without skipping the battle scenes, as I used to do. I see her memorizing the poems of Lermontov and Pasternak and reciting them flawlessly before speechless groups of stunned relatives and friends.

When she is nine, we sell the Nutley house because we want a better school for Sasha, the school that glimmers in my childhood memory, radically refurbished by the crafty team of nostalgia and time. What was that school really like, the place I remember with such fondness? Did I feel any true affection for Leningrad school number 238 when I studied there, or is this the tenderness cultivated by looking back through the deceptive prism of so many years? This was the school that sharpened our minds and softened our hearts, my memory murmurs. We read Pushkin in fifth grade, it whispers; we read Dostoyevsky in ninth. We solved algebra formulas in seventh grade and mastered trigonometry and calculus in eighth. We studied world history, from the Bronze Age to the ascent of capitalism everywhere except in our Motherland. We memorized and recited poetry—all of us, including class hooligans and perennial failures with blank eyes who always sat in the last row and were kept back to repeat the year.

In search of that illusory school, we decide to move to Ridgewood, hoping that Sasha will be as enthusiastic about the prospects of a better education as Andy and I. In the middle of all the contracts and inspections, of packing up what Mama, who is moving with us, has managed to accumulate, we fail to notice that our daughter has developed deep friendships with Megan from her grade and Chris from her dance class and Marl from our block. Years later, I will find one of the letters she wrote to Megan that summer:

*I can't believe school is already out. I think you should forget about the hair club, OK? I think we should have the spy club. If we have the spy club, we'll have to have a spy school at someone's house who is in the spy club. You can't tell anybody about the spy club cause then it won't be a spy club if everyone knew about it. I don't know if we should have a mystery club. If you say yes to the mystery club I'll be very happy because we have a mystery to solve. The mystery is, why are we moving from Nutley to some place called Ridgewood? Why didn't my parents ask me? Cause if they did, I would definitely say no.*

I try to convince myself that we are moving to a place where she will quickly make new friends who will be more like her. When we find Sasha hiding in her closet clutching Puffy and gouging her name into the Sheetrock with a ballpoint pen, it is too late to alter the plans.

On the morning of the Nutley house closing, we sit in the attorney's office, Andy and I and the young couple who just bought our house. I know I should feel happy: we sold the house without a broker on the second Sunday when we led scores of strangers up and down our stairway with its chestnut banisters, past the stained-glass windows, up to the third floor we built for my mother, back down to the living room full of built-in bookshelves, and out the hallway with the fireplace we had lit, on the advice of a neighbor, to give the house a more homey feel.

I should be happy, but I sit there straight as a stick, trying to breathe deeply and swallow whatever is rising up in my throat. The swallowing doesn't work, and I realize I've clapped my hands over my face because I am weeping. A moment later I scrape back my chair and race out of the room. In the blurry hallway I find a bathroom and collapse on the tile under the sink. I crouch on the floor, sobbing and wailing, completely blindsided by this sudden eruption of grief. What am I crying so bitterly about? I know I should go back and sign the contract, but I cannot stop bawling. There seems to be an endless supply of tears being pumped out of the dark inner pool, and the faucet gurgling over the sink does not have enough water to wash my face clean of salt and snot. What am I just about to lose? The first house I've ever had? The built-in bookshelves, the crystal chandelier, the place that made my mother realize that every Soviet bureaucrat had lied to her? The kitchen cabinets we stripped by hand, the deck where Sasha learned to walk?

There is a knock, and I hear Andy's voice. He opens the door, hesitantly, and fits himself under the sink, scooping me into his arms.

"I'm so embarrassed," I mutter between gasps for air. "I don't know where this came from."

"We have to go back," he says, but I don't move. I can't go back yet. I can only crouch in a ball in Andy's arms, sobbing into his chest, leaving wet spots on the good shirt he wore to the lawyer's office.

Sasha goes to fourth grade at the new elementary school in Ridgewood, where it turns out she is no longer the top student in her class. She is surrounded by children with sharper math skills and better reading comprehension, children of parents described by acronyms: CEOs, CPAs, and DMDs. Andy and I have acronyms, too: MSW and EdD, but they might as well be Cyrillic symbols that do not blend into the alphabet of our neighbors' Tudors and sculpted shrubs.

My daughter is nine, and she is already an experienced complainer. No one else in her school is required to do the extra work of Russian reading, she points out every time I open a book of children's verses from my Leningrad days of elementary school.

"Why am I the only one?" she demands, looking wistfully out the window to where a neighbor is tossing a ball to his dog. "It's not fair," she laments, her invariable refrain to anything she does not want to do.

"Because I want you to speak two languages, like me," I say, in what I don't yet recognize as my mother's teaching voice.

∽

But Sasha doesn't want to be like me. She wants to be like everyone else. Everyone else in Ridgewood plays lacrosse and soccer, so she joins a local soccer team and for a while we spend weekends driving back and forth to games. When Sasha is tired of sitting on the grass, she announces that she wants to try swimming. Instead of sitting in lawn chairs, Andy and I now sit in the chlorine fog of the pool, waiting several humid hours for a thirty-second match.

None of her friends speak a second language, and she draws tic-tac-toe squares on the page designated for declining nouns when we bend over an old book with pictures of Young Pioneers feeding chickens. I enroll her in a Russian class in Fair

Lawn, the town where Russian immigrants move up from Brighton Beach after they learn how to write CVs and program computers. Sasha hides in the last row, pretending to listen to the teacher, who sprinkles the six or seven bored American children with bits of our imperial history told in a language they barely understand.

I sit by the door on the outside of the room, privy to every detail about the life of Catherine the Great and the beginning of the Hermitage collection, making believe—when Sasha emerges from the lesson—that I haven't heard a word. On the way to the car, I ask my daughter what she has learned today. Nothing, she says, and invariably shrugs.

ဢ

When Sasha is eleven, we buckle under pressure and yield to her incessant demands to get a dog. We research the breeds: the size, the health, the character, affinity to children. Andy narrows down our search to a Lakeland terrier, a sturdy sixteen-pound dog as difficult to find in the Northeast as it is to describe to anyone we know. It's like Asta in *The Thin Man*, Andy explains to anyone who asks, only instead of black and white it is one color, sand. Few people seem to know who Asta is—or the *Thin Man*, for that matter.

In July the three of us drive to Maryland, where a litter of Lakeland terriers reside in a garage adjacent to the breeder's house. There are three puppies, the color of apricots, and Sasha scoops up the smallest one and holds him in her arms the way she still cradles her stuffed dog, Puffy.

"Deema," she coos over him, short for Dmitri, the name of the Russian counselor in her summer day camp, and I am foolishly happy that, after all, my Russian efforts haven't gone to waste.

ဢ

"Tell me a story," Sasha says from the backseat.

"What kind of story?" I ask. We are in the car, driving home from a Russian lesson, or maybe from swimming class.

"A story about your life."

I am glad she wants to know about my life, and in my mind I quickly scan my Leningrad years for a satisfying tale. The Young Pioneer initiation when we turned nine? Dimka the Hooligan and his girl-terrorizing campaign of braid pulling? It seems appropriate to start in third grade, and I begin, in Russian, with our homeroom teacher, Vera Pavlovna. She is tall and sharp-elbowed, I say, and a brown cardigan trails from her shoulders like from a clothes hanger. We called her Veshalka, I say.

"What's *veshalka*?" Sasha asks, and I realize she doesn't know the Russian word for a clothes hanger.

I translate the word, but its English equivalent feels false on my tongue, altering the story I barely had a chance to start. If Sasha doesn't know the word *veshalka*, how many other words doesn't she know? My next sentence comes out artificial and clumsy because I now try to monitor myself for simple vocabulary and syntax. As I strain the words through the filter of my mind, I feel as if I were speaking to my students at Leningrad University's Russian Program, where this whole American adventure started almost twenty years ago. By now the story is so stripped of any heft it isn't even a story.

When I glance in the rearview mirror, I see that Sasha twirls a strand of her light brown hair around her finger, losing interest. As I turn into our driveway, I am depressed by the thought that my daughter and I do not share a native language.

More and more often I switch to English when I speak to Sasha. It is much easier for her, I reason. Is it also easier for me? In English, I don't need to monitor myself, trying to avoid the words she may not know; I don't have to force the stories into simple sentences and first-grade grammar she will be able to understand. Yet the more I switch to English the more I viscerally resent it. In my heart, English—just as Russian—is a barrier between us.

Like a spy, I live with two identities, American and Russian—two selves perpetually crossing swords over the split inside me. My American self is freshly cheerful and shiny as a newly minted coin. My Russian self is stale and dark, a week-old brick of sour Leningrad bread. It broods and ponders, as it always has, about questions that have no clear answers.

Something deep inside myself does not let the American me take over raising Sasha. The American me is for Andy, his family, and our mutual friends. It is a costume, a disguise. The Russian me is my inheritance, rooted in my veins from birth. The Russian me is for my mother and my sister and my daughter, my blood.

# Thirty-Six

A ndy is on the phone, and I can't put together what he is saying. I understand each word separately, but they blend into nothing reasonable, nothing that makes sense. His voice is unrecognizably hollow, as if he hasn't yet begun to believe his own words. He tells me that his younger brother, Frankie, has suffered a seizure and has been taken to a local emergency room in Ellenville.

I have trouble seeing Frankie in an emergency room, incapacitated and sick. My mind still harbors the last image of him in his Catskill kitchen, standing as tall and unfailing as the main support beam of the house behind him. In what feels like an attempt to block Andy's words, I conjure up a picture of Frankie's house, where we have spent every Christmas and many weekends in the summer since Sasha was born. I think of its creaky steps, sagging in the middle, that descend to the living room; of pots with wilting plants among mismatched pieces of furniture topped with dusty knickknacks that his wife, Jen, has picked up at yard sales over the years. I think of how rarely we saw Frankie in the house during our visits to the Concord Hotel, where he worked, and how Andy suspected that his brother's long hours were a choice rather than a requirement of the job.

I think of last December, when Frankie's daughters, Heather and Amy, adopted Sasha like a younger sister, teaching her about their make-believe world of decaying luxury that flourished in the Concord Hotel, especially around the holidays. The three of them explored the endless hallways and gigantic lobbies, whose blue carpets absorbed the din of festive crowds; they snacked at the coffee shop, where waitresses, who all know and love Frankie, brought them platefuls of free food; they took dips in the pool and wobbled on skates around the rink to the sound of Christmas music. They spent long days at the hotel under the protective gaze of all the people who work there, who watched over and took care of Frankie's girls the same way Frankie watched over and took care of them.

Now Heather and Amy are in Florida. Jen moved to Boca Raton several months ago, while Frankie, after a few weeks of helping the family get settled, went back to the Concord, presumably to keep his job. When my mother-in-law heard that Jen had left, she simply raised an eyebrow and sighed. Andy's father was blunt, making her wince when he sliced the air with the sibilant sounds of the word *separation*.

Maybe it was the stress of that separation that brought on the seizure, Andy and his parents hoped, tiptoeing around the emergency room and speaking in whispers as though any sound could skew the diagnosis in an undesirable direction. They stayed with Frankie all day, dismayed to see him disoriented and exhausted from a battery of tests, anxious in their wait for the results.

Later, an emergency room doctor peered at the scan pinned to a lighted screen, examining every inch of the X-ray, trying to delay what he had to say to the waiting family. His face stiffened as soon as he glanced at the picture, but he pretended to need more time to evaluate what looked like a golf ball with tentacles on the left side of Frankie's brain.

"Look, I'm only an ER physician—I could be wrong," the doctor finally said. He shook his head, as if deciding whether he should continue. "But it looks to me like a glioblastoma." The doctor peered at the screen, not able to glance at Andy or his parents, the name of the lethal cancer bursting out of his mouth like a grenade. "If it is what I think it is"—he paused and drew in a breath— "there's no cure." The doctor removed his glasses and held them to the light of the X-ray screen, staring at the lenses. "The survival rate for a glioblastoma, even with surgery, is around twelve months," he said finally and hooked the glasses back behind his ears.

∞

At home that evening Andy and I sit on the couch in the living room, shell-shocked and numb, staring into space. Unwilling to accept the diagnosis, we type "glioblastoma" and send it into the galaxy of cyberspace, clutching at straws of information scattered online. The Internet is even less forgiving: six months, we read silently, ten at the longest. There is one legendary blogger, who has survived the disease for a year and a half. We feverishly click on the link and pore over the story of his life. The man writes in confident sentences that coalesce into hopeful, even optimistic paragraphs. It is the only good news we have heard all day.

"Do you remember the last time we were in Ellenville?" I ask Andy as we sit in our bed, unwilling to stay awake in the presence of such terrible news yet unable to sleep. Of course, I know he remembers—and I bite my tongue, regretting the word *last*, which seems to certify that there will be no more trips to Frankie's house. I ask about Ellenville because I want to conjure up Frankie by the Christmas tree, the children ripping up the festive paper that only a few hours earlier was meticulously wrapped around the gifts. I want to see my mother and my mother-in-law in their best dresses straightening up the living room, making small talk neither one could understand; to watch my brother-in-law toss logs into the wood-burning stove at midnight, when he is back from work, and feel the room instantly warm up. I want to go back to the Ellenville of ten months ago, where everything was all right, where we drank champagne, dressed up for dinner, and saw a performance of a famous Russian comedian named Yakov Smirnoff, someone Mama and I had never heard of.

In my mind, I see us piling into our Toyota, Doris and me shivering in high-heeled shoes, wisps of frozen breath dancing around our faces. Jen had come down in a sweat suit half an hour earlier, saying she was tired and wanted to stay home to rest. Rest from what? asked my bewildered mother, who had trouble understanding how anyone could turn down an offer to watch a performance of something—anything—at such a *prekrasny* place as the Concord.

"What a country!" exclaimed Yakov Smirnoff in heavily accented English in front of an audience softened by dinner and drinks. He was about my age, and I suspected his accent was nothing but a stage prop because even my sister Marina, who has never studied English, delivers her broken sentences with less phonetic mangling than I heard from the Concord stage. "In America you break law. In Russia, law breaks you!" said Yakov Smirnoff, and I realized he was cleverly capitalizing on the fact that Russians ignore articles because our native language doesn't have them. "In America you assassinate presidents. In Russia, presidents assassinate you." Artie looked at me to confirm that what the comedian said was true; I was, after all, an expert on all things Russian. I nodded, since his statement, I had to agree, was the essence of what my Motherland believed in.

"In America, you can always find party. In Russia, Party always finds you!" declared the famous Russian, and I saw that my father-in-law's face—more often confused lately—widened in a rare smile. The girls were all laughing because the oldest, Heather, had decided it was funny, and I didn't know if Sasha had any idea what party Yakov Smirnoff was talking about. My mother, sitting next to me, was the only one with a serious face, since she didn't understand a single word that came out of the mouth of this comedian, who ironically became a famous Russian by leaving Russia.

I looked at the three girls, still giggling; at their fathers next to them, fathers whom they took for granted. I thought of my own father, who died when I was ten, and of my sister Marina, who never even knew her father. He left three weeks before Marina was born, on medical advice from Mama's former infectious diseases professor, because he had an open form of tuberculosis and couldn't stay with a newborn in the house. He died in his hometown on the other side of the Ural Mountains five years later, never having seen his daughter.

When Marina was young, Mama said her father had died during the war. She never specified how he died, and in my sister's mind this vagueness created a vacuum that had gradually filled with plots of varying dramatic intensity and men of progressively ascending valor. They all had blond, wavy hair, but some were more heroic than others, tossing a grenade at a tank and dying in the explosion of flames, while others perished more slowly, like Soviet partisans living in the woods in the middle of the winter, sleeping in log-reinforced trenches hidden under a meter of snow.

At six years of age, Marina already knew that no matter how brave and noble her father appeared in her plots, he was not coming back. If she wanted a father, she decided, she had to take matters into her own hands and find one. So one Sunday, when Mama took her to the Ivanovo town park, my sister didn't waste time in the sandbox or on the swing. Leaving Mama on a bench under a tree, she took off to find a handsome, brave man who could become her father.

It took her ten minutes to discover that there weren't many handsome men in the park. Another few minutes revealed that there weren't many men of any kind: an invalid with an empty sleeve smoking on a bench, a drunk with a purple nose sleeping under a tree. But Marina was not interested in invalids or drunks. She took a path that ran past a kiosk where a woman in a stained apron presided behind glass containers with fruit juice, and that was where she saw him.

He stood by the kiosk with a mug of golden liquid in his hand, his military uniform cinched by a belt with a shining buckle, his black boots reflecting the sun. Two women on a nearby bench undoubtedly saw him, too: they whispered to each other, covering their faces with their hands as they spoke, gave him quick, furtive glances, and burst into hushed laughter. But Marina was already on the path, skipping toward him, pretending to be drawn by the multicolored drinks sparkling in their vats.

When she was about a meter away, she paused. Out of the corner of her eye she saw that the women had stopped whispering and laughing.

"*Zdravstvuite,*" Marina said politely, as if addressing her teacher. The man swallowed what was left in his glass. He smiled, his gaze golden and liquid, as if the juice, instead of flowing down his throat, had ascended and lit his eyes from within.

"Do you want to be my father?" she asked, and from the way his smile spread across his face she knew he did. "Come," she said and grabbed his hand. "I'll take you to Mama."

They walked past the two women on the bench, stiff and silent, past the empty-sleeved invalid and the drunk sleeping under a tree until Marina saw Mama on a bench near the sandbox, where a bunch of nursery school girls in berets were digging what looked like a war trench.

Marina clasped Mama's hand and set it down on the man's broad palm. "Here," my sister told her. "I want him to be my father."

His name was Aleksey, Lyosha for short, and he was a military pilot. But despite Marina's lucky discovery that day in the park and her subsequent efforts to keep Lyosha around, he never became her father. When my sister was eight, Mama married Ilya Antonovich Gorokhov, a stomach ulcer patient at her Ivanovo hospital, and the three of them moved to Leningrad, where my future father's party duties had dispatched him.

I looked at Heather, Amy, and Sasha whispering and giggling, secure in the knowledge that they have fathers, a simple certainty that always hangs around them, as unnoticed and essential as air.

# Thirty-Seven

O n the day after the surgery we all sit in the hospital cafeteria
staring into bowls of untouched soup. My mother-in-law looks
as if she'd shriveled into her cardigan, its padded shoulders propping
up her ears. Her hair, usually set in a careful wave, sticks out side-
ways like straw, and there are black streaks of makeup under her
eyes. I imagine her at home this morning staring at her face in the
bathroom mirror, swiping a mascara brush over her lashes with her
shaking hand, summoning a routine to remind her why she should
go on. Andy's father, Artie, tries to emit authority, but his lips keep
shaking and his fingers have trouble grasping a spoon. We don't yet
know how deeply he has already plunged into the vortex of dementia, something Doris has been trying to hide from us, blaming stress
or exhaustion every time he repeats himself or fails to remember
what he told us only a few days ago.

Frankie's wife, Jen, who has flown in from Florida, is arguing
against our plan to have Frankie treated by a prominent neuro-
oncologist in New York. Maybe she feels we are ganging up on her,
all of us except Doris, who silently stares into her soup, so Jen turns
to her mother-in-law in an attempt to find an ally.

It was only last December, before our Christmas dinner at the
Concord, that she chatted with Doris about her latest yard sale

trophies, lifting porcelain gnomes and flowery cups from a shelf. Jen was wearing a yellow dress, the only time she allowed herself to put on anything but linty sweaters and jeans found at garage sales, and a touch of rouge on her cheeks gave her face an almost happy look. Artie, who always felt that his younger son should have married better, sat on a couch seething at how oblivious Jen was to the torn paper and empty boxes from all those carefully selected gifts now scattered over the rug, how undistracted she seemed by the mess in the living room. Maybe she simply didn't see all the things that were difficult for everyone else to miss. Heather, then in the eleventh grade, had told me only a few days earlier that her mother hadn't seen their cat sleeping in the laundry basket when she tossed the whole thing into the dryer. Heather's face tensed into an ironic smile, as if she wanted me to know that the cat incident was only one small comical example of many crazier, unfunny things my niece had to endure when no family members came to visit.

Now Jen is staking her position at the head of the cafeteria table, loud and illogical, pushing her glasses up on her nose in an incessant defensive movement, acting as if our plan involved shoving Frankie off a cliff to relieve him of further suffering. "He needs to be with me," she shrieks, leaning over the table on her forearms, spitting the words into Andy's face. "It's my husband and I know what's right for him."

I listen to her frothing with idiotic examples of the medical advantages of Florida, wondering if Andy and his father were right in their assessment of why Frankie didn't move south with his family months ago. Jen wants to take him to Boca Raton, she shouts, to the homeopathic doctor they both trust—to their life before the word *divorce* crept into their dinner conversations.

Andy, who is used to dealing with hysterical outbreaks, insists that Frankie's treatment should be in New York, and his logical calm makes Jen even more livid. Artie leans on his elbows, slaps his hands against his ears, and begins to hum. Doris pulls out a tissue and dabs at her nose, although it is her eyes and the two black tears crawling down her cheeks that need to be wiped. Andy says that it has all been decided and he has already made an appointment for Frankie at NYU. Jen scrapes back her chair and calls us all fucking bastards. As the most distant relative, I remain the only one who is visibly unperturbed and silent.

We leave our uneaten lunch and go upstairs to Frankie's post-surgery room, which blooms with flowers and visitors. A chef Frankie hired at the Concord six months ago—after the man had been blacklisted from all the Catskills kitchens because of his drinking—sails in, distressed but sober, with a tray of smoked fish on his shoulder. A Dominican waiter I remember from our visits to the hotel squeezes in between the bed and the IV stand. A fragile-looking woman with red hair and an American Airlines tag still attached to her duffel bag, her eyes holding back tears, overzealously rearranges the roses on the bedside table. I wonder if any of them know that Frankie's given name is Fred and that he changed it to be like his middle school friends in Queens, who were all Italian. Three of them are trying to con their way past the head nurse, insisting they are immediate family, all brothers. They don't have a single feature in common with one another or with Frankie. The middle-aged nurse with steel-colored eyes, who has undoubtedly heard all this before, gives them a harsh stare and lets them through.

Perhaps not yet willing to face what is in front of me, I think again of Frankie and last Christmas. I see him in a tuxedo and black tie, tall and more narrow-boned than Andy, with a head of dark, wavy hair hemmed in by a conservative haircut required for the job, standing next to the silver-haired maître d' in the Concord dining room the size of a football stadium. The dining room was replicated in miniature on a blackboard behind the two of them, with circles surrounded by thumbtacks of different colors the maître d' would rearrange as people walked in. I wondered about the color significance of those pins the maître d' was sticking into the board. Did red denote customers who were nuisances, who always asked for more than what you offered them? Did green stand for agreeable? Did yellow mean too unpredictable or too loud?

Frankie led us to a big table somewhere in the center of the dining room, under a complicated chandelier—white tablecloth, starched napkins, real flowers.

"Bring us everything on the menu," said my father-in-law, grandly pounding the table with his palm. We all knew that Artie didn't really want every item on the Concord's titanic menu. What he wanted was to be able to say those words and watch his younger son, the softer and more obedient one, deliver tray after tray in a demonstration of Artie's continued importance in the family.

I didn't need to translate for my mother since dishes arrived at a dizzying pace. Melon with prosciutto, green salad with hearts of palm, grilled calamari, onion soup, roasted vegetables, mashed potatoes, pasta with seafood, and the weekend special, prime rib. I watched Mama try a bit of every dish set down on our table, praising the tenderness of the beef, giving the plate with calamari a suspicious look. I watched Frankie sail around the dining room, talking to guests, making sure that the waiters and busboys—who have been his friends since he began working here—didn't get blamed for the diners' quirks or the mishaps of the kitchen. I watched him taking care of his friends the same way he took care of his family.

Now Frankie's friends are here in this postop room, looking helpless, wishing they could do something—anything—to take care of him.

"Hey, is this a party or what?" says Frankie as he opens his arms to us. Aside from a patch of padded gauze covering the back of his head, he looks like the same old Frankie I remember from his house in Ellenville. Maybe he is even more handsome with his hair shaved off. "Come on in, everyone. Have some whitefish. It all comes from this man," he says, pointing to his chef friend, who has set down the tray on the windowsill and is serving portions of fish on paper plates that emerge from a hefty plastic bag he has brought with him. The bag also dispenses forks and knives, napkins and crackers, and I am afraid wine will begin to flow next.

We talk and mingle, as if we were in his Ellenville living room, as if we were his invited guests. Frankie is our host, sitting tall in bed, cheering us all up, telling us everything will be all right—as though we were the ones who needed to be consoled.

ॐ

After six weeks of radiation, there will probably be a remission, says the doctor from NYU. He is one of the best neuro-oncologists in the country, but even this top expert with charcoal hair and a starched lab coat cannot twist the prognosis into a good outcome.

"Go travel," he tells Frankie, stacking his most recent MRI into the file with the others. "Now is the time to do what you've always wanted to do. Don't wait too long," he adds and shakes his head as if to emphasize his words.

I think of a picture of Frankie we have in our family album. It was taken during one of the summers when he was still in college, standing barefoot in the grass, tall and skinny in rolled-up jeans, his curly, thick hair falling down in a lush, dark triangle, touching his biceps. He wanted to go to India then, he told me, to learn meditation and yoga, to hike in the Himalayas, to try to figure out the meaning of life. He has wanted to go to India ever since.

When we get home from the doctor's office, I am ready to accompany Frankie to Bombay. In my mind, I can see us immersed in the energy of a wise yogi who knows everything about life and who may possess powers to cure the lethal tumor American doctors are helpless to approach. There are always reports of medical miracles, I think, especially from faraway places that no one can reach to verify the facts. I stare at the scuffed paperback I bought a week ago at a sale in our local library, an ode to a Buddhist monk with the power to cure incurable ailments who practices healing somewhere among the Himalayan mountain peaks.

"Look," I say to Andy, knowing how ridiculous I sound, pointing to a testimonial on the back cover of the book signed by someone from North Dakota. "American doctors had given him three months to live. That was ten years ago."

Andy squints, making a skeptical face, and shakes his head.

Of course, I know that Andy is right. But since my mind is unable to scrape together any hope for Frankie, I hold on to the paperback a little longer, leafing through the dog-eared pages of miracles Frankie's oncologist has never heard of.

ॐ

When it is clear, even to me, that we are not going to the yoga sanctuaries or Buddhist monasteries of India, I ask Frankie if he would like me to take him to Petersburg, my hometown. "It is a beautiful city," I say. "I promise you'll love it." I don't know why I have just volunteered to take my brother-in-law to see where I grew up, but maybe I do know. Petersburg, in my mind, is the most precious thing I hold inside me, and I want to offer it to Frankie as a gift.

But Frankie doesn't want to go to Petersburg. He wants to go to Florida to spend time with his girls.

Andy arranges for him to get on a flight with the Corporate Angel Network, a program for cancer patients who need to travel between different parts of the country. I drive him to Teterboro Airport, and we sit in the waiting room, watching small private planes take off and land behind a wall of glass.

"You can stay at our house for as long as you like," I say. "I hope you know this."

It is strange, I think, that we were nothing more than distant relatives until only a few months ago, that I barely knew my brother-in-law before his illness flung him into our life. It is even stranger how close we have become since he spent two months in our house after the surgery, how protective, almost possessive, I feel of Frankie now. I look at his face, still as handsome as the pictures in our photo album, but there is a melancholy in his eyes, even when he smiles: they seem to be set deeper in his head and the whites have become darker, as if Frankie were now privy to some ancient wisdom.

"I can do some catering in Boca Raton," he says, but we both know it isn't the prospects of catering that are summoning him to Florida. His older daughter, Heather, who is finishing high school this year, signed up for ROTC and has now volunteered to join the Army. A few months from now, after the prom and graduation, she will disappear into boot camp. His younger daughter, Amy, as tall and lanky as her father, wants to try to become a model. Frankie is going to Florida to find a good modeling school for her. He wants to sit on the porch of their house when she comes back from class and watch her walk toward him slowly and gracefully, with a newly acquired gait of confidence and poise, then run and clumsily throw her arms around his neck, the way she has always done. He wants to be there to watch her awkward charm gradually mature into quiet graciousness. I know all this without Frankie saying a word.

A young woman gets up from her desk with a phone and walks to where we are sitting. "Your flight is ready, sir," she says and points to the door that opens onto the airfield. We walk outside, into the December wind and the fumes of Route 17, where a tanned, uniformed pilot next to a small plane, as experienced and dependable as any pilot in any magazine ad, greets Frankie and shakes his hand.

We say good-bye and embrace. I think of my father, of the last time I saw him being carried to the waiting taxi that took him to the hospital, but I shake off all these thoughts and hold Frankie in my arms a moment longer.

"He's in good hands," says the pilot, and I smile and nod to confirm that I know.

# Thirty-Eight

In May a second seizure catapults Frankie back north. We spend two weeks driving back and forth, first to his NYU oncologist and then to his surgeon, who suggests another operation. In his office, he taps on Frankie's knees, tells him to touch his nose, and makes him walk across the room.

"You're in very good shape, young man," says the surgeon, who is in his sixties and has a paternal air about him. "Now go and tell my secretary I want her to schedule an operation as soon as she can find an opening."

When Frankie is on the other side of the closed door, the doctor tells us he will remove as much of the tumor as he can get to, which will grant my brother-in-law a few more months. "It's not curable, no false hopes. You understand this, right?" he asks, his eyes stern, his fatherly demeanor vanished. Andy and I nod. We understand.

Behind her desk, the secretary, a young woman with a black ponytail and gold hoops swinging from her ears, drags her finger down a sheet with days partitioned into hours. "I can find a slot for you tomorrow, I'm almost sure of it," she says, her consonants made more sibilant by her Spanish accent. "This person can be moved," she mutters, "and I can call Mr. Jackson and see if he can make the same time next week. He'll be thrilled." The badge on her lapel reads ARACELY NUNEZ. She is efficient and focused, a twenty-five-year-old in charge of life.

၈၁

We spend the summer sitting in our kitchen and drinking wine, despite the no alcohol sticker on the bottle of Frankie's steroids. Every few days his friends drive in to visit, and I throw together big dinners that make us move from the kitchen to the large table in the dining room. We carve into whole chickens and plow through salad bowls full of pasta; we dig into pots of boiled potatoes and strip lamb down to the bone. It almost feels like a never-ending party.

During the day, I drive Frankie to local MRIs and then to NYU, where his oncologist squints at the film pinned up against the lighted screen and points out the encroaching swell of white. Andy and I and sometimes my mother-in-law, who seems to have shrunk even more in the past ten months, crowd around the screen, staring at the pale, expanding stain—an aggressive void, a sea of sickness in the middle of Frankie's brain. Artie remains in his chair, leaning down and staring at the floor, spared remembering why he is sitting in an oncologist's office because his mind has already begun to close the window into what he knew only the day before.

"Is it any better, Doctor?" Doris invariably asks, her voice high and thin, as if the words came not from her lips but from someone else's, someone whose eyes were able to hold more hope.

The neuro-oncologist, who has been trained to deal with such unanswerable questions, returns to the lighted screen and encloses the white blur in Frankie's brain between his palms, repeating what he already said a few minutes earlier, knowing that this is not what Frankie's parents are able to hear. I watch him stagger through the second presentation, wondering why anyone—with so many specialties in the medical field—would deliberately choose neuro-oncology as his occupation.

Frankie, who sits in a chair in the corner of the room, is always undaunted by our intense peering. "It is what it is," is all he ever says.

∽

In September, another seizure quakes through Frankie's body.

"You call his doctor this time," says Andy. "Please." He sits on our bed, looking down at the floor, and I know that, from now on, I will be the one making these calls. Andy has been arranging surgeries and subsequent appointments, maintaining his brother's health insurance, talking to distracted clerks, keeping in touch with Frankie's friends scattered all over the area, all wanting to spend time with him—making calls, compiling lists—which may be the only way you can get through a year of watching your brother die.

I dial the NYU oncologist. It is Saturday, and when we get connected, I hear children's voices in the background, the sounds of a family event outdoors. I imagine them in a meadow full of flowers behind the house, the doctor's daughters in dresses from Laura Ashley, their arms extended like wings of small airplanes, sailing through the grass away from their father and then back. I imagine the doctor frowning at the ringing phone, an unwelcome intrusion that for a few minutes will divert his attention from this sunny afternoon, from life. I tell him about the seizure; I recite Frankie's medications from memory; I scribble down what the doctor says. I am the most distant relative, the only one in the family who can muster the composure to describe the new symptoms of paralyzed fingers, slow-paced speech, a weakened right arm. I am the only one who has the audacity to ask how long he has left.

After I hang up, I go to my brother-in-law's room and do what the doctor tells me. I fill a syringe with blood thinner, let out the air bubbles as my mother has taught me, and clumsily jab it into

Frankie's stomach. He makes a joke, praising my injection skills, pretending it doesn't hurt.

෨

Amy calls to say she is on Interstate 95, on her way from Florida to our house in New Jersey. She arrives radiant and fresh, as if she has just stepped out of the ocean instead of an old Toyota she drove for twelve hundred miles. We kiss and embrace; she is so reedy that hugging her feels like holding a birch tree.

Aren't you supposed to be in school? Andy asks.

Amy smiles, throwing back her head—Jen's blond hair, Frankie's green eyes—and shrugs. She informed her high school counselor she was going to go to New Jersey to take care of her father, she says, then simply got into Frankie's car and drove from Boca Raton to Ridgewood.

She runs into the house and into her father's arms. Frankie has moved from his bed into a chair to greet her, and they hold each other silently, his failing body sheltering her healthy one.

෨

For the next few weeks, Amy helps with grocery shopping, makes elaborate salads, and drives to a local trattoria to pick up orders of the fried calamari Frankie loves. The steroids he takes have rounded his face and his middle, making him permanently hungry.

We rent a hospital bed, and the picture of those few weeks I hold in my mind is of Amy sitting by Frankie's side, feeding him the crispy golden rings.

This is when a rabbi, Frankie's friend of about five years, starts coming to the house. As we have found out since his diagnosis, my brother-in-law boasts a whole battalion of unexpected friends: waiters, short-order cooks, stewardesses, actors turned caterers, real estate agents who are part-time hairdressers, busboys with the skills of investment brokers, and now a rabbi.

The rabbi drives all the way from Monsey, where I imagine him presiding over a congregation of men dressed in black, women in wigs peering out from behind a curtain. He wears a black coat and a long beard, and when I offer him a drink of water on a ninety-five-degree day, he politely declines.

"Where did you meet him?" Andy asks.

"In Aruba, of all places," says Frankie. "I was catering a group of singles who wanted a kosher Passover with sun, and Rabbi Kaploon was my overseer. It's been a good gig for both of us ever since. We've even become friends."

When the rabbi judiciously calls to say he is on his way to our house, Frankie orders Amy in an urgent voice to hide the calamari.

"Why should I hide the calamari?" Amy giggles, lifting another golden piece from a take-out tray.

From now on, "hide the calamari" means the rabbi is coming for a visit.

While they talk in Frankie's room, Andy and I go online and try to find the blog of the man who has survived glioblastoma for over a year and a half, the only website that offered a glimpse of hope on that dark day when Frankie suffered his first seizure. We punch in all the possible word combinations; we scroll up and down the screen. It's all inconsequential. The blog is gone.

෨

Jen now calls the house every week from Florida to get a report on her husband's health. I tell her about our doctor visits and the MRIs, and she tells me that the airfares are still too expensive for her to travel north. She also cannot leave her part-time job that involves reading to patients in a local hospital. Her voice makes me want to materialize in her Boca Raton kitchen armed with a blunt object and club her. But I simply give her the report. Frankie's whole right arm now refuses to move, and I can see the frustration in his eyes when he has to search for words. He asks his friend the rabbi to teach him how to pray.

∞

Words are slipping away from Frankie's mind, strangled by the ravenous blob of cancer, by the insatiable tentacles that have all but paralyzed his right side. It is time, he tells us, to think of saying good-bye. On a late November day, when naked branches etch a filigree pattern against the frosty sky, one by one we go into Frankie's room. Heather is here, too, on an emergency Army leave. The Army physician who read her father's chart, she says, signed her documents required for a leave without asking a single question.

First Frankie's friends disappear behind the door, then his relatives from Florida, then his parents. They come out stooped and humbled, mouths tightened, eyebrows mashed together. Sasha runs out sobbing, her hand over her wet face, and I realize this is her first experience with grief. Andy goes in and stays what seems like a long time, although time has warped and become as unreal as everything else. When he leaves the room, he hurries outside, his head down so no one can see his eyes.

Then it is my turn. Frankie is half-sitting in bed, not able to say much. His language has become tentative, making every word sound significant because it takes him so much effort to produce it. How ironic, I think, that of all human faculties it is language, the only thing I know something about, that Frankie's cancer has chosen to plunder.

I have a bracelet in my hand made from honey-colored chunks of Baltic amber, one of the few pieces I brought with me when I arrived in Washington on an Aeroflot flight. I put the bracelet into Frankie's good hand, and, as he closes his fingers around it, it glows inside his palm like a tiny sun. I say it has been a privilege taking care of him. I say it was he who, in a strange way, has looked after the rest of us, his grace and dignity binding us all together.

He says, "It is what it is."

છ

Andy and I are in a hospice, where we brought Frankie two weeks ago. For three days now he has been in a coma, we are told; his consciousness has turned off, no longer willing to fight. We walk along a hallway glittering with shiny stars and tinsel, past a Christmas tree decorated with birds and angels. The festive lights blink on the walls, the holiday celebrating birth so incongruous with the purpose of this place.

Frankie is in an auditorium full of windows seeping in the gray light of a December afternoon, among a dozen other people reclined in wheelchairs. His eyes are closed, his head tilted to the right. Jen is standing by his side. She is wearing a coat, ready to leave, her round face resigned, her curls limp on the pink shoulders of her parka. She has been here since morning, she tells us.

We take her post and sit with Frankie for a while. His face is a mask; not a single muscle moves. His breathing is even and quiet, almost inaudible. A young man in a blue uniform asks if we want to move him back into his room; it is time for a sponge bath, or for some other procedure Frankie will not be aware of.

For half an hour we walk around, past some doors open and others closed, past the Santa Claus hunched under a glittering sack of presents, waiting for the procedure to be over.

In his room, Frankie lies on his back, sleeping. We know, of course, that he is not really sleeping, that what looks like sleep is a stand-by mode before his system shuts down completely. There are chairs on either side of his bed, and we sit down. Andy takes his right hand, and I take his left, with an amber bracelet on his wrist, his palm cool and soft and completely pliable. We sit like this for some time, holding Frankie's hands, the only way we can connect to him right now.

"Do you think he can feel that we're here?" I ask.

"Don't know," says Andy. He has been pragmatic for this year and a half, rational and full of common sense, celebrating with Frankie's many friends the last months of his brother's life.

I think of a photograph hanging on the wall of my in-laws' apartment: Andy's young mother, in makeup and a pretty dress, with an obligatory photographic smile radiating from her face, on a 1950s couch with six-year-old Andy and three-year-old Frankie. Andy is already old enough to register the significance of the moment, so he is sitting up straight, a little crimped by his new suit, smiling into the camera. Frankie is still in the stage where conventions don't matter, so he is stretched across the sofa, resting his head in the lap of his brother.

I look at the two brothers now: the younger one in a hospice bed, in a coma; the older one hunched over, holding his hand. I see the muscles in Andy's face tighten. I tell him we should stay. He says we need to go.

&

The phone in our house rings at 5:20 in the morning after we return from the hospice. I know what I will hear. I try to imagine what went on in Frankie's ravaged brain. I try to imagine his body light and almost suspended, flooded with the sensation of wholeness, as if every part of him ceased being separate and coalesced into one.

# *Thirty-Nine*

When Sasha is thirteen, she takes a test and gets accepted into the Johns Hopkins Center for Talented Youth, a summer camp at Siena College in Albany, New York. Before departing for her four-week program, she bleaches her hair to the color of endive. As part of their camp experience, every participant is required to spend two hours a day at the library, in addition to a daily four-hour class on the history of philosophy. Her voice on the phone drips with sarcasm when she asks what kind of summer camp has a library, but we hear no snide remarks about the class itself. Her teacher is a twenty-something PhD whose arms are covered with tattoos from wrist to shoulder. The tattoos are called a sleeve, she informs us, hinting that she might choose philosophy as her major in college. Yet when Sasha returns home, instead of analyzing Descartes and Kant, she spends a year poring over books on tattoos.

ഔ

At fourteen, Sasha secretly puts in a nose ring, judiciously hiding it when we are around. I glimpse it accidentally when she is in a dentist's chair. Strangely, the sight of her pierced nose revives the images of summers at my Russian dacha, of the Gypsy bull tied to a pole with rope threaded through a metal ring hanging out of his nostrils, which, I know, is a sad and unfair juxtaposition I shouldn't share with anyone but Andy.

From my Russian trip, I bring back a black-and-white film called *Wild Dingo*, the movie I remember from my own adolescence, thinking that actors on the screen may wield more power than pages in a book. Sasha watches it to the end, maybe because the introverted characters do not engage in a great deal of talk. The protagonist is a sixteen-year-old girl who has trouble connecting to her mother and her friends, not being part of the collective, according to the blurb. For a day, I resuscitate my hope that Sasha will express interest in my background. Then *Wild Dingo* is tossed into the box with the rest of the books and tapes I have lugged back from many trips to Russia, a sad linguistic graveyard where the abandoned relics from my former life have been collecting dust for years.

Because I can no longer fight Sasha's rejection of my linguistic heritage all by myself, I decide to hire a Russian tutor to come to the house and inject my daughter with a weekly dose of Russian classics and declensions.

Sasha suffers through the lesson, being polite to the stoical tutor. But when we are alone, she is blunt and unforgiving. "I hate reading Chekhov," she spits out. "I hate declining adjectives and nouns. You can't make me do what I hate."

I grapple for an appropriate response, clutching at the few wisps of sanity I have left, trying to prop up the argument so it doesn't devolve into a shouting match, like the fights I remember so well from my own childhood. Was I as stubborn and impossible? Did my mother have a point when she yelled at me in our Leningrad kitchen?

I don't know the answer to these questions, and my fumbling for a good response to Sasha produces nothing. The only action I can think of is to retreat to the garage, where I try to shake a cigarette out of the emergency pack I have stuffed in the rafters, spilling the whole contents to the ground I cannot see. Half an hour later, when Andy comes home, he finds me leaning on the inside wall of the garage, sniffling.

∞

A month before her fifteenth birthday, my daughter announces she has become a vegan. I am not sure what a vegan is, and she rolls her eyes and obliges to explain.

"I eat nothing that comes from an animal," she says. "Nothing."

"Not even milk?" I ask. "What about yogurt and farmer's cheese and the butter we buy at the Russian store in Fair Lawn? You've always loved them. And what about ice cream?" I demand, not really believing she can part with dessert.

"Nothing," she insists, staring at me with the white, angry eyes of an annoyed true believer. "Not even honey."

"Honey?" I say in the limp voice of someone who has just been electrocuted. "Why not honey?"

She looks at me with bemused contempt, not gracing my dense question with an answer, then walks away to release herself from the kitchen and this senseless conversation.

I start after her, as if I could keep her here, chained a little longer to all the animal protein so shamelessly exhibited on the shelves of our refrigerator, the protein, I am convinced, her body still needs to grow and form. How ironic it is, I think, that of all the ways to express herself my daughter has chosen to remove from her life the comfort of food, the most visceral thing that tethers me—and every immigrant—to my homeland. I think of all those hearty soups and stews that simmer on the stove for hours, and those countless *kotlety* from Marina's Leningrad recipe, and *syrniki* Mama molds by hand from a gooey mix of farmer's cheese and sugar. I think of the recipes from the iconic *Book About Tasty and Healthy Food,* which adorned every Russian bookshelf, the leathery navy tome we read for entertainment because none of the necessary ingredients for its recipes could be found in Soviet grocery stores. The pictures from that book rise before my eyes—whole baked bass in butter sauce, casseroles with beef goulash and lamb pilaf, rows of stuffed cabbage and trays of rabbit stewed in sour cream—all those mouthwatering manifestations of pleasure that have now turned into a wall separating my daughter and me, the highest one yet between us.

છ

After years of my mother's unsought advice followed by fights and sulking, there finally comes a confrontation. Mama and Andy are in the kitchen, getting ready for dinner. She has made a pan of *kotlety*, oval-shaped hamburgers I remember from my childhood. One slips off the spatula and falls to the floor; Andy picks it up and throws it into the garbage. When I come downstairs, I see my mother fish the *kotleta* out of the trash, then carefully wipe it off with a sponge we use to clean the sink, and from Andy's tensed back I know what he is thinking. "No dirty, clean," my mother says. This is not the first time she has picked the food off the floor, or reused paper napkins, or insisted we eat leftovers while fresh chicken or lettuce sit patiently in the refrigerator turning old.

Andy's eyes swim with rage. "You have to stop interfering, do you understand?" he says to her. She doesn't understand. She thinks she is protecting us from all this American waste. "*Kotleta* clean," she says, "no dirty."

I could step in between them as I have done so many times before, but I don't. I could tell my mother to stop saving us, in Russian. I could take the hamburger from her hands and give it to the dog. But I don't move. For the first time, I refuse to be a buffer: between my old country and my new one, between the benefit of saving and the harm of wasting, between how I was raised and how I am living now. What is happening in the kitchen has ceased to be about a dropped *kotleta*. It has crossed the border of civility; it has crossed the limit of Andy's patience.

My mother wraps the cleaned *kotleta* into a paper towel, opens the refrigerator, and carefully places it on the upper shelf. Andy grabs the pan off the stove and flings our entire dinner into the garbage. The glass top hits the wall and shatters into shards on the ceramic floor. "If you don't stop meddling in our life, I'll send you back to fucking Russia," he yells, as if my mother could understand what he is saying.

She understands perfectly. Her mouth is pinched; her eyes fill with tears.

"I leave," she says, sniffling, shuffling down the basement stairs. "I go soon," she mutters, a threat I heard so many times in Leningrad.

# *Forty*

Andy and I are in our kitchen, finishing a bottle of wine, which has become a routine ever since I realized that Sasha was never going to open the tomes of Russian classics weighing down my office shelves. Our daughter, almost sixteen, is at the mall with her eighteen-year-old friend Kate, who goes to the same high school and who drives. The phone rings, and from the way Andy's shoulders droop when he picks up the receiver, I know it isn't my sister from New Orleans calling to share a new recipe she has just invented.

"We'll be there as soon as we can," I hear him say, and the worst images every parent has stored in the recesses of her mind—easily accessible at a moment like this—readily align themselves for a hideous viewing.

"She is at the Hackensack police station," Andy says. "Arrested for shoplifting."

None of the available images in my head carries the label "arrested," and I feel relieved. At least, she is uninjured and alive.

Andy calls a cab, and, five minutes later, we are inside a Lincoln that smells of old, cracked leather, sailing, like a big boat, through the June dusk. A week from today, we have three tickets to fly to Paris for a week, as we do almost every year in early summer. Only this time Sasha has convinced us that she is mature enough to stay home and take care of the dog. She was so adamant in her desire to remain home and spend a week by herself that she has persuaded me to manipulate her pediatrician into writing a letter to the airline pleading a medically necessitated refund for her ticket. The letter is now waiting on my desk, ready to be presented to an Air France official at Newark Airport tomorrow.

As we walk into the police station, we see Kate, sobbing, being led by her parents to their car. Inside, Sasha is slumped in a chair, with puffy eyes and a wet face, avoiding looking in our direction.

Sergeant Dutton gets up from behind the desk to greet us. He is in his fifties, short and paunchy, his ears almost perpendicular to the graying hair sprouting out of his skull. I don't know why I notice his ears.

"Sasha and Kate were arrested in Neiman Marcus," he says. "They stole a two-hundred-dollar pair of jeans. Kate has admitted that she stole the jeans, but your daughter was waiting outside the dressing room and agreed to hide the jeans in her backpack. That is a crime, too," he says.

I conjure up Sasha's room, with jeans tangled in knots on the closet shelves, with more jeans strewn across the bed and rolled into balls of denim on the bathroom floor. More jeans than all the students in my whole high school in Leningrad could ever dream of. More jeans than all the actors in Marina's theater, even counting those with lucrative film careers, could manage to procure.

"What were you thinking?" Andy asks, his voice so full of anger it is almost a shout. "Were you thinking at all? In my whole life I've never been arrested." He leans forward in his chair, his hand stabbing the air in Sasha's direction. "You're not even sixteen, and you are in a police station. What the hell were you thinking?"

Sasha folds into a ball and bursts out sobbing.

Sergeant Dutton takes a few steps in front of his desk as my daughter wails. "Since she is a minor, the case will be transferred to

a juvenile court," he says. She'll have to see the juvenile court coun-
selors and follow their instructions.

I am grateful I have two glasses of wine in me to soften the edge
of this disgrace. How could you do this? I want to ask my bawling
daughter, although I know that this is a stupid, rhetorical question.
Why would you try to steal what is so readily available to you? My
eyes wander from the scuffed linoleum floor to the beige walls devoid of any pictures, as if the generic blandness of this police station
could provide the answer.

The sergeant stops in front of Sasha, now quieted in her chair.
"You know, you could have worked part-time and made the money,
if you really wanted the jeans," he says. "You could've earned the
money yourself."

Sasha sniffles, looks away, and says nothing. The irony is glaring
us in the face: everyone in this room except Sergeant Dutton knows
that Sasha didn't have to work. The pathetic truth is that we would
have bought the Neiman Marcus jeans for her, if she had asked us.
They would have been one of those dozen presents Andy still insists
we get for Christmas and her birthday.

Andy gets up, and Sergeant Dutton motions for him to sign the
release form. Behind the window, the headlights of the taxi waiting
to take us home light up the empty parking lot.

I can see how furious Andy still is. I feel the same disappointment
and humiliation sloshing inside me, overpowering the wine. "This is
it," he says, facing Sasha, drawing the confines of the imminent punishment. "Don't say a word, not a single word. You are going with us
next week. Do you understand, young lady? You're going to Paris!"

I know how ridiculous this must sound to a stranger. Our
daughter's punishment for shoplifting, a trip to Paris. As we walk
toward the door, I pass Sergeant Dutton, whose features have
scrunched into a confused, bewildered look. I don't even dare to
imagine what he must think of our parenting skills, or our sanity.

∞

Sasha is seventeen, and her hair is now in dreadlocks. One look at her should be enough to banish my fantasy of our traveling to Petersburg together, yet I attempt what I think is my last pitch in favor of learning Russian.

"Someday you'll be glad you can speak another language," I say. I know I sound like my mother, but I cannot stop because I pushed off the top of this slope a long time ago and am now sliding down, pulled by the force I can't control. "You'll have so many opportunities others don't. You already have the base. Now it's just a question of not losing it. It would be such a shame to lose what you already know. Look at me: I struggled through two years of German at the university, and now I can't say a word." I deliberately speak rationally and calmly, so that the logic of my arguments will be so obvious even Sasha can't dispute it.

"I am not you," she spits out, and no matter how hard I search for an appropriate parent-like response, I know there is nothing I can say to contradict her.

She is succinct and to the point, my daughter. She is just as ruthless and honest as I used to be. Isn't this what I said when my mother bought me a flowery polyester skirt I called provincial; or when I applied to the English department of the university instead of medical school, as she had insisted; or when her face froze in panic as I announced I was going to marry an American?

I feel hopeless and old. How can I possibly know anything about raising a child when I still live with my mother? The mother I have always kept at an emotional distance, rarely telling her anything of any importance; the mother who followed me to a different hemisphere to keep an eye on me, to make sure I was all right. Is this what has made me so myopic and inept: remaining a child, never having to grow up?

I am as disconnected from my daughter as I have always been from my mother. We speak different languages: Mama does not know English and Sasha does not know Russian, all because I have been unable to teach them.

# Forty-One

After her freshman year at the small liberal arts college in up-state New York, Sasha drops out and spends the fall driving cross-country with a couple of tattooed friends we never met. They are defending animal rights, she says, and I imagine young men in baseball caps with blue and red dragons on their biceps loading signs and posters into a car trunk. She doesn't really need college, Sasha tells us on the phone. She can learn everything she has to know without going to school.

Andy carries on long phone conversations with her, and I can only envy his patience. He offers evidence in defense of higher education, so obvious it makes my ears wilt, arguments Sasha resolutely refutes with examples of friends we don't know who have done just fine without school.

She calls us from Pittsburgh, then Detroit.

"You need to be careful with what you're doing," Andy says into the receiver. "You know you're breaking the law."

I hear Sasha's angry voice on the other end. "It isn't *my* law that I'm breaking," she yells.

"Whether it's your law or not your law"—I hear Andy's voice climb higher—"it's your ass, and they're going to throw it in jail. And when they do throw you in jail, I won't be able to help you."

"You're right, it is my ass, and no one is going to throw me in jail for protesting cruelty to animals," she shouts, self-righteous and angry. I imagine her furiously clutching the phone, her hazel eyes narrowed to slits. "And anyway, all we're doing is standing on lawns and holding up signs."

"And just whose lawns are you standing on?" Andy asks.

"If you must know, we stand on the lawns of the corporate presidents and the scientists who kill dogs and cats to test for hair color or some bullshit. Isn't it obvious to you *this* is what the real crime is? Isn't it painfully obvious, even to you?"

"What's painfully obvious is that we have a nineteen-year-old daughter who dropped out of college," Andy shouts back. "With one arrest already under her belt and now going for number two."

There is an angry exhale on the other end, then a loud intake of breath. "Oh, I was just waiting for you to bring that up. I was fifteen when that happened. And it wasn't even me who took the fucking jeans." Sasha is screaming now, so I can hear every word. "I knew you were holding on to it, waiting to use it against me as ammunition." There is a pause, and I can sense my daughter is reloading her own weapons. "I hate you! And I never want to talk to you again," she yells, her voice precise as a well-aimed gun.

છ

In the evening, Andy and I sit in the kitchen and stare into our glasses of wine.

"I really blew it, didn't I," he says in a quiet voice. "I shouldn't have brought up that stuff about her arrest."

He walks over to the phone on the wall and I know he is dialing Sasha's number. He waits as I hear the rings, then a voice-mail recording.

"Maybe I should tell her about my lab assistant job in Leningrad," I say. "Then she will hate me, too, and will never want to talk to me again."

As a university student, I worked in Mama's anatomy department at the time when the Soviet Union launched one cosmonaut after another into space and we were required to produce research on weightlessness. My fellow lab assistant, Luba, and I pulled rabbits out of their cages in the basement, strapped them to a centrifuge, and spun them at a speed that blurred the rabbits into circles of gray and white. If they were still alive after the centrifuge stopped, we had to kill them with ether, because the researchers needed the rabbits' spinal cords. We had to carefully break the vertebrae, remove the soft cord of spine in one piece, freeze it, and then slice it into thin translucent chips that would fit under a microscope. I hated holding a rag full of ether to the rabbits' faces, while Luba hated breaking the vertebrae, so we delineated the labor in a mutually agreeable way.

"Our humble rabbits from the anatomy department basement sent many humans into space," I tell Andy to make him smile because I see that his eyebrows are still knit together in one droopy line.

We both know, of course, I will never repeat any of this to Sasha; I will never initiate that battle. I wonder if there are any battles I am prepared to fight with my daughter. I fought so hard for her to get A's in algebra, to finish her papers on time, to memorize irregular verbs in French. I confiscated the phone line she used to connect to the Internet and chat with friends instead of researching literary lives or the dates of important historic upheavals. Before she took the practice SATs, we hired a geometry tutor, who sat with her at our dining room table every Thursday solving three-dimensional problems that thirty years earlier I could never understand myself. During the year of real SATs, we saddled Sasha with a three-month course of make-believe test taking, driving her twice a week to a sad-looking brick building in the center of Ridgewood, where I sat in the car waiting for her stooped figure to emerge from the back door.

It was at the end of that year when I saw a mark on Sasha's hand, a small purple circle that looked like a cigarette burn. Andy told me what it was, but I didn't believe him. "Why would she do that?" I asked. "Why would she scar herself?"

"She's under too much pressure," he said, "and she wants us to notice the pain she's in. She burned her hand just below the sleeve line, just where we would see it, to let us know she's on the verge of breaking." We were sitting in our living room, an absurdly bright day streaming through the windows, and Andy said we had to back off and no longer push her.

We stopped urging Sasha to revise papers or enroll in AP classes, and yet, in the pit of my soul, where no one could see and instantly condemn me, I still couldn't understand what made her feel so pressured. She had a sharp mind, a house full of books, a school that taught world history and looked like a French château. She had a pair of relatively normal, sometimes overly protective parents, usually calm and sober. Her mother didn't demand that she become a doctor, and there was no older actress sister to dread and envy. Her father was alive and well. All Sasha had to do was turn off instant messaging.

During my first spring in the United States, I was insanely envious of the eighteen-year-old Russians in my SCS Business and Technical Institute class, those lucky immigrants who had so many American universities still ahead of them, spread at their teenage feet. They compared the scholarships they had already been offered and casually gabbed about premed studies at Columbia or fine arts programs at NYU. Fine arts, I repeated in my mind, a field whose name alone made me melt.

Now, almost three decades later, I don't understand what Sasha is thinking. I don't understand how anyone could reject a chance to study at a school where no one makes her drill the tenets of Scientific Communism or History of the Communist Party of the Soviet Union. I don't understand anything, it seems, and this makes me feel like an outsider in my daughter's life, an ignorant and clueless immigrant, again.

# Forty-Two

In Chicago, Sasha is arrested. She calls from the police station, her voice defiant and high, struggling to speak over the background din. I feel as if someone with a big fist has just punched me straight in the solar plexus.

"We didn't do anything," she shouts into the receiver, but I can hear her voice is cracking. "We were just standing on a lawn and holding up signs."

I tell her to keep her cell phone on so we can call her as soon as Andy gets home.

"My phone has been confiscated by the cops as evidence," she yells in response.

Evidence of what? I want to ask, but don't.

When Andy gets home, I tell him about the arrest and the confiscated phone. We find a number Sasha gave us before she left, a number to call in case of an emergency, in case we couldn't reach her on her own phone.

A boy our daughter's age answers, and there is a moment of silence on the other end when Andy identifies himself as Sasha's father. We wait again and then we hear our daughter's voice.

"Tell us what's going on," Andy says. "I don't want to hear any hysterics, I don't want to hear about animal rights. Just tell us if you're all right. Tell us where you are."

"With a friend," says Sasha, in a voice no longer shrill but still defiant. I know that her notion of a friend is much broader than mine, allowing a dozen people into a space where I would fit only one. I try to conjure up this friend, a fellow protester with unwashed hair and tattoos. She tells us the police have released her, so she can now leave the state and come home.

Come home, I repeat in my mind, longingly. Andy and I look at each other and take a deep breath.

"So can I come home or not?" Sasha asks, her voice louder and more resistant.

"Of course you can come home," says Andy. "But things have to change."

"I'm not going back to school, if that's what you mean," she snaps.

If it were I talking to my daughter, I know I would fall straight into the fighting trap again, reaching for arguments in defense of higher education that had already been flogged to near death in our kitchen. But Andy is wiser and more patient with Sasha than I will ever be.

"I can't force you to go back to college," he says. "But if you're old enough to quit school, you're old enough to earn your own money." He walks out of the kitchen with the phone, and I hear his voice behind the door gently arguing with our daughter.

When he comes back, he looks down and shakes his head. "I don't know how she did it," he says. "I've just agreed to give her an allowance. But only until she starts making her own money," he adds hastily. "Oh, and I've also agreed to pay her cell phone bill."

∞

A week later, Sasha is back and looking for a job. She says she will answer the phone in Andy's office, but only on a temporary basis. She is obstinate and proud, and she wants to find a real job, not a sinecure offered by her father. Andy pays her ten dollars an hour, more than the minimum wage—or any wage she would get in a job without experience—but our daughter finds this arrangement too easy and unsatisfying.

She applies to Trader Joe's and comes back from her interview with a stack of uniform T-shirts she must wear to work. I have trouble seeing Sasha in a uniform, so it is a surprise when two weeks later she is still holding the job. When Andy and I ask her about work, she pouts and says nothing. A few days later it turns out that the manager has assigned our vegan daughter to a meat locker. Sasha doesn't talk to us about work. Every morning she silently puts on a Trader Joe's T-shirt and gets into my old Volvo with a manual shift I taught her how to drive.

In May, her meat locker sentence ends when she upgrades herself to folding shirts at Urban Outfitters. At her invitation, Andy and I go to visit her at the Garden State Plaza mall, where we see her walking around the store with confidence, making sure the belts are coiled into perfect circles and the scarves are arranged in rainbow patterns. Instead of the Salvation Army sweatshirts that are still spilling out of her closet, she now wears the same outfits she arranges on the shelves with such masterful care. Looking at Sasha expertly folding a pair of jeans, I think of my daughter's room at home, pieces of clothing scattered all over the unmade bed, wet towels crumpled on the floor, and orphaned shoes poking out of the open closet door in search of their missing mates.

∞

"You know, I respect you for sticking with these jobs," Andy says to Sasha. She is in the living room, fumbling through her bag, getting ready to go to work. For three months, she has been packaging meat at Trader Joe's, then folding shirts at Urban Outfitters for eight dollars an hour. "But we both know this isn't going to be your life."

"So what should my life be?" she says, the old defiance back in her voice. She lifts her chin, speaking in machine-gun spurts, as if expecting someone to clamp her mouth shut. "Do you think I should get a doctorate, like Mommy, and spend my life teaching kids who don't want to be there? Is that what you want me to do?"

"Look, you can do whatever you want to do," says Andy. "But you can't do anything without a college degree. There's got to be more to your life than stocking shelves. A college degree is your fall-back position. If nothing goes right in your career, at least you will have a higher education."

I see Sasha turn away from him, her shoulders slumped. She looks as fragile now as she was belligerent only a minute earlier. Her hands clasp her elbows; her lower lip curls forward as it used to when she was a baby ready to start crying. "That's all you ever talk about, that's all that matters to you, that I finish college," she says and sniffles, and even from where I am standing in the kitchen I see a tear rolling down her cheek.

Andy wraps his arms around her and pulls her into his embrace. "No," he says softly. "All that matters to me is you."

⁓

When Mama asks about Sasha, I say she has taken a year off to find a better school. I know my mother will accept this lie because she can relate to a search for academic excellence. I also know I should grow up and talk to her as an adult would do, as she talked to her own mother, letting my grandma in on every hurdle put up in my way by life. I can almost see Babusya's soft face behind her round glasses as she listened to Mama's laments about my father, who refused to have a child, or about my sister who refused to go to technical school because she wanted to become an actress. I know Grandma heard every intake of breath and every stumble in my mother's voice; I know she heard and understood everything. So why am I so stubborn in keeping my troubles from my own mother? Why can't I go down to her basement, sit on her bed as she watches news from Moscow, and allow her to worry with me?

# Forty-Three

At the end of the week Sasha announces she is going back to college. She has chosen the University of Vermont, she tells us.

"Why Vermont? It's so far away," I question feebly, suspecting it may be precisely the distance from home and from us that drives Sasha's choice of school.

"It's a good university," Andy says, and I know I shouldn't say anything because any school, even five hours away, is better than no school at all.

In June the three of us pile into Andy's Saab and go to Burlington. Sasha has already informed us she doesn't want to live in another dorm. The dorm at Bard College was awful, she tells us. Her dorm mates spent their days guzzling beer and nights staggering aimlessly through clouds of pot. I instantly feel guilty for not having known this earlier, for not being able to rescue my vegan, teetotaler daughter from a year of social torture. I know she is as absolute about drugs and alcohol as she is about milk, and when on New Year's Eve I poured an inch of champagne into her glass, she barely let it touch her lips.

After a day of searching, we find the first floor of a house for rent on a main street, twice the size of my Leningrad apartment. The house has no dishwasher or window blinds, but it has eleven-foot ceilings and tall, enormous windows that are certain to present us with an exorbitant energy bill from October to May. I will never tell my mother that we have put up a twenty-year-old in this grand apartment with a separate dining room big enough to give formal dinners for twelve, but we are ready to do anything to have our daughter finish college.

She has chosen sociology as a major because she has already taken enough courses to allow her to cram three years of studies into two. When she signs up, on her own volition, for an advanced Russian course, my heart seizes with joy. After the first semester, she takes two more courses in the Russian department: Tolstoy's *Anna Karenina* and Bulgakov's *Master and Margarita*. I am so thrilled I am afraid to make a sudden movement or breathe audibly. I already see us strolling on Nevsky Prospekt together; I imagine her in Petersburg carrying on conversations with my friends about poetry, asking people on the street for the directions to my courtyard.

Sasha stoically struggles through the text of both novels, and I proofread her final papers to make sure she is rewarded with A's.

⟨⟩

The fantasies of our reading Russian literature and going to Petersburg together are again premature and short-lived. Sasha, I have learned, has joined the university's shooting club and bought a gun. Andy, while not happy about it, says that owning a gun is legal in Vermont. It dawns on me that this may have been the reason she chose to study in a state so far away from home, a state so lax about firearms.

She is back in school, but she owns a gun. One step forward, two steps back—the title of Lenin's article I had to memorize for the state exam on the History of the Communist Party. I don't know why Lenin's words from my student years have floated up in my memory and are now bobbing in my head as the refrain of an annoying song.

When Lenin's quote retreats, like a fetid tide, it leaves behind the hideous knowledge that my daughter now owns a gun.

"What gun?" I ask in horror, imagining Sasha pulling a revolver out of the inner pocket of her jacket to hold up a 7-Eleven.

There is a pause on the other end. "An AK-47," she says hesitantly, knowing that I won't take it well.

I don't.

&#8451;

"A vegan with a military rifle!" I moan to Michelle, whose daughter, Lindsay, and Sasha were lukewarm friends in high school. We are sitting in Michelle's marble-floored kitchen the size of our house, clutching glasses of wine. I ran into her in Whole Foods as we were eyeing containers of Ben & Jerry's frozen yogurt, and we both squealed in delight as if we were best buddies who had suddenly reunited after years of painful separation. Michelle's two daughters have both left the house for small, exclusive schools, and she no longer has anything to do but walk the dog, she tells me. The dog she has to walk is a stately borzoi with long, silky hair the color of rust parted around its sad, elongated face. Except for the sorrowful expression, the dog, whose name is inexplicably Natasha, looks very much like the owner of this stone palace.

I question Michelle, desperately and rhetorically, about why a girl raised in a middle-class, professional family would want to own a gun.

"What does Andy think?" she asks, looking up at me from the wineglass, her face framed by the golden borzoi hairdo.

When Sasha recently came home for a holiday recess, Andy suggested she take lessons at a local shooting range. As long as she has a gun, she should know how to handle it safely, he reasoned. He called the Bullet Hole in Belleville and paid for a day of classes and target practice. My daughter came back with a paper target of an outlined torso and hung it on the wall of her room. All twenty-five shots were clustered within a two-inch-wide circle in the middle of the paper chest. I didn't know how to feel because two incompatible emotions rose inside my own chest almost simultaneously: nausea and pride. It made me feel sick that my daughter's long, exquisite fingers—the fingers I had hoped would make her a pianist before she refused to continue playing at thirteen—pressed the trigger of a gun, releasing deadly bullets into a paper target; yet her accuracy impressed me and made me proud.

My laments about Sasha's love for guns seem to inspire Michelle, and she gets up and walks around the table. "And I cannot even imagine what you must think of those tattoos," she says in a voice both concerned and catty. "They are all over Facebook, Lindsay tells me."

I feel like someone hit me in the chest with a four-by-four, crushing my lungs so that for a moment I cannot breathe. I turn away to face a wall and steel myself because I don't want to fall apart in Michelle's perfect kitchen. I gulp down the remnants of wine in my glass as my cluelessness comes into focus, like a photograph in a developing tray. How could I not have questioned all the long-sleeved sweaters Sasha wore on ninety-degree summer days, all those times when she refused to go to the beach with us?

"All over her arms," says Michelle, dragging her manicured fingers from her shoulder to her wrist.

I mutter something about having to grade papers for tomorrow's class, then get up and stagger to my car. The inside of my Volvo is airless and stale, but it is all irrelevant now in the shadow of such monstrous news. The AK-47, with all its hideousness and its hazards, has instantly retreated to the rear of possible threats: no matter how much my daughter loves it, its metal barrel or its trigger or its handle of polished wood will never fuse into her skin and mar her body for the rest of her life.

I turn the key to the Volvo and back out of Michelle's endless driveway, then pull over in the middle of the block and switch off the ignition. I sit in my car and breathe deeply, as if before a plunge underwater. Although my mind registers the surroundings and my eyes pass the images to my brain—a patch of lawn in front of a wrought-iron fence, a line of cement squares called a sidewalk—none of them seems to fit into this new reality. Next to my car is a pole with a No Parking sign. STREET WEEPING, says the sign, the only part of the landscape that makes sense—until I see that the letter s in the second word is hidden behind a bolt holding the sign to the pole. Nevertheless, with the encouragement from the parking regulation, I open the window and do some street weeping of my own, grateful to the darkness and the late hour and the suburban emptiness.

When I am finished, I decide I am not going to upset Andy if he doesn't already know about Sasha's tattoos. What can we do now anyway, when she has already done what she has done? I think of the time when she had chicken pox at five, when she accidentally pulled a scab off her forehead and I felt desperate because I thought she would be scarred for life. Is it my fault that she now feels a need to scar herself, to brand her body with a permanent mark—of what? Of my rejection? Of my impossible demands? Of her failure to be Russian enough for me?

It makes me nauseous to think that my daughter is just like all those miscreants in Soviet jails we used to despise back home, those societal dregs who couldn't string words into a grammatical sentence or find Europe on a map. When I was eighteen, my friend Roman and I took an overnight train ride from Arkhangel'sk to Leningrad, a ticket with the unbelievably low fare of five rubles. As soon as the train departed, it turned out that the car we were in was full of convicts being moved between prisons, and I spent the entire night facing the wall on the upper berth, a threadbare blanket pulled over my head. All I saw was a man snoring on the berth across from mine, his bare arm hanging off the side, skin full of blue anchors, smudged lines of sailor wisdom, and naked women with balloon-like breasts.

At home, I go straight to the computer and try to get onto Facebook to see Sasha's pictures, which I dread even to imagine. I know nothing about Facebook, but I realize I need to make up a name to become my daughter's friend. "Chekhov," I type frantically, as if she wouldn't figure out instantly this friend seeker's deafening identity. I hunker down in front of the computer screen in a feverish effort to channel my desperation into the vacuity of busywork, of senseless key striking that leads to nothing. I am a failure, again, already rejected by Sasha as a mother and, now, as a Facebook friend called Chekhov.

ॐ

At night I dream that Sasha has tattooed her face. I don't know that I am only dreaming, so in my mouth it tastes like gall. She is outside, tall and leggy in her skinny jeans, standing with her back to me. When she turns, I see that her beautiful face is branded with wiggly blue lines and dots, the permanent scars no time will be able to erase.

I dream—a dream I've had several times in the past—of getting on an Aeroflot flight to Leningrad. There is always a ticket waiting for me, even when I call only a few hours before departure time. Both my passports, Russian and American, are in order, and the cabin of the plane is luxurious, vaster than any airplane I have ever seen. The flight attendants disperse un-Russian graciousness, their faces lit with seemingly genuine smiles. We eat and drink and languish in the splendid lounge, but no matter how long the jet flies eastward, I never arrive home.

# PART 4

# *Mama*

# Forty-Four

There was a time—those first few years of my life that do not leave an imprint on the memory—when Mama and I were one. When I was still attached to her by so many invisible strings, when we shared one soul. When she woke up in the middle of the night to check if I was breathing in my crib, when I somehow knew that she was bending over me, smelling of sleep. We were one: she was in me and I was in her, and she knew what I wanted at any given moment, and I knew what she was ready to give: everything. I can glean this from old photographs, those snapshots taken at home where I used to melt into her arms, burrowing into her chest, curling up in her lap. At five or six I would roll into Mama's bed because my feet were cold. I would press into her with my entire body, squeezing my feet under her soft thighs, stealing her warmth. "They're cold like frogs, your little *nozhki*," she used to murmur, warming me with her embrace.

Then we separated. Was it in first grade, when no one picked me up on the first day of school because of a miscommunication between Mama and the teacher, when I walked home alone, surrounded by clanging streetcars and rumbling trucks, basking in my power to be able to cross streets by myself? Was it when the three of us—Mama, Marina, and I—stood in a phone booth, rain streaking down the glass, my wooden fingers dialing my father's hospital number, the indifferent voice on the other end of the line saying that he had died?

When did Sasha separate from me? I remember looking at her standing in our living room holding on to the side of the coffee table. She had just learned how to walk, making little steps, wobbly and tentative yet resolute. She ambled forward on her own, refusing help, and I had an intense, almost physical sensation at that moment that our paths had begun to part.

℘

Every week Mama speaks on the phone with the mothers of my two Leningrad girlfriends, Tania and Julia. Tania, with whom I shared the last two years of high school, has two grown sons and now lives near Princeton, an hour and a half away, with her husband and mother. Julia, who studied with me at the English department of Leningrad University, lives with her husband and mother in Nutley. Mama did not know Faina or Irina—Tania's and Julia's mothers—when she lived in Leningrad, but here they are her close friends, in the absence of the real friends she left behind. Since she was the first mother to arrive in this country, she gives them survival advice and teaches them what is expected here.

Mama introduces them to *Wheel of Fortune,* which she turns on at seven every evening, sometimes guessing the words before the contestants do. She tells Faina and Irina to watch the Weather Channel, easy to understand because it has pictures of little suns and clouds. She explains the idea of coupons and the necessity of taking calcium. But most important, she tells them how to behave around their sons-in-law. She is shrewd, my mother, steeled by famine and war, trained by the decades of Soviet doublethink, so she has already mastered this strategy. She has learned not to say anything even when her daughter and son-in-law go to a restaurant, ignoring a pot of stew waiting in the refrigerator, even when they buy a brand-new television and throw out the old one simply because the remote control no longer works. She has learned to be silent about all the waste she witnesses in this country: lights she has had to switch off, unused leftovers she has clandestinely removed from our refrigerator and relocated to her tiny icebox downstairs, plastic shopping bags she has rescued from the garbage.

Now, with the authority earned by time, she shares the skills she has acquired with my friends' mothers, her new audience. From the height of her American experience, she teaches them not to criticize their sons-in-law in front of their daughters.

"Don't say anything," she advises in her teacher's voice into the phone. "You can think anything you want, but keep it to yourself. After all, the husband is the one who works, who brings home the money. He takes care of everything in the house; he takes care of you."

She gives examples of how she has learned to keep the commentary to herself, despite her disapproval. "My daughter and her husband—ours—have been dressing Sasha as if they lived in the tropics." Mama always calls the family and relatives *ours*, *svoi*, as opposed to all those *chuzhoi*, unworthy of our sympathy and our telephone time. "It came from Andy, I'm sure of it—this American disregard for cold seasons, this obsession with ice and air-conditioning. And Lenochka, by now, has become infected with this silly nonsense, too."

Lenochka, she calls me, the diminutive of my name she has used since I was born. As usual, I am annoyed at Mama for making comments about my life, but her Lenochka rolls off her tongue like a piece of caramel, softening and melting the edges of my resentment.

"But do I say anything when they rattle ice out of the freezer or turn the air conditioner on full blast?" she questions into the phone.

"I know that Sasha and I are sure to come down with a sore throat from all that frozen water and cold drafts, yet I say nothing. Not a single word."

She has said nothing since Andy, usually self-possessed, flung that pan of *kotlety* at our kitchen wall a few years ago. My mother cried and sulked and occupied her time by reading Russian thrillers and watching news from Moscow in her basement. But after a week of silence, she came up to the kitchen and made *chanakhi*, Andy's favorite Georgian soup with eggplant and lamb, letting us know by her cooking that she understood and accepted our changed roles. After all, as one of her favorite sayings advises, *When things are good you don't search for better*.

I hear her phone conversations with my girlfriends' mothers when I am in the kitchen by the basement door, and I often stay there for a minute or two to listen, just as I did in Leningrad, when Mama and Marina talked behind the door about something I was not supposed to hear.

"Of course, you and I know what's right," says Mama, to give a bit of consolation to herself and her new friends. "Americans are so carefree and naïve. They never had to struggle, never fought an enemy on their land, like we did. But we're living in this country. We have to adapt because things are different here."

Things are different here. I am the one who teaches at a college. I am the one who shops and cooks. I am the one now who worries about scarves and schools, soup and order.

I want to think that Mama no longer feels she needs to control and protect, as she did in Russia. There are no commissars here and no lines bristling with elbows. There are no party cells and mandatory meetings, no shortages of mayonnaise or winter boots. But old habits linger, and when I load her shopping cart with buckwheat and farmer cheese, she still scrutinizes the receipts in search of errors, just as she did back home. Like most Russian immigrants, she frowns at gays, illegal immigrants, and the Democratic Party, despite the fact that she is on Medicaid and SSI.

But she is also practical, my mother. She knows her life is good here. On holidays, she buys us cards with puppies and roses. To help me, she cuts out quick dinner recipes, photos of new fashions, and horoscopes, piling them up on the kitchen counter, along with advice on college majors for Sasha from the Russian-language newspaper published in Brooklyn.

# Forty-Five

Every two months I take my mother to the doctor. He is the same doctor who treated her when she complained about dizziness during her first visit here, in 1983, the doctor who almost fainted after he checked her blood pressure.

"Two thirty over one ten," he announced in a grave voice and checked it again, to make absolutely sure. "I need to send her to the hospital," he said, frowning, and it took me some time to convince him not to. I promised I would keep her resting on the couch, faithfully taking the medicine he had prescribed and measuring her blood pressure at regular intervals with the portable machine I bought at Rite Aid. "Here is my home number," said the doctor, scribbling it on a piece of paper. "Call me tonight if things get worse."

The next day, Saturday, Mama's blood pressure came down, and since that first encounter, Dr. Klughaupt's office has become a regular destination.

"How could she have lived in Russia with untreated hypertension?" he asked when we returned for an office visit.

From the slight curl in her mouth, I knew Mama was pleased and grateful that Dr. Klughaupt asked about her past. She laughed and told him her blood pressure story, which I translated bit by bit.

She went to a clinic in Leningrad just before her trip to the United States. The doctor, a woman in her fifties, with small eyes empty of compassion and thin, graying hair pulled back into a bun, sat behind the desk. She took my mother's blood pressure and wrote down the numbers in her logbook in neat, bureaucratic handwriting. No muscle twitched in her face: in her thirty-year tenure at the Central Cardiology Clinic, she had seen it all.

"How is my blood pressure?" my mother asked. "Is it still high?"

"How old are you?" said the doctor and put down her pen.

"Sixty-eight."

"Well, of course your blood pressure is high. What did you expect? It should be high at your age." The doctor's voice had an accusing tone as she trained her eyes on my mother's face. "You should know this yourself, you're a physician," she said, glancing at my mother's chart. "We don't treat sixty-eight-year-olds for hypertension. There is absolutely nothing we can do." It was my mother's fault. She had the nerve to trudge to the clinic, climb to the fifth floor, and take up the woman's valuable time with a problem as untreatable as old age.

"Ten flights of Russian stairs," Mama says. Dr. Klughaupt's eyes stare out at her in disbelief from behind his glasses when she tells him that the cardiology clinic in Leningrad is on the fifth floor of a building with no elevator. "The doctor was right," she adds, smiling. "If you made it to her office, you had a strong heart. There was nothing she could do."

෨

Is there anything that I could do? I have been living a life—teaching ESL classes, making soups, walking the dog—in which my mother, always there, in the basement of my house, has become little more than a parenthesis. In the morning I hear the exhaust fan go on in her bathroom; in the afternoon I hear a knife drumming on the cutting board as she chops vegetables for salad. Her Russian TV programs used to boom all the way up to the first floor, but when she began to lose her hearing, we bought her a pair of headphones, and now I barely hear her at all. As years pass, we talk less and less frequently, and when we do, it is about the most trivial things: dinners, television news, birthday cards from our Russian family.

ॐ

Every year Dr. Klughaupt gives my mother a flu shot. "Everyone older than sixty should get one," he says, and I believe him, as I believe everything he utters. For several years, before my mother became a U.S. citizen and eligible for Medicaid, he treated her for free.

But this fall the flu vaccine is in short supply, and even Dr. Klughaupt cannot help us. I try to explain to Mama that the shortage has to do with last year's insufficient orders by the government, but all she sees is what it means to her. There is a new anxiety in her eyes, a fear that for a whole year she is going to be at risk, vulnerable and unprotected, at the mercy of a freshly invigorated virus.

I call a local hospital that directs me to the community health services of Ridgewood. They say the few doses they received have already been assigned to newborns, the aged, and the sick. My mother is aged, I say to the woman on the other end of the phone line, who says in a practiced voice that she is truly sorry. She advises me to call the health services of the neighboring towns. You never know, she says, offering a sliver of hope; there may be a cancellation.

When I explain the sequence of my flu-related calls to her, Mama does not try to find a culprit or offer criticism of the vaccine-related bureaucracy, as she would have in the past. She is in her new survival mode, which instructs her to keep things to herself, but I can see that she is worried. I try to reassure her, trotting out arguments that I know won't convince her. You're almost never in a crowd, I say, because you mostly stay home. You'll simply hibernate with a book, I joke, like a bear in a lair. She smiles, but I can see her smile is strained.

I call more hospitals and community service centers, and finally one says that a few days from now they will administer flu shots at a local church. If we arrive early, I am told, we may be able to get on the list of those lucky enough to get an injection. I tell Mama, and the news makes her beam.

We arrive early. I go up to the three administrative women and the male nurse who run the show. They take Mama's name and age and tell me to wait. We sit on a pew in the middle of the church and watch a panel in front of us call other names. They look omnipotent and authoritarian, like the presidium of the Central Committee in the Palace of Congresses we so often saw on television—only instead of a hammer and sickle there is a stained-glass cross hanging behind them.

Every ten minutes or so my mother looks at her watch and shakes her head in dismay, as if she were going to be late for an important appointment, a meeting she couldn't miss. Her frowning brow and the bitter look in her eyes betray fear and make me get up and walk to the pulpit, where they again tell me to wait.

Only a couple of years ago we sat like this, waiting, when Mama needed her passport renewed in the Russian Consulate on the Upper East Side in New York. On a January morning, after two hours' driving from New Jersey, inching along in rush-hour traffic, we elbowed our way through a thick crowd around the consulate's front door, eliciting glances of resentment because Mama held a World War II veteran's card that allowed her to enter without waiting on line. As we pushed through the human cordon besieging the consulate, I thought of an overnight line for Finnish boots at the main department store on Nevsky Prospekt, where a woman with henna hair or a man in dark blue trackpants brandished the list of those who had spent all night on the street and could now be allowed inside the store for a chance to own a pair of European footwear. Inside the consulate building, in the entranceway to the once exquisite brownstone with columns and complicated moldings, we joined another line. The consulate, it seemed, processed its expatriated citizens like an intestinal tract would process food: by holding them all in one small space to be marinated in frustration and discomfort, then—in a slow peristaltic movement—pushing the group into the next room, where nothing was going to be done, again.

"Sir," I said in Russian to the official in a suit and tie who seemed in charge of the human peristalsis, "could a Russian war veteran please have a chair to sit down?" He winced and looked around, as if the word *sir* could not possibly refer to him, as if inside this Russian fortress in the middle of capitalist Manhattan they all still remained comrades. For the next two hours, as Mama sat waiting and I stood behind her chair like a guard, she glanced at her watch every few minutes just as she is doing now, and frowned when someone else's name was called.

We sit and wait inside the church until there are only a few people left, until finally our waiting pays off. They call Mama's name and we walk to the almighty flu presidium, where she rolls up her sleeve and gets a shot.

Outside, as we make our way to the car, I see that her face has softened and relaxed. We are both basking in the moment of release: the tension is over and the burden is off my back, at least for another year.

"I can't believe I got the vaccine," Mama says, happily. Her shuffle seems to have vanished, and her steps are again in stride with mine. "What gods should I thank for this?" she asks, looking up into the pewter autumn sky, a nonbeliever who seems to have been transformed by two hours of sitting on a pew.

I am immune to pews, so my answer is, as usual, irreverent and selfish.

"Thank me," I say.

I am in the basement of my Ridgewood house—Mama's apartment—emptying the washing machine and tossing wet clothes into the dryer. The laundry room is next to Mama's bathroom, and every week when I bring down a basket with dirty shirts and underwear, a smile rises to her lips. Our laundry gives her another chance to see me.

She is watching a figure-skating championship on a direct channel from Moscow. This is what used to occupy our evenings in Leningrad: we watched figure skating together. We knew the broadcasting times of every national, European, and world competition; we could both recite the name of every gold, silver, and bronze medal champion in the past five years. Granted, aside from *News from the Fields* and the *TV Travelers Club*, there was little else to watch on Soviet television. But figure skating was special. There was something poetic in those inhumanly high, effortless lifts, when the man glided on the ice with his arms raised and his partner slowly circled in the air above his head, hovering like a big, weightless bird, unensnared and untethered to the earth.

The skaters are all new now, and gliding over the ice in free flight is no longer sufficient to win. I linger to watch a couple crocheting a lace of steps on the ice in some European capital, dancing to a song from *West Side Story*. I wait to see their scores as they clump on their skates into the contestants' box and sit down next to their coach, a balding man with a Mediterranean mustache. Are they from Italy, I wonder, or maybe Bulgaria? The girl is still bursting with adrenaline after their dance, her arms flying as she tries to explain something to her coach. She rolls up the sleeves of her dress, and the camera freezes on a tattoo on her forearm, a starlike object with a ribbon of words we don't have a chance to read before the camera abandons them in favor of the scores that have just been posted.

"What a beautiful tattoo," Mama says.

I register her words but do not know how to react to them. My mother, who has always worshiped uniformity and order—how could she possibly attach the word *beautiful* to a tattoo? She may think that living in the West has corrupted me into liking tattoos, and this may be her way of sidling up to me, of making me want to linger in the basement, to spend more time with her than I normally do. If I allow her to breach the wall I so assiduously erected after my father died, will I lose the self I have struggled to create?

Instead of asking her what she likes about this tattoo, I let her remark float past my ears as if she had never said it. It glides into the air, just like an old, legendary figure skater we both remember, and then it is gone.

I go back to my laundry, feeling guilty for shutting her out, resenting that she is always here, a constant witness to every moment of my less than perfect, tattooed life.

# Forty-Six

My driving Mama to doctors becomes our usual outing, our time spent together. Every two months or so we drive to Dr. Klughaupt, her internist; and Dr. Miller, her ophthalmologist; we drive to Dr. Sevano, her cardiologist; and Dr. Stahl, her retina specialist. Every six weeks, we drive to Dr. Phillips, her podiatrist.

Mama likes going to doctors. For fifteen minutes, she is the center of attention, stepping on the scale, rolling up her sleeve for a blood pressure cuff, steadying her chin on the shelf of an eye scanner. After we leave the office, she wants to know what the doctor said about her health. They all say that for her age she is doing fabulously well, but she does not believe me. My legs don't want to walk, she laments. My head spins when I get up, she grumbles. My heart hurts when I wake up at night.

I want to tell her that my heart hurts, too. It hurts to watch her slowly deteriorate: to see her shuffle around the basement in her slippers, holding on to the bed railing; to have to speak to her in short, loud phrases that always sound demanding because she can no longer hear well; to see her tread cautiously across the parking lot, propping herself on a cane. Her face has collapsed in a cascade of wrinkles; her body fat has melted away, making her skin hang off the bones like an ill-fitting suit; her spine has bent, robbing her of a few inches of height.

Is this the reason why I don't go down to the basement as often anymore? She seems so needy—for manifestations of love, perhaps, for more attention from me, for buckwheat with onions I am too busy to cook. I seem to punish her by letting her read and watch TV instead of leafing through our family photo albums together, instead of drinking black currant tea, my grandma's favorite, with her. She has become so humble and quiet in the last few years, yet I don't seem to muster enough generosity to forgive her—for what? For living with me, inadvertently turning me into a spoiled child? For never allowing me to grow up?

I am always one floor above her, close enough to be there in an emergency but distant enough to be able to deny the inevitable a little longer.

❧

We have her cataracts fixed, one eye after the other, and the world opens up to her, she says. She can see the smallest branches on the trees along the parkway as we drive back home, she marvels, able to make out their tiny leaves curling open. She can read the letters on the signs and the numbers of the exits. She can watch Russian movies without the blurry background and the pellicle of gauze over the picture. For the first time in many years, she can read her Russian books without a magnifying glass.

Before we leave the eye surgeon's office, he checks her one more time to see that everything is fine. It is.

"How old is she?" he asks.

"Ninety-six."

He shakes his head, impressed. "It's good she is still here with you."

I vigorously nod in agreement. It has only recently occurred to me that she would ever not be here.

છ

Sasha is back home. She has just graduated from the University of Vermont, magna cum laude. Her hair is back to her normal light brown color, and she is now dressed in clothes not exclusively found in the Salvation Army stores. I notice her carefully lined eyes, her emerald-painted nails, her high cheeks touched by rouge. When she moved back from Vermont, she sold her gun. The tops she wears around me are all long-sleeved.

"What's her specialty?" Mama asks. Many decades ago, my mother graduated with a specialty in medicine; later, on my diploma from Leningrad University, my specialty was listed as English philology. Every Russian graduate had a specialty, written in a calligraphic handwriting into the blue passport of a diploma.

"Sociology," I say. "She is into humanities, just like me." I don't mention that, as useless in terms of employment as a degree in sociology may be, Sasha has just announced that she wants to try something altogether different, something even less commercial and practical, if this were possible. She wants to try to become a photographer, she has told us, maybe because she took a year of photography at Bard College before she decided that she no longer needed higher education.

I say nothing about photography to my mother because I need time to digest this new development. I need to present the new career prospects calmly, arguing that photography is as lucrative as accounting, as promising and reasonable as teaching. I don't want my mother to get worried about Sasha's future. I don't want her to give me advice on how to change Sasha's mind or on the best way to switch to a more profitable career, something she heard on a commercial watching one of her Russian TV channels. This is how I have communicated with Mama for years: always presenting the summary of the outcomes, never the curves of the process. Always putting her in front of a decision already made, never asking for any input I may have needed earlier.

Is this what Sasha has just done by announcing her photographic aspirations? Does she communicate with me the same way I have been communicating with my own mother? After all, she didn't ask me whether she should try to be a freelance artist in the most unforgiving place, New York; she simply placed me in front of the fact that she was going to do it.

I coax Deema—our terrier, who is already twelve and prefers sleeping to running outside—out of his bed in the kitchen and take him for a walk. He stops and looks around, trying to stall being dragged into the drizzly afternoon, but I pull on the leash toward the street because I need time to think, to have the rain cool my face. I know I am supposed to feel worried about this unforeseen course of events, about the questionable prospect of an introvert breaking into one of the most competitive fields in the world. I am not sure if Sasha has the gift to be a photographer, but I know she doesn't have the technical skills, and it will cost her time and fierce dedication to learn them. My mind tells me I should try to dissuade my daughter from stepping on the risky path she is trying to chart for herself, unless Andy and I are willing to support her for the rest of our lives.

Instead, as Deema and I plod under the drizzle around the block, I feel relieved that Sasha will not have to sit in a cubicle eight hours a day, five days a week, for the next forty years. This is the decision I made when I was twenty-two, after a year of forty-hour weeks behind a secretary's desk. Just as Sasha, I couldn't see my life erased by sameness. And now, by the time my dog and I reach our driveway and escape the rain under the patio roof, I am thrilled, perhaps foolishly and irresponsibly, that every day of my daughter's life, no matter how hard-earned, is going to be a new adventure. By the time I unhook Deema's leash from his collar, I feel proud of her decision to discard all those sociological hypotheses she spent years mastering. I am glad that, of all the possibilities rolled out before her, she has chosen to become an artist.

Knowing how I feel, I am now ready to face my mother. We go

downstairs together, Sasha and I. Mama is bent in front of her small refrigerator, taking out vegetables for the daily mountain of salad she chops up. One by one, she slowly and meticulously removes a bag with radishes, half a pepper, quarter of an onion, a long cucumber sheathed in plastic skin.

"Sashenka!" Mama beams when she sees us, and for a moment her eyes almost sink into small waves of skin. She holds out her arms and presses my daughter to her chest. I haven't hugged Mama in a long time, but I can still feel the pillowy softness of her breasts, the visceral sense of comfort that has stayed with me since I got lost in the woods on a mushroom hunt when I was ten. She smelled of kitchen and the woody inside of our armoire then. Later, she smelled of valerian drops and mothballs, of autumn apples and raspberry jam. She smelled of perfume called Red Moscow and of the old leather address book she always carried in her purse. Now she smells of dry skin, the Jergens moisturizer I buy her at the A&P, and the special diabetic herb tea I bring from my Russian trips.

We tell Mama that Sasha has graduated "with excellence," using the Russian expression for all A's. We tell her about photography.

"Very good," Mama says, without hesitation. "You will be great at it, Sashenka, if that's what you like." She has become easygoing, my mother, ready to accept anything from Sasha or me or Marina or Andy because we are the only *ours* left in her life here.

The phone rings upstairs, and I turn to go back into the kitchen. Mama is still holding on to Sasha's wrist, gently making her stay a little longer.

When I hang up on a recorded sales call, I go to the open basement door and listen. I hear Sasha saying something; I hear her beginning to climb the stairs.

I step over to the sink, pretending I wasn't craning my neck by the doorframe, pretending I am busy with the dishes.

"Babusya asks if you could go back down," Sasha says, emerging from the basement.

"I just came from there. What does she want?"

Sasha regards the basket with fruit, takes an apple, peers at me for a few seconds.

"She wants *you*," she says, and I know that my daughter sees and understands everything, just as I thought I did when I lived in Leningrad.

# *Forty-Seven*

"I'm living for Yuva and Sima," Mama often says, referring to her two younger brothers, and this is why I believe in her immortality.

Yuva, the youngest in her family, had been stationed on the border with Poland before the war began, writing only one letter home, a triangle of gray paper my grandma kept on the bottom of a drawer for the rest of her life. "They feed us well here, thick soup and boiled potatoes," he wrote for her sake. "Yesterday the sergeant said they might soon issue us guns." Mama could never understand why soldiers on the Polish border, right before the German blitzkrieg into Russia, did not have guns. After the war, the family filed numerous inquiries about Yuva's fate, but until today no one knows exactly what happened to his unarmed battalion stationed to protect the country from invasion.

Mama tells me that, for many years after the war, my grandma ran outside the house at every creak of their front gate to see if it was Yuva returning home. Maybe he had to walk all the way back from Berlin, she reasoned. Or maybe he was wounded and had amnesia, and is now living in another town under a different name, just as she remembered him, a nineteen-year-old boy with blue eyes and unruly copper hair. Until her death in 1968, Grandma refused to believe what Mama had known since the end of the war, that, along with thousands of other youths, Yuva had been plowed into the warm earth in the first hours of the blitzkrieg, when the army of German tanks crossed into the Soviet Union on June 22, 1941.

Sima, three years younger than Mama, was wounded at the front and made his way back home to Ivanovo in 1942. This is how Mama tells me she remembers that day: It was January, and there was a knock on the door. When Grandma opened the latch, there stood Sima—in a military coat with burnt bullet holes, on crutches, in a torn *ushanka* hat tied under his chin. The hospital could no longer do anything, so they released him. Sima decided not to write home because he wanted to surprise everyone with his arrival. My grandma, wiping under her eyes and making happy sniffling noises, boiled water for him to wash, as Grandpa ordered Sima to take his clothes off immediately—everything down to the rags inside his boots—so he could throw the dirty heap outside, where it was minus twenty degrees Celsius, to save the rest of them from typhus and lice.

Mama says she was furious that a doctor at a front hospital failed to operate properly, leaving a shard of a grenade lodged in her brother's lung. Her voice is low and even now, but there is still a quiet sadness in the rhythm of her words, a regret that her brother hadn't been brought to her own front-line hospital, where she would have removed that last piece of metal from his lung and made him live. That sliver caused a metastatic abscess in his brain, Mama says, and I imagine slow tentacles worming their way from Sima's lung into his head, slithering into his eyes and ears, robbing him of hearing and sight. I imagine Mama sitting by his bed, taking his temperature and peering into his throat, pretending that whatever small medical procedures she performed could make a difference. She kept pretending for Grandma, who still ran outside at every creak of the gate, hoping that Yuva, her youngest son, would walk in, miraculously alive.

Before the war, Sima graduated from the Leningrad Art School, and two of his paintings have made it across the ocean and now hang on the walls of Mama's Ridgewood room. Above her bed is a portrait of my young mother, her lips curled in a happy smile I rarely saw when we lived in Leningrad, the smile that had been wiped off by the war and, later, by the slightly less deadly injuries of Soviet life. Above her table is an oil painting of a soldier throwing a grenade at a tank, the man's uniformed back tense and determined, the tank halted by yellow tongues of flame leaping into the sky.

Every year, Mama reminds me of the day when Sima died, three weeks before my sister's birthday, two months after the birthday of my father. The cemetery was about a kilometer away, where two men with unshaved, veiny faces helped Grandpa lower the coffin into a grave they had dug earlier in the day for a liter of moonshine. Grandma bent down, scooped a handful of wet, heavy dirt, and tossed it into the grave; it hit the lid of the coffin with a thump. My grandfather had to hold her and lead her back since she couldn't see where she was going, tears spilling from her eyes and clouding her glasses. She felt numb, her insides parched and shriveled up, and she leaned on Grandpa's arm, blindly following his lead, wondering why there were any tears left in her at all.

Mama is living for her younger brothers, she says, the two who didn't have a chance to live. Yuva was nineteen when German tanks rolled over the Soviet border. Sima was twenty-four when he died from a wound in his childhood house in 1942. There are a lot of unlived years for my mother to claim.

∞

Mama is lying in bed at Valley Hospital in Ridgewood, hooked to an IV and an oxygen tank. She had grown frail prior to her scheduled departure for New Orleans for an annual three-month winter stay at my sister's. The day before her flight she had difficulty breathing and could barely get out of bed. I was at work on the morning I called Dr. Klughaupt, who told me to call 911.

When I got to the hospital, my mother was just being admitted to the cardio unit. "Congestive heart failure," said a soft-spoken woman in her thirties, whose badge identified her as Dr. Sharma, a hospitalist. The words *heart failure* sounded so daunting, so distressing. There is a skinny brochure on Mama's blanket, "Living with Heart Failure," a title that sounds like an oxymoron. I try to find a suitable translation of the term *heart failure* for Mama; in Russian, it turns out, they call it heart deficiency, a more merciful term, with room for a less drastic outcome.

Mama smiles when she sees me, relieved. She looks tiny in the middle of the tangle of tubes, her gnarled fingers over the cover, like a small bird's claws.

"Lenochka," she says, "I'm so glad you're here."

She tells me how they brought her to the hospital, how she spent several hours in the ER, speaking to doctors through a translator. She shows me her IV and her oxygen tubes; she points to a special blue phone behind her bed that connects her to a Russian speaker if she needs to ask a question. She is feeling better, she says, with the oxygen and the nitroglycerin patch pasted to her chest.

I sit on her bed and listen, watching the nurse check Mama's meds by the computer screen, helping her out of the bed and into an armchair when a man in a chef's white hat brings dinner at five. I listen and utter short, meaningless sentences as sharp, uncomfortable questions scratch around in my head. How did this all happen, these oxygen tubes and the IV bag slowly emptying into her arm? Did I ignore her complaints about dizziness, her wheezing on the basement stairs, her frequent refrain that her legs refused to walk?

I come back home from the hospital and go down to the basement, where a packed suitcase is still sitting on her bed. Her cup is on the table, filled with chamomile tea, now cold. Her shoes are neatly lined up under the nightstand; they must have taken her to the emergency room in her slippers. I look at the Russian detective mystery she has been reading, bookmarked on her bed next to the portable blood pressure machine. I look at the dozen photo albums—different styles and sizes filled with pictures from her American life—stacked on the shelf; at her last war medal framed on the wall, the one she received from the Russian Consulate in celebration of the fiftieth anniversary of victory in World War II.

With Mama not here, her room looks eerie and sad. I go upstairs, dial Sasha in Brooklyn, where she now lives, and tell her Babusya has been taken to the hospital. I want to tell her to come here as soon as possible, but my daughter seems to be able to read my mind. She will be here tomorrow morning, she says, then pauses. "Do you need me to come over tonight?" she asks, and I hear a little girl voice I hadn't heard in years—the voice of a good daughter—the voice my mother should have heard earlier today.

ॐ

We hire the Ukrainian aide, Sveta, to come to our house three times a week to help Mama with a shower and meals. Quick and efficient, Sveta is done with the chores in an hour, and for the rest of the time they watch Russian television together or lean over family photo albums, with Mama pointing out every relative and every occasion that necessitated a shutter click. I stop by the basement door and listen to their soft banter, to Mama's voice explaining the family connections.

This is what I should be doing, I think: sitting next to her, the two of us looking back on our past.

ॐ

My home phone rings at eleven at night, and my heart seems to stop when I see my mother's number downstairs.

"I fell," she whispers into the receiver, her voice almost unrecognizable. I run down the stairs and see her lying on her side, in her blue and white nightgown, stretched between the bathroom and the bed.

I carefully pull her up to her knees; then she helps me seat her on the bed. She doesn't cry out in pain, and I hold on to a little hope that she didn't break any bones. "What happened?" I ask.

"My legs just gave," she says, "I don't know how. Thank god I was able to reach the phone."

There is panic in her eyes—something so uncharacteristic of my tenacious, survivor mother—a fear of what would have happened if she couldn't call me.

Her eyes brim with many fears lately: a fear that she won't be able to walk or hear, that the birthday we marked last week will be her last, that her heart will fail her and I won't be there, by her side, to hold her hand.

&#8450;

It is the end of March, my spring break, and Marina comes to stay with Mama while Andy and I take a five-day trip to Chicago. I go over Mama's medications with my sister; I show her how to paste a nitroglycerin patch on Mama's chest.

I say good-bye to Mama. She gets up from the bed and we kiss each other on the cheeks three times, the Russian way. Her eyes are pale blue, smiling: it doesn't happen too often that she has a chance to see both daughters together.

"We'll be back on Tuesday," I say. "Will see you in a few days."

"Rest well in Chicago," she says, holding me in her arms a little longer. "Rest from me," she adds, a smile spreading to her lips.

I smile. I know I should tell her I have nothing to rest from, but I don't.

"*Schastlivo vam.*" I wave to both Mama and Marina from the door. It's a Russian going-away saying, a sort of *may fortune be with you* wish.

# Forty-Eight

Marina tells me how it happened. It was nighttime and Mama was in bed, watching her favorite figure-skating program. "I'll come down again," my sister said, "to say good night." An hour later, when she got to the basement, Mama was unconscious. Marina yelled her name and shook her. When she didn't respond, my sister called 911.

We want to think that Mama simply fell asleep, simply glided off to another world.

An ambulance came and took her to the emergency room. This time she remained there for only twenty minutes. Then she was gone from the hospital, gone from our house, gone from life.

Andy and I spent that night in Chicago on the phone with United Airlines. They got us on a flight back the next morning, at the alarming price of $1,137. It was almost a relief to argue with a ticket agent, then her supervisor, in a futile attempt to understand how, under the circumstances, they could charge us eight hundred dollars in excess of the flight we booked originally. For half an hour, asking in vain for logic and compassion from a corporation distracted us from allowing the truth to sink in. With a cell phone pressed to my ear, I paced the room of our hotel, my arguments circling as desperately as my feet. As long as I held on to the agent on the phone, it seemed, our return home—the reason for our unplanned departure—was not yet final.

Marina met us outside; we hugged and tried not to cry. Andy made the necessary calls. Sasha drove from Brooklyn, and the four of us sat in the living room all day, talking a little, staring at the floor, eating food from a local restaurant sent by Frankie's daughters, who know what to do when someone dies. The sun crept in through the curtains and painted saffron lines across the floor; then the air became grainy and thickened into dusk. At night, my Leningrad girlfriend Tania drove in from work, and we sat and ate some more. There was comfort in our common passivity, in letting hopelessness and grief swaddle us, make us as helpless as infants, reduce us to nothing at all.

છ

The next day we go to a funeral home to say good-bye. The undertaker opens the doors into a room, and we reluctantly creep in. It smells of flowers, a sickeningly sweet smell I remember from my father's funeral. We don't want to be here, but we know we must be here. We take a deep breath and look.

Mama is in the front of the room, on a table, dressed in her usual gray pants and a wool cardigan she liked to wear at home. We cluster in the corner, six feet away, humbled by the presence of death. Sasha turns to Andy and begins to sob. For a few minutes, we huddle together before approaching the table one by one.

As Andy is standing before Mama, I wonder what he is thinking. What is he saying to her in his mind? Whatever it is, I know she can't understand it. Or maybe she understands it perfectly. No matter how hard she tried, she never learned enough English to be able to speak to her son-in-law. For many years, she diligently wrote down exercises and listened to tapes until she succumbed to the realization that, in her own words, she simply had no ear for foreign language. Maybe that was why Andy was a good son-in-law to my mother: they spoke in broad gestures, devoid of the nuances of intonation. Unlike me, Andy never lost patience with my mother during the last few years, when she shriveled and turned weak.

He lays his hand on hers and then walks away.

Sasha approaches the table tentatively, wiping her eyes, trying not to look straight ahead at Babusya, bereft of life. I imagine her summoning all those years of Russian to her rescue, fishing for words she never said to Grandma while she was alive. The words the three of us—Mama, Marina, and I—were too tough to say to one another in Leningrad, as we were so preoccupied with survival, with the never-ending struggle to carve out our own slices of privacy.

Marina takes Mama's hand and stands still for a few minutes, looking down. She has lived longer with Mama than I have, a life that started in Ivanovo during the war, continued in Leningrad, and concluded on the other side of the Atlantic. Does she regret that all those years she took Mama for granted, as I did? That she sometimes aimed her stage voice at Mama, over the phone from New Orleans and in person during the winter months our mother stayed there? That's how I speak, she would always say to defend herself. That's what they taught us in acting school. This morning Marina told me of an odd coincidence: in her last film role the character she played tried to wake up her dead mother shaking her by the shoulders, just as my sister had to do two days ago. The scene had made her sink to such murky emotional depths that she wailed for hours after the shoot was over, sobbing on the Petersburg bus all the way home. "Was it a premonition?" asked Marina before we came to the funeral home, and I knew that in her mind it wasn't really a question. "My last role," she said quietly and shook her head. My sister's face looks older, and she lumbers out of the room looking down.

They all leave the room, and I know it is finally my turn.

I stand over my mother, so familiar and already such a stranger. Her hands are gnarled with arthritis, but the sharpness of joints has dulled, leaving the skin thick and white. Her face is white, too, cheeks and lips touched slightly by the undertaker's rouge. I look at her chest, as I have done many times when she would fall asleep in her bed, only now it doesn't move. I lean down and kiss Mama on the forehead. Her skin, so soft and warm, so permeated with the smell of our Leningrad apartment, is now cold as stone. I wipe away the sobs and snot with a bunch of napkins Andy stuffed into my hand before he left the room.

"Forgive me, Mamochka, if you can," I whisper, hearing this last pathetic plea dissolve in the emptiness of the echoey room. But as soon as the words leave my mouth my request invalidates itself: I know, of course, that she can. I know that, despite her strict façade and her Russian toughness, she always forgave me everything.

∞

When I wake up in the middle of the night, the enormity of loss presses on my heart, constricts my temples, drives my head deeper into the pillow. I lie in bed with my eyes closed and wait for morning. Once in a while I fall back to sleep and have dreams. An old woman is walking toward me, her head down, slowly and meticulously measuring the ground with her cane. *Tuk-tuk*, the sound in rhythm with her plodding steps. The contours of her body and her movements are so familiar that I am certain it is my mother. One more *tuk* toward me and I know it is Mama. I feel so light-headed and happy that I have been granted one more chance to see her and to hold her, a final opportunity to say to her I love her. She will look up and see me any moment now. Lenochka, she will say, and her papery skin will crease in a smile. The woman lifts her head and looks at me, a face I've never seen. I hastily turn away and run, a single thought bouncing around in my head: Who will ever be as happy to see me as Mama was? Who will call me Lenochka now?

∞

I have kept stacks of Mama's letters from when she still lived in Leningrad, and I am sitting in her basement apartment, unfolding the lined pages filled with her squared handwriting. I read each letter, lingering over every page, scrutinizing every sentence, in an attempt to glimpse something that eluded me when she was alive but that would surely stand out now. For over a half century—my whole life—I have defined myself against her, and now, with Mama gone, I have to figure out who I am. I read letter after letter, beginning with 1982, when Andy and I moved to our Nutley house.

*My dearest Lenochka and Andy*, she wrote carefully many times over the years, followed by the descriptions of holiday and birthday celebrations, of bouts with Soviet bureaucracy, of fights with drunken plumbers, of colds, play openings, and chores. She diligently wrote of her numerous trips to Kineshma to see her younger sister, Muza, to go to the graves of her parents and her younger brother Sima, to visit, in Mama's words, both the living and the dead. She documented the gradual disappearance of food from Leningrad stores: *there is nothing but bones on meat counters*, she wrote in January 1982; *cheese has vanished entirely and there are lines for butter*, she told me in March 1983. Then she consoled herself with this: *Kineshma's stores are even emptier, and no one there has died of hunger yet.*

Among the letters I stumble onto a note Mama must have left in our Leningrad apartment for my sister. *Marisha, here is a ruble,* her squared words spell. *Buy two bottles of milk and see how things are with bread. Please water the plants.* I put down the note; I stuff the letters back into their airmail envelopes. Again, it is bread and milk and chores, the things that make up a life. There are no revelations—just a series of ordinary moments, too humble for redemption.

# PART 5

# *Petersburg*

# *Forty-Nine*

I am in Leningrad, now St. Petersburg, my former home. I come here every year, like a felon drawn to the site of the crime. I zip my American passport into the inner pocket of my handbag and pull out my Russian one—the red identification replacing the blue—as the plane taxis past the edge of the northern forest and stops at one of the eight gates of Pulkovo International Airport.

But this trip is different. Next to me is Sasha, on her first voluntary trip to Russia since we dragged her across the ocean, screaming through most of the twelve hours of the SAS flights, when she was eleven months old. Mama was with us, happy in her new role of a babushka visiting from overseas, and our bags were filled with Pampers, bottled water, and little jars of Earth's Best baby food.

This time, when my daughter asked me if she could come along, she looked anxious for the few moments it took me to respond, as if she entertained the possibility that I could have said no.

On our arrival at Pulkovo Airport we found out that, in addition to the school graduation festival, the week we chose to visit my hometown was the week of the International Economic Forum, when police-escorted motorcades whip through the city center, closing roads and clogging streets. Still, it was the prime week of white nights, and for the graduation fireworks Vladimir Putin had guaranteed a clear sky: clouds not complying with the dry executive order would be immediately shot with storm-dispersing chemicals.

I knew I was home.

Nina and her second husband, Sergei, were waiting for us at the airport, waving from behind the glass door that still separates Russia from the rest of the world. It took us two and a half hours of Nina lamenting and Sergei swearing under his breath to get from the airport to their apartment. We inched forward in maddening traffic, jammed amid creaky Volgas, gleaming BMWs, and trolley buses tethered to electric wires overhead. In disbelief, Sasha stared out at a Mercedes SUV that veered onto the sidewalk for a shortcut, its horn blaring at pedestrians to get out of the way.

Our room at Nina's apartment, with eleven-foot ceilings and a faint smell of wool coats and warm tea, makes me instantly home-sick. The window looks out onto a square of asphalt and an island of rickety trees amid unmowed grass—one of the many courtyards familiar to everyone who was born here. I think of my own court-yard and of a quiet stretch of the Neva embankment a few blocks away from the apartment building where I used to live, the two main destinations of this trip. Their images rise in my mind—sharpened by the anticipation of what my daughter and I have come here to do—and make me feverish and restless.

∽

For a week, Sasha and I enjoy guest status at Nina's apartment. After a day of walking with my daughter on the paths of the enor-mous Field of Mars hidden under the froth of blooming lilacs, of standing on the hunchback bridges over the canals that crochet the city into a lacework of 101 islands, we climb the stairs to Nina's fifth-floor apartment for a nightly feast. The table in her tiny kitchen brims with cucumber and tomato salad, boiled potatoes with wild mushrooms that Nina and Sergei have picked on their trips to Finland, pan-fried zucchini with onions Nina made for Sasha, and chunks of hot-smoked salmon, wrapped with thick ropes, from a local farm market. We sit on the balcony and drink Argentinean wine from a supermarket called Okay until the brief dusk lifts and light begins to spread through poplar branches rising all the way up to our windows.

I take deep breaths, as if inhaling pure oxygen, as if I were a consumption patient bathing my scarred lungs in the city's healing breeze. This luminous air, and the arms of open bridges, and the atmosphere of sleeplessness, and the vague anticipation that invariably hangs in the dusk of a June night are still here as they have always been before. Only now—maybe because my grown-up American daughter is here—it finally dawns on me that they are no longer mine. They belong to Nina and Sergei and their few remaining family and friends—to all those who have stayed here.

∽

When I look at Sasha, I see Andy's length of bone and my young mother's inner luminosity that makes her skin glow from within in the sleepless sun of Petersburg's white nights. She is twenty-four, the age I was when I left this city. She is a photographer now, the most unlikely career, short of being an actor, I could have conjured up for my self-conscious and introverted daughter. Like every child, she is—and may always remain, at least to me—a mystery.

She began as an intern in New York City, graduating to a photographer's assistant after eight months of unpaid work; then learned—pretty much on her own—the complex intricacies of digital technology and professional photo retouching. She has assisted on many photo shoots and retouched a number of pictures for major glossy magazines that I proudly lift off the Barnes & Noble shelves. Andy and I no longer have to support her. Just a few months earlier, she completed her first freelance photography assignment for one of those gleaming issues. Her work is now published, with her name in the byline following her title, photographer. She can read Russian, and she tries to speak my native language to Nina and Sergei—in simple phrases but with almost no trace of a foreign accent.

As we walk around Petersburg, she looks for interesting shots, and my city is always ready to oblige. She captures images of a pack of homeless dogs crossing a major street, six motley mutts with torn ears and patches of missing fur following their leader, a German shepherd mix with a limp. She trains her camera on two enormous ravens perched in the poplar tree next to Nina's apartment building, cawing loudly—a sinister omen, according to my mother—and I whisper the magic words Mama used to utter to protect me from bad luck every time she heard a crow's cackle.

We pass a student dorm, and my daughter kneels on the sidewalk to snap a shot of a message sprayed on the wall: I'VE BEEN DEREGISTERED. CALL ME AT 114-2875. OLGA. Sasha doesn't understand what this means, and I tell her that we all had to be registered with our district militia at the address of our residence when the city was called Leningrad, a requirement that has survived all the historic upheavals of the last three decades. Olga must have failed out of school and been ordered to leave the city. I tell Sasha that I, too, was deregistered from Leningrad over thirty years ago, but there is no number left where anyone can reach me.

We walk around my city until our feet hurt, adding our footprints to the dust of the streets that I hope will remember every prodigal resident of this subarctic marsh abuzz with mosquitoes. We walk and walk through the limpid air of day and night, as though the constant, untiring movement could convince the city to take me back, as though I could fool the bronze horses and the cobblestones of Palace Square—the place where wars and revolutions happen with eerie regularity—that, after more than a quarter century living on a different continent speaking another language, I still belong here.

# *Fifty*

The street under the windows of my apartment, which was Maklina Prospekt when I lived here, is now called Angliisky, or English, Prospekt. It is ironic, I think, that only after the fall of communism did they rename my street after the passion I had harbored for as long as I lived in this city.

Sasha and I walk away from where Griboedova Canal makes a sudden bend, past the building where my high school friends Tania and Nadia used to live, across a small bridge where the street stops, as though astonished by the sudden expanse of the river that springs before our eyes. This is the unglamorous part of the city, too ordinary to be included among the glossy snapshots of bronze statues and golden domes, a shipbuilding district with construction cranes stretching their necks into the sky.

My old school, where I deciphered the mysteries of the English language, is just around the corner, and the previously abandoned historic triangle called New Holland, wedged between the two sleeves of the canal where Peter the Great built the first vessels of the Russian Fleet, boasts newly restored brick gates and expanses of shaved grass. The view of the canal's wrought-iron banisters juxtaposed against the Neva with the university buildings in the distance, as if etched into the low pewter sky, is so familiar it wrenches my heart.

We stand by the granite banister and look down on the lazy waves that lick the stone when a boat passes by.

"Would you like to do the honors?" I ask Sasha.

"Not really," she says. "I'm not sure I can do this."

"I thought you'd have the honor as the youngest in the family," I say, a cowardly attempt to get out of doing myself what we have come here to do. "But you're right. We should do this together."

She takes a breath and steadies herself. Out of the zipped compartment of my pocketbook I take a small plastic bag. Before Mama's ashes were buried at a cemetery in Fair Lawn, I asked for a few ounces to take with me to Russia, so that part of her would stay where she lived most of her life.

She lived three lives, my mother: first, in her native town of Ivanovo, where she lost two brothers and gave birth to my older sister; then in Leningrad, where she gave birth to me and where she buried my father; and finally, in my house in New Jersey, where she raised my daughter and wrote down the story of our family.

Sasha and I hold our arms over the water and release Mama's ashes into the salty Baltic wind she knew so well. For a few moments, they dip and swerve with the air current over the surface of the river; then they are gone, the breeze carrying them away in its gentle palm, out of our sight.

I think of what Mama must have felt when she moved here from Ivanovo, when she took the first breath of the Neva brine. It was the first big city she had ever seen, with its baroque, mint-colored curves of the Kirov Opera and Ballet Theatre only two blocks from her new apartment. I wonder what she felt walking past the eighteenth-century mansions and the golden needle of the Admiralty, what she thought of the broad avenues in the city center and the mazes of its courtyards. I wonder if she had felt as I did on my first visit to a supermarket in Princeton when she saw Leningrad grocery stores with their sawdust-covered floors and sweet smells of bologna and cheese, a gastronomic heaven after the four hundred grams of war-rationed bread in her native Ivanovo.

I think of how difficult it must have been for her to leave this northern capital of gauzy light, of how sweet it must be now to return.

&

Sasha and I are at the last stop on our Petersburg itinerary, the final destination of our trip. My childhood courtyard has been emptied by the summer: most children are in their dachas, tending reluctantly to their mothers' patches of tomato seedlings, shivering on the windy beaches of the Gulf of Finland between the watering and weeding. My old nursery school is no longer here, but hopscotch squares are still chalked on the asphalt. In the center of the yard five poplar trees, tall and creaky, rise around the playground, and tufts of their fuzzy seeds float through the air like snowflakes.

Sasha walks around the courtyard, snapping pictures of those arches between the buildings leading to other quads that tantalized me when I lived here, of crumbling bricks and little puddles pooled in cracks of asphalt. I sit on my old courtyard bench and see ghosts. They parade out of my head onto the sidewalk—preserved by time, as ageless as I am never going to be.

I see my nursery school friend Genka, who dares me to explore the vaulted hollows under the buildings—enticing, scary, and forbidden. While our teacher is distracted, Genka and I hide behind aluminum garbage bins and dive under an archway, a damp tunnel that leads to another courtyard and then to the street so maligned by our parents for its dangerous streetcars and speeding trucks.

I see the building garbageman, a gnome with black stubble sprouting through his cheeks who works in the cellar shoveling raw garbage dropped from each apartment through chutes. On rare occasions he climbs up the stairs and crouches on the ledge to smoke a hand-rolled cigarette, his smell hanging in the air long after he is gone, the smell of rotting potato peels and fish skeletons and his whole underground pool of decomposing trash.

I hear Aunt Polya—not really my aunt—in a stained apron over her round stomach, shouting at me as I am standing in the nursery school corner, punished. In her kitchen voice, she warns me about my bleak future in real school, where everyone will know not to trust me because I dared to disobey the teacher, because I am the one infamous for placing the interests of the collective beneath my own.

I look at the courtyard metal gate and see a taxi waiting to take my father to the hospital. He hangs between my mother and Marina, his arms around their shoulders, an open coat thrown over his long underwear, as if it no longer matters what he wears, as if his relevance to the world dressed in street clothes has ceased to exist. I see him through the glass recline across the backseat, reedy in his blue underwear, ashen as the sky.

Strangely, I see Frankie. When he was granted several months of remission, I offered to take him to Petersburg, and for a minute a spark ignited in his eyes before he chose to do what he had always done, take care of his daughters. I know Frankie would have liked my city, its pale façades and pearly domes the color of the overcast sky. I see him walking through the gate into the courtyard, still carefree and healthy, his head full of dark, wavy hair down to his shoulders.

"Mom," calls Sasha and shakes my arm. "Are you all right?"

I am all right. I nod, and from her smile I know she is beginning to understand something about ghosts. She is beginning to understand something about other things, too, the deeply personal and guarded things. We both are.

I think of my mother, and her face comes together before my eyes, as if my mind, like a camera, brought her features into focus. I think of our watching figure skating in her Ridgewood basement when she made a comment about a contestant's tattoo, smiling at the girl on the screen, saying the tattoo was beautiful. Was she able to sense what I never told her about my own daughter?

Sasha has finished with her photos and sits down next to me on the bench. I turn to her and take her hand. It feels like the right time, and I hope I am ready.

"So let me see those tattoos of yours," I say in Russian.

She winces at first, but then the whiff of panic in her eyes fades and I can see relief. She is glad that I've finally asked her, that I am interested in the deepest part of her, the most flawed compartment of her soul. Or maybe it is my own flaws that have drawn me to the edge of this revelation. I steady myself as she rolls up the sleeves of her shirt.

Her arms bloom with the intricate red and green design of the *matryoshka* nesting doll Marina painted for me soon after she moved to the United States, the doll that still adorns the prime space in my home, the kitchen. I think back, to the time when Sasha became interested in that doll, taking it apart and lining the pieces up on the kitchen counter, asking me all kinds of questions about my sister's design. I was thrilled by her sudden interest in Russia back then, unable to figure out the reason for her unexpected curiosity. Now, of course, everything makes sense.

I force my eyes to stay on the *matryoshka*'s red scarf amid the pattern of violets and leaves inked into my daughter's arms. Black clouds rush through my head, but I take a deep breath to steady myself and shoot them down, just as the Russian government did, dispersing rain clouds on the night of the graduation festival. I think of how Mama always loved me—despite a million things I had done to gouge more lines into her face and turn her hair as white as this courtyard in January—a sadly belated moment of recognition that makes me move closer to Sasha and drape my arm around her shoulders. I swallow what I would have said only a year ago; from now on, those words will be hidden on the lowest shelf of my soul, where they belong. My eyes are now directly above the long, wheat-colored braid of *matryoshka* my sister painted, as complicated on Sasha's skin as the original still sitting above my American refrigerator.

Russia is tattooed on my daughter's arms as permanently as it is tattooed on my heart.

We sit on the bench without moving, without saying a word.

The wind tosses the poplar snow against the playground fence, and little blizzards are whirling under the bench, around our feet, just as they did every June for the twenty-four years I lived here. The breeze brings the smells of city dust and traffic fumes, so familiar they itch my eyes. I still know this place and its people to the marrow of their bones, to their soft, unguarded core, which had once sustained my own life, yet I am as much of an outsider here as I am on the other side of the world, in my adopted country. The truth is that there is no bridge between the two lives—the past and the present—that would conveniently span the memory of loss and the promise of an onward search. There is only a wound, the inner divide of exile. A daughter of an anatomy professor, I should have known that sliced hearts do not become whole, that split souls do not mend. Along with all those who left their countries for other shores, I belong in neither land. We are unmoored and disconnected, like these poplar seeds blown into the crevices of the buildings, into the corners of the world.

I look up and see another ghost: Mama walking home from work with a string bag full of groceries, our dinner. Her hair, still brown, is brushed back away from her face and held up in a bun, as she arranged it every morning of my childhood, with me watching her patient fingers dip and twist expertly at the back of her head she couldn't see. I want to run toward her, but my legs, like in a dream, are filled with lead. When she makes another step to turn the corner, she sees me. She smiles her younger smile and opens her arms.

"Lenochka," she says, my name as soft as her cheek. "I'm so glad you've come."

Again, she is as tall as I am, and I press into her neck, into the pillows of her breasts. She smells of our Leningrad life, of the life I lived here with my mother and sister and father: of wild mushroom soup, of the dusty straw of our barn loft at the dacha, of our evening tea with bowls of black currant jam, guiltless and sweet. Tears course down my cheeks, leaving wet spots on Mama's dress with a red apple print I remember so well, and the warmth of her embrace heals and makes me feel forgiven.

# Acknowledgments

I am deeply grateful to my agent, Molly Friedrich, whose generosity and insight have guided me through the painful process of writing this memoir; and to my editor, Priscilla Painton, for her wisdom, exacting eye, and sharp scissors.

My appreciation goes to my early readers Mervyn Rothstein, Irina Veletskaya, and Sydney Tanigawa, for their support and honesty. I thank Lucy Carson for always being there when I needed advice. A special thank you to Jeffrey Brown for his writing suggestions, generous heart, and mushroom pizza. My gratitude to Loretta Denner for her rigor and style.

*Spasibo* to my sister Marina for her stories and her artistic soul. She is the only one left from our small Russian family.

And finally, this book would not be possible without the two closest people, whom my mother would have called my American "ours": my husband and my daughter. To you, my love.

# A Mountain of Crumbs

Elena, born with a desire to explore the world beyond her borders, finds her passion in the complexity of the English language — but in the Soviet Union of the 1960s, such a passion verges on the subversive. Elena's home is no longer the majestic Russia of literature or the tsars. Instead, it is a nation humiliated by its first faltering steps after putting up appearances for the sake of its regime and fighting to retain its pride.

In this powerful and affecting memoir, Elena re-creates the world that both oppressed and inspired her. Through her captivating voice, we learn not only the personal story of Russia in the second half of the twentieth century, but also the story of one rebellious citizen whose love of a foreign language finally transports her to a new world.

'Enthralling'
J. M. COETZEE

'This is a rich experience — a personal journey paralleled by huge national changes and ending in a deeply satisfying portrait of peace in America'
FRANK McCOURT

'Rich with honesty and insight . . . a stunning memoir: subtle, yet brimming with depth and detail. It leaves you wanting more'
DAILY TELEGRAPH

'An exquisitely moving memoir . . . Her story of oppression and hope is described in distinctive poetical prose'
MARIE CLAIRE